Family life in western societies

Offering a masterly review and synthesis of the currently available literature on family life in western societies – primarily in Britain and the United States, although with comparative reference to other western countries, as well as to eastern Europe and the Soviet Union – this book presents a distinctive new approach to family sociology. Focussing on two related questions: Why did we have the kind of family life we did when we did? and why did we have the kind of sociology of family life we did when we did?, Goldthorpe employs a doubly historical perspective, in which both 'family life', as opposed to 'the family', and sociological thought about family life, are alike seen as processes in time and in relation to each other. He draws on the findings of historical research to show continuity and change in family life over the centuries, as well as on those of earlier sociological studies, which he uses as historical evidence both for more recent changes in family life and for the evolution of sociological thought on the family. A discussion of more recent research brings the picture up to date.

Meticulous in presenting both sides of controversies in family studies, and forthright in taking a clear position on all of them, Goldthorpe challenges many widely-held preconceptions about family life. The book assumes little previous knowledge of sociology, and is easily accessible to students and other readers interested in understanding this fundamental aspect of human experience.

Family life
in western societies

A historical sociology of family relationships
in Britain and North America

J. E. GOLDTHORPE

Honorary Lecturer in the Department of Sociology
University of Leeds

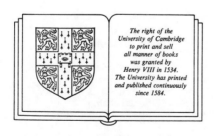

The right of the
University of Cambridge
to print and sell
all manner of books
was granted by
Henry VIII in 1534.
The University has printed
and published continuously
since 1584.

CAMBRIDGE UNIVERSITY PRESS

CAMBRIDGE

LONDON   NEW YORK   NEW ROCHELLE
MELBOURNE   SYDNEY

Published by the Press Syndicate of the University of Cambridge
The Pitt Building, Trumpington Street, Cambridge, CB2 1RP
32 East 57th Street, New York, NY 10022, USA
10 Stamford Road, Oakleigh, Melbourne 3166, Australia

First published 1987

Printed in Great Britain by Billings & Sons Ltd., Worcester

British Library cataloguing in publication data
Goldthorpe, J.E.
Family life in western societies:
a historical sociology of family
relationships in Britain and North America
1. Family – Great Britain
2. Family – United States
I. Title   306.8'5'0941   HQ614

Library of Congress cataloguing in publication data
Goldthorpe, J. E.
Family life in Western societies.
Bibliography.
Includes index.
1. Family – Great Britain – History.
2. Family – United States – History.
3. Social change.
I. Title.   HQ613.G65   1987   306.8'5'0941   86–26413

ISBN 0 521 33174 9 hardcovers
ISBN 0 521 33752 6 paperback

55,405

Contents

Preface

This book represents an attempt to synthesize some of the material available in the early 1980s on aspects of family life in western societies, namely (as explained more fully below) those of north-western Europe together with those derived from them by overseas migration. Limited as my survey has been to English-language sources, within that major culture area systematic attention has been given primarily to family life in Britain and the United States. With that limitation, however, I have tried always to place the material on these amply-documented English-speaking societies' family life in a wider setting, at the very least by including references to other western countries for purposes of comparison, if not at every point in a more fully integrated discussion. Where appropriate material has been available, too, some comparisons have been drawn with aspects of life in eastern Europe and the Soviet Union.

For reasons set out in chapter 1, I refer throughout to 'family life', not 'the family'.

If there is anything distinctive about this book, I should like to think it lies in a doubly historical perspective in which both family life itself, and sociological thought about family life, have been seen alike as processes in time and in relation to each other. As far as possible throughout I have drawn on the findings of historical research along with those of sociological studies. Some early sociological research, indeed, was carried out long enough ago to have passed into history, affording evidence which when compared with more recent studies gives us direct indications of changes in family life. In reviewing this literature, I have been able to trace continuities and changes in western family life as it has evolved over the centuries, and as it

vii

has been shaped especially by the 'four revolutions' identified in chapter 2. In other words, the prime concern has been with the question why we had the kind of family life we did, when we did. At the same time I have tried also to review the evolution and development of sociological thought about family life at different periods, especially of our recent history, and to relate that thought to the salient characteristics and leading issues of family life at those periods. In other words (again), from a slightly different but converging viewpoint I have been concerned with the question why we had the kind of sociology of family life we did, when we did.

Not much previous knowledge of sociology is assumed in the pages that follow. Where technical terms occur I have tried to explain them, while occasional references to social scientists' various research methods will, I hope, be intelligible in their context to the general reader. Rather than a particularly detailed substantive knowledge of the subject, what may prove helpful is a general appreciation of the sociological enterprise, its nature and purpose, and its distinctive cast of mind and style of thinking.

While writing this book, however, I have been interested to find how often Sigmund Freud and the psycho-analytical school of thought come into the story. To explain them in adequate depth would have involved cumbersome and probably unnecessary digression; they have surely been among the most powerful influences shaping 20th-century western thought as a whole, and have had a direct bearing on our ideas about family life, even though many have come to regard them as profoundly mistaken.

J.E.G.

Leeds
February 1986

Acknowledgements

I am grateful to colleagues in the Department of Sociology, University of Leeds, for continuing to afford me a niche in an academic environment as an honorary lecturer and to let me use the departmental facilities after my retirement from university service. This has contributed materially to the progress of this book, and I am particularly grateful to Professor Zygmunt Bauman for his never-failing encouragement. Peggy Holroyde introduced me to the world of south Asian families in Britain, and Jennifer Murdock to that of step-families. Library facilities are indispensable to an academic author, and it is a pleasure to thank the staff of the Leeds University libraries for all their help. Janice Leaman typed my drafts with meticulous care, and also introduced me to her own delightful family life. I am grateful to the staff of Cambridge University Press for their help at all stages.

For permission to use copyright material etc., I wish to thank: The Population Reference Bureau, Washington, DC, for permission to reproduce fig. 1; Professor C. C. Harris, and Messrs George Allen and Unwin, for permission to base my fig. 2 on works of which they hold the respective copyrights; The National Schizophrenia Fellowship for permission to quote from the pamphlet *Schizophrenia: the family burden*, of which they hold the copyright: The Statistical Office of the European Communities for kindly supplying the data represented in my fig. 3; Messrs Routledge and Kegan Paul for permission to quote table 2.

1

First principles

Everybody is somebody's daughter or son. Many if not most of us are sisters or brothers; nearly all of us marry, and most of us become parents. Nearly all of us know what it is like to be somebody's grandchild, and many of us live long enough to be grandparents in our turn. Most of us are nieces or nephews, and go on to be aunts or uncles; most of us are cousins. Unlike working in a factory or office, belonging to a political party or a religious sect, family life is a well-nigh universal part of human experience.

There is therefore both a particular need for a sociology of family life, and particular problems about it. So universal an institution clearly requires prime attention – and, it may be contended, seldom gets it – compared with other institutions such as occupations, organizations, religion, and social class. On the other hand, in a sense everybody is a sociologist of family life, for everybody has some idea, some cognitive map, of what family life is like by which to orient his or her own actions in relation to other family members. In this field more than most, therefore, sociologists have a challenging task to show that they are doing more than state what everybody knows from personal first-hand experience. Moreover, of all the social worlds that sociologists study, the family is one of the hardest to observe. The idea of a sociologist sitting in on a family during the hurly-burly of the family evening meal, children's bedtimes, and the like, solemnly and silently recording it all in a corner of the living room, is obviously absurd; and clearly the kind of interaction that would be observed in such circumstances would bear little relation to what normally happens unobserved. About the only family life which a sociologist can study by direct participant observation is his or her own. Personal experience has indeed prompted some sociological studies; but one sociologist's family life may not be typical, and the same can be said of anyone's family life. How are we to know if our own experience is typical, or if the taken-for-granted assumptions of our own cognitive map have any validity outside our own family?

With every respect for his genius, I question what Tolstoy wrote at the beginning of *Anna Karenina*: 'All happy families are alike, but every unhappy family is unhappy after its own fashion.'[1] Happy or unhappy, family life may be more diverse than we think, and we can easily generalize too readily from limited personal experience. If the sociology of the family has any justification, therefore, it must be that of a wider vision, a deeper understanding of the conditions that affect family life generally and make different families resemble one another in some respects, along with a heightened appreciation of the diversities that make each family's experience unique.

'FAMILY LIFE', NOT 'THE FAMILY'

As the German sociologist Norbert Elias long ago pointed out, all that we study in sociology are human actions, which are processes in time. True, much action is patterned and predictable, giving rise to expectations as people learn how things are usually done. Stable expectations about how others will act in their various roles give rise to institutions and structures, the study of which is essential to sociology. However, to present human society as if it were a set of static objects – structures, institutions, groups – is to make a category-mistake that fundamentally falsifies the reality of human social life. No action is ever exactly repeated; and changes in the way actions are performed, even if they are slow, subtle, and even almost imperceptible, can continue and cumulate over centuries of social change, as Elias himself showed in his study of changing patterns of eating and excreting in western European societies, with concomitant changes in family life and the upbringing of children.[2]

Accordingly, I take the view that to represent 'the family' and 'society' as if they were things existing in their own right, capable of exerting pressure on people to act in particular ways, would be to commit such an error as Elias warned us against. What we are concerned with are events, processes, and experiences, whether they are those of individual development, or the formation and dissolution of families ('the developmental cycle in domestic groups'[3]), or the processes of change in whole societies. That is why I refer throughout to 'family life', not 'the family'.

Further, as the anthropologist Meyer Fortes wrote, events and processes in the domestic field of social relations, viewed from within as an internal system, are simultaneously events and processes in the external, public domain of political, jural, ritual (and I would add economic) institutions.[4] Thus in our kind of society births, marriages, and deaths are events of prime importance for family life; they are also announced in the papers, marked by civil and religious ceremonies, and officially registered, so finding their way into published statistics. Such information about the public aspect of family life is far more accessible to the social scientist than are social relations 'in the domestic field, viewed from within as an internal system', as Fortes put it, or what others have called 'the psycho-social interior of the family'. For these, as already noted, the evidence tends to be partial and indirect; and though central, they are the most difficult aspects of family life to study.

Family as household –

Like many words in common speech, 'family' is an imprecise term. At the outset we must distinguish family as household from family as kin. Often the word family refers to a married couple and their young children who live together in one dwelling and share catering and cooking arrangements. Even though at any one time only a minority of households correspond to that 'cereal-packet image' of the family, probably most people spend half their lifetime or more in such households, first as children for their first fifteen to twenty years, then again as parents for a similar period, with or without a spell of independent life between. Later in the developmental cycle of domestic groups, when their children have grown up and moved out, middle-aged couples who stay together form two-person households, and later still when one of them dies a single-person household. In addition to the households of couples with dependent children, then, there are others differently composed, including couples without dependent children, and single, widowed, divorced, and separated people, some living alone, others as lone parents with dependent children.

– and as kin

Kinship relations are also recognized, however, with others who do not live together in the same household. (The word 'relations' in everyday English is unfortunately ambiguous here: how are your relations with your relations? To avoid confusion, I refer to related people as kin, to the relationships among them as relations.) In western societies, kinship relations are recognized equally on the mother's and the father's side, and this is reflected in a bilateral kinship terminology in which, for example, mother's sister and father's sister are alike called aunt. Married people also recognize affines, or spouse's bilateral kin, commonly called 'in-laws', who are their children's kin. From the point of view of the individual, bilateral kinship extends outwards in a series of concentric circles. At the centre, the kernel of the whole system, is the nuclear family, the intimate group of parents and children, conventionally forming a household. Outside this, and not usually co-resident, are grandparents, uncles and aunts, and from the point of view of an older person, nieces and nephews and grandchildren. Next come cousins; first cousins have common grandparents, second cousins common great-grandparents, and so on, while those of different generations are 'removed'. For instance, if two people are first cousins once removed, the grandparent of one is the great-grandparent of the other. But effective kinship in western societies generally stops at first cousins, and though less closely related kin may know each other it is usually as little more than 'ascriptive friends'. Nonetheless, a person's kindred, or circle of kin, is usually quite numerous, as many have found to their surprise when they begin systematically to list them. Thus the anthropologist Sir Raymond Firth found that Londoners typically recognized between 100 and 200 people as kin, and could name up to 150 of them.[5]

The family as kindred, therefore, is not a group but rather a network. An individual's kindred seldom assemble except for the great ceremonial occasions, especially weddings and funerals: as the Cumbrian villager said, 'If tha wants to know who folks' friends and relations is, Maister, tha'd best wait on 'em being buried.'[6] Collectively the kindred have neither power nor property, and when they meet they make no decisions. They constitute rather a set of people to whom an individual may properly turn for help and support, whether emotional, personal or financial, and who may reciprocally look to him or her for help when they in turn need it. This is the prime importance of kinship in western society; whereas people look to neighbours for immediate help in emergencies, and to friends for variety, companionship, and advice, it is to kin they turn for more substantial support and help in the longer time-perspectives of a lifetime.[7]

WESTERN SOCIETIES

This book is about the events, processes and experiences that have come to characterize family life in the societies of north-western Europe and those derived from them through overseas migration, especially in north America. Over the centuries, family life in these western societies has exhibited a number of enduring features marking it off very distinctively from other major culture areas in Africa, Asia, the Islamic world, and even southern and eastern Europe.[8] They centre on bilateral kinship and the monogamous marriage of consenting adults.

As I have stated above, and explained more fully elsewhere, bilateral kinship reckoned outwards from the individual 'ego' takes the form of concentric circles of nearer and more distant kin. Each individual's kindred, so delineated, is different from every other individual's except his or her brothers and sisters. Unlike the unilateral kinship to be found among many other cultures, bilateral kinship does not lend itself to the formation of descent groups such as clans or lineages, the living descendants of a common ancestor.[9] Where clans are found in western countries at all, as in Scotland, it is as little more than picturesque survivals. Generally, in western societies, ties of kinship are recognized between grandparents and grandchildren, and extend laterally as far as first cousins, but outside a three-generation kindred they are weak or non-existent.

With no organized descent groups to exert pressure,

marriage takes place on the initiative of the couple themselves. If there is family influence on the individual's choice of marriage partner, it is generally informal and even tacit. Arranged marriages, though not unknown in western history, are not characteristic of these societies in which marriage has long been regarded as essentially based on the freely consenting choice of adult men and women.

Further, as the demographer J. Hajnal pointed out, for many centuries in 'Europe to the west of a line running roughly from Leningrad (as it is now called) to Trieste' comparatively late marriage at ages well over twenty for most men and women was associated with a sizeable minority of men, and even more of women, who never married, proportions of the order of 10 to 20 per cent compared with under 5 per cent in non-western societies.[10] The social and economic organization of western societies seems always to have made independent singlehood a viable option for women as well as men. Together with the late marriage of consenting adults, this has made for egalitarianism (not necessarily equality, but a tendency towards it) in relations between spouses, and between the sexes generally, and contributed to the comparatively favourable position that women have always enjoyed in western societies.

Marriage based on adults' choice and consent has characteristically led to the formation of autonomous nuclear family households, regarded indeed as the basic building-blocks or constituent cells of the whole social organization. While there are generally strong ties of affection, and a good deal of helping-out in times of need, between married adults and their parents, the latter have no rights either to interfere in their offsprings' autonomous nuclear family households, or to claim support from them. The maintenance of the aged has never been regarded as wholly a family responsibility, and has always involved some community provision.

Generally speaking, too, there have always been rather few children. Although the average number born to each married couple has varied somewhat in different western societies at different periods, usually it has not been very large. In former times fertility was checked mainly by marrying late or not at all. Since about 1880 (earlier in France), however, married fertility has been reduced by the adoption of deliberate family limitation practices.

Consequently, western families have always been small in two senses: few children, and few co-resident kin. In this respect the Austrian sociologists, Michael Mitterauer and Reinhard Sieder, noted a broad historical contrast between eastern and western European patterns; whereas large multi-generational households predominated in pre-revolutionary Russia and elsewhere in eastern Europe, households were much smaller in western countries such as the Netherlands, Germany, and Austria.[11]

But how long is 'always'? and how did our family life come to be marked by these very distinctive characteristics? These are questions to which I turn in the next chapter.

SUGGESTION FOR FURTHER READING

Michael Mitterauer and Reinhard Sieder, *The European Family: From Patriarchy to Partnership from the Middle Ages to the Present*, trans. Karla Oosterveen and Manfred Hörzinger, Oxford, Blackwell, 1982

2

Family life in the past:
continuity and change in four revolutions

Few subjects have received more scholarly attention since about 1960 than the history of our family life, and for a number of reasons it has proved to be a controversial subject. This is partly because historians have discovered new materials and made fresh use of previously neglected sources such as, for instance, parish registers and listings of inhabitants, diaries and autobiographies. These directly-recorded observations and first-hand accounts of events and experiences by people in the past have upset many earlier interpretations based on the impressionistic use of secondary sources, as will appear below.

Further, social scientists have taken different sides on different issues in the debate. Thus Alan Macfarlane disagreed with earlier writers including George Homans and Eileen Power about the nature of English mediaeval society in general, but he nonetheless cited their support for the supposition that it included many women who never married; and while he agreed with Hajnal about that distinctively European pattern of late marriage and a substantial minority who stayed single, he could not accept Hajnal's tentative suggestion that it originated with the Reformation in the 16th century, and insisted that it prevailed much earlier.[1] Almost all authorities have viewed north-western Europe as a whole, including Hajnal,[2] Peter Laslett,[3] Jack Goody,[4] Michael Drake,[5] and Edward Shorter.[6] Macfarlane's has been the dissenting voice, maintaining that England was quite unlike France, Germany, Ireland, and even Scotland in never having had a peasant economy and society, and stressing the singularity of the English in all respects including family life.

Some authorities have placed prime emphasis on change,

including Philippe Ariès,[7] Shorter, and Lawrence Stone;[8] others on continuity, including William J. Goode, Goody, Laslett (and the Cambridge school generally), Macfarlane, and Linda Pollock.[9] Over one particularly important cause and period of change there has had to be a fundamental re-appraisal, namely the industrial revolution in the 18th and 19th centuries. So profound, far-reaching, and rapid a trans-formation did that bring about of most aspects of our social and economic life that it was natural to assume that it had transformed our family life too. Our latter-day focus on the autonomous nuclear family household was therefore assumed to be the result of the industrial revolution, which, it was supposed, had broken up extended family groups and stable, integrated rural communities in the process of migration from country to town that industrialization entailed.[10] Since 1960 it has become quite clear that those assumptions about 'the classical family of western nostalgia'[11] were false. Kinship ties prove to have been no more 'extended' than they are today; and as for rural communities in our agrarian past, they were nothing like as 'stable' or as 'integrated' as they were assumed to have been, but subject rather to a constant rapid turnover of population as people moved in search of wage work and oppor-tunities for small-scale private enterprise. It would be wrong to rush to the other extreme and assert that the industrial revol-ution made no difference to our family life, and I go into more detail below about the changes it did bring about, though they are not those that are generally supposed. Suffice it to say here that it was not the formative period of the kind of family life whose distinctive characteristics I set out at the end of the last chapter. That, it now seems clear, was the Christian revolution of the 4th and subsequent centuries AD.

THE ANCESTRAL SOCIETIES AND THE CHRISTIAN REVOLUTION

With the conversion of the Emperor Constantine in AD 313, Christianity was transformed from a persecuted minority sect into a Church, the officially established state religion of the Roman empire and later of its successor states the empires and kingdoms of Europe. It became an immensely wealthy and powerful corporation, or set of corporations, which dominated European society and largely shaped our family life through its

control of marriage and the very considerable influence it
exerted over inheritance.

Some features of our family life no doubt have even earlier
origins in the ancestral societies of the Roman empire and the
Germanic tribes of north-western Europe. Thus it is clear from
Lorraine Lancaster's account that Anglo-Saxon society was
marked by the primacy of the nuclear family.[12] Kinship was
bilateral, and an individual's kindred consisted of a circle of kin
whose extent varied according to circumstances, not a closely
delimited and structured group. Further, marriage was monogamous throughout the period covered by her study from the
7th to the early 11th century AD, though it is open to question
whether it had always been so before Christian influences were
as active and pervasive as they evidently were during that
period. Writing of the Germans at an earlier period in the 1st
century AD, Tacitus stated that single marriages were universal. He also hinted that the European pattern of late marriage
was already in evidence – 'the young men were slow to mate . . .
the girls, too, are not hurried into marriage' – though according
to Goody he may have been moralizing, and holding up the
supposed practices of the tribes as 'noble savages' to criticise
the actual ways of the Romans.[13]

By contrast very early marriage seems to have been general in
ancient Rome; an analysis of tombstone inscriptions, cited by
Hajnal, indicated that 74 per cent of Roman women were
married before they were twenty, including 39 per cent before
they were fifteen. However, according to Goody, 'plural
marriage was not a general feature of the Mediterranean world,
certainly not of Rome', though monogamy was softened in
practice by concubinage.[14]

We may conclude, therefore, that these features of western
European family life are pre-Christian in origin: almost certainly,
the primacy of the nuclear family, bilateral kinship, and a lack
of organized kin groups such as clans or lineages; probably
monogamy; and just possibly late marriage, especially of
women.

While it is difficult to be sure which features of family life in
the ancestral societies persisted unchanged, it is possible to be
more confident about those which the Church insisted on
changing. Some of them were set out quite explicitly in an
exchange of letters between Augustine, the Roman missionary

in England, and Pope Gregory in AD 601: the marriage of close kin, the marriage of close affines and the widows of close kin, adoption and fostering, and concubinage. All of these had been widespread (according to Goody) in Mediterranean and Middle Eastern societies, all were to be found recorded in the Old Testament, and there seemed little or no scriptural warrant for prohibiting them. Included among the prohibitions was the levirate, or marriage to a deceased husband's brother, a means of providing for widows positively encouraged in many cultures including that of ancient Israel. Another issue was divorce, which had been permitted under Roman law and was practised also by the ancient Greeks, Hebrews, Egyptians, and Irish. The Church raised no particular difficulty about separation, especially on the ground of adultery, but divorce with remarriage was specifically forbidden; however, nullity afforded an escape route under strictly ecclesiastical control. More positively, the Church insisted that the mutual consent of the parties was essential for a valid marriage. As already noted, marriage based on the freely consenting choice of adult men and women has come to be an integral feature of western family life, and it accords well with modern liberal ideas, though according to Goody it also 'ran directly up against the secular model' and, no doubt, an older tradition that allowed for parental authority, family alliances, and arranged marriages. Ruling out concubinage, the Church made itself the sole arbiter of the validity of marriage, and consequently of legitimacy. That had a powerful bearing on the inheritance of property and succession to title, including claims to the thrones of European kingdoms. The Church's influence over inheritance was further advanced by the changes it promoted in land tenure, from 'folkland' to 'bookland', that is, from land held in customary tenure and transmitted by customary inheritance to the family of the deceased, to land held under a 'book' or written title deed; and a concomitant increase in the use of written wills, written in most cases by the clergy, who were among the few people who could read and write.[15]

Goody acknowledged that like any large organization the Church needed resources. Besides clerical stipends there were buildings to maintain, while the Church also supported learning and the arts, and made some provision for the care of the sick, the poor, orphans, and widows. Thus according to the 5th-century Pope Gelasius I gifts to the Church were to be divided into four parts among the bishops, the other clergy, church buildings, and the poor – who therefore got only a quarter of the offerings often made in their name. However, it was Goody's central contention that the changes brought about by the Church had the effect of increasing its own wealth and power, and weakening family and kinship influences. Especially during the most rapid build-up of the Church's property from the 5th to the 8th centuries, Christians were enjoined to put the Church's needs before family affections and loyalties. Leaving property to kin outside the immediate family only encouraged in them the sin of avarice. Adoption was even more vehemently condemned as perjury, falsely representing such a one as your child in order to cheat the Church of an inheritance; and this may even partly explain the emphasis on consummation, natural procreation, and consanguinity in the Church's whole treatment of marriage and family relations.

Goody went on to argue that by blocking many of the ways in which in man might provide himself with an heir, for example, divorcing a childless first wife and remarrying, or fathering a child by a concubine, or adoption, the Church limited the 'strategies of heirship' a family might pursue to retain their property, and so increased the possibility of its alienation. Widening the prohibited degrees – at one period in the Church's history as far as the seventh collateral degree, that of sixth cousins – must have made it quite difficult, in theory, to find an eligible marriage partner in the small-scale rural communities in which most people lived. In practice, however, the Church could and did grant dispensations from its own laws – at a price; so deriving an income from, as well as control over, the marriages of large number of people. The sale of dispensations, indeed, was denounced by Martin Luther and by the English Parliament under King Henry VIII, and became a major issue in the Reformation. Under the doctrine that husband and wife became 'one flesh', the Church went on to identify affines with kin, so that for instance a woman's husband's brother was literally her brother in law, that is, in the Church's law. In later centuries that was to give rise to anguished debates about whether a man should be allowed to marry his deceased wife's sister. Unless dispensed, the 'one flesh' doctrine restricted even more narrowly the remarriage choices of widows and widowers by barring all their late spouses' kin as well as their own. This was likely to increase the numbers of people who died unmarried, and could be persuaded by the clerics who wrote their wills to leave some or all of their lands and moveable property to the Church. Allegations of undue influence upon the dying were another source of bitter complaint at the time of the Reformation; thus one of the grievances set out by the Diet or assembly held at Worms in 1521 was that 'they prevail upon the old and the sick to withhold their estate from their rightful heirs'.[16] The increasing use of written wills, already noted, accorded with the maxim, *Nemo est heres viventis*, no-one is an heir to the living. Although wives were protected by the rule entitling them to one-third of their husband's property, children had no rights to inherit, and those who regarded themselves as the legitimate heirs to land and other property could very well find that a dying parent had willed it away, in whole or in part, to the Church.[17] Further, by making it more difficult for a widowed person to remarry, the Church increased the number of people for whom the celibate monastic life in an abbey or nunnery might be a viable option – especially widows with property; and those who in this sense entered the Church took their property with them.

And once in the dead hand or mortmain of the Church and its constituent foundations, property never came back into circulation, either through family inheritance or through the market. The irreversibility of the Church's acquisitions so alarmed the landed gentry, nobility, and royal families throughout Europe that in a number of kingdoms Statutes of Mortmain were enacted to try and halt the process; but they were not of much effect. This, then, was a third issue in the Reformation, and it is significant that in England the first and most drastic step taken after the final breach with Rome was the dissolution of the monasteries and the dispersal of much ecclesiastical property among the gentry.[18]

➤ The fourth issue in the Reformation with a bearing on family life was, of course, divorce. This came to a head in an atmosphere of high political crisis in England in the 1530s, where the Great Divorce had a double meaning: the annulment of King Henry VIII's marriage to Catherine of Aragon, and the severance of the kingdom from the papacy. The details of

Henry's fascinating and important case have been amply recounted elsewhere; suffice it to say here that it had much to do with 'strategies of heirship'. The outcome was that in 1533 Henry assumed supreme authority over the Church of England, and asserted the power of the sovereign in Parliament to make laws concerning marriage. Parliament did in fact proceed in 1540 to legalize the marriage of first cousins; and while that had the immediate effect of removing a possible impediment to Henry's fifth marriage, it had a greater and more lasting importance in narrowing the prohibited degrees. [19]

The Reformation in England achieved some important Protestant objectives in the translation of the Bible and the liturgy into English, with profound implications for freedom of thought and expression. But church government remained hierarchical, not presbyterian or congregational, with archbishops, bishops and clergy exercising authority from the top downwards, and the archbishops and a number of bishops sitting in Parliament as members of the House of Lords, where they long continued to impede the further reform of the divorce law – until our own times, indeed. The power of the sovereign in Parliament to dissolve marriages was not delegated to the judiciary until 1857, and before that date a divorce could be obtained only through a cumbersome and inordinately costly procedure involving both the civil and the ecclesiastical courts and finally a private Act in the House of Lords. I return to this point below.

Elsewhere too the Reformation made very little difference either to the doctrine of the indissolubility of marriage, or to ordinary people's chances of divorce. When the Bible was translated into the peoples' own languages, and widely disseminated in printed form, as it was for the first time in the 16th century, Protestant churches had to acknowledge that there appeared to be scriptural warrant for divorce, at least on the ground of adultery; but they did so with the utmost reluctance. Thus in Sweden under the Ecclesiastical Ordinance of 1572 the clergy were expressly charged with the duty of watching over the people's married lives, and according to Max Rheinstein the Lutheran state church adopted a heavily disapproving, even punitive attitude towards 'quarrelsome couples'.[20] Only gradually were the grounds of divorce extended from adultery to include desertion (especially 'beyond the borders of the realm') and later incurable insanity, alcoholic addiction, crimes involving moral turpitude and plots against the life of the other spouse, habitual wastefulness, and finally 'deep and lasting discord'. In 1686 the secular courts were brought into the process of investigating and proving the facts of adultery or desertion, though the church long continued to issue the final letter of divorcement enabling the petitioner – not the respondent – to remarry. In Denmark matters took a different course, as the powers of the sovereign in Parliament were exercised through administrative rather than ecclesiastical or judicial decisions, and the great majority of Danish divorces in recent times have been granted by local authorities with recourse to the courts only in contested cases. In Scotland, however, as early as 1560 the courts were granting divorces under the common law to men and women alike on the ground of adultery, to which desertion was added by an Act of 1573; while legal aid (as we should now call it) was available under an even earlier Act of 1424.[21] The position in Scotland was therefore quite different from that in England, and it continued to be so until well into the 20th century, when the differences narrowed mostly as a result of changes in English law and administrative practice.

In some European countries, including Austria and Portugal at various dates, divorce was permitted only to non-Catholics. In France and Belgium divorce was introduced in a hot flush of revolutionary fervour in 1792, but in France it was abolished again in 1816 and not re-introduced until 1884. In Italy civil divorce was first enacted as recently as 1970, while at the time of writing there is still no provision for divorce in the Irish Republic.

Almost equally wide diversity prevailed in the New World, reflecting the different religious attitudes that prevailed in the colonies, later to become the states and provinces of the USA and Canada respectively. In Canada it was not until 1968 that uniform provision for divorce was made in all provinces through special family courts; before that date residents of Newfoundland and Quebec could obtain a divorce only through a private Act of the Canadian Parliament, as in

England before 1857.[22] In the USA, according to Clifford
Kirkpatrick there were marked regional differences, with
church control more evident in Virginia and Maryland, while in
the northern colonies, where the sentiment was 'keenly anti-
papist', divorce was sanctioned and remarriage was accepted.[23]
Judicial procedures for divorce appear to have been introduced
first in Massachusetts in the early 1700s;[24] but adultery was long
the sole ground for divorce in New York, and there was no
provision at all in South Carolina till 1950. Wide differences
persisted until after 1969 when, led by California, most states
enacted 'no-fault' divorce laws doing away with the old
doctrine of the matrimonial offence; I take up the story below.
So it took more than 400 years for the principle first conceded
at the time of the Reformation to be widened sufficiently to
open the way for the divorce revolution of the late 20th
century.

     Although I have called it the Christian revolution, perhaps it
was more like a great glacier, advancing across the European
landscape from the 4th century onwards, reaching its
maximum extent in about the 10th to the 12th centuries,
beginning its slow retreat in the 16th century with the Reformation, and continuing to recede in the climate of secularism
and rationality that prevailed in the 19th and 20th centuries,
but leaving behind it untidy moraine hillocks, a confusion of
inconsistencies and anomalies about important issues concerning our family life. In that retreat, some of the practices of the
ancestral civilizations have (as it were) surfaced and been
restored, particularly divorce, adoption, and the marriage of
cousins if not closer kin and affines; but at very different dates
in different states, and still not yet in all. And though the glacier
may have retreated it has not melted away. Christianity remains
a powerful influence, even though since the Reformation it has
been represented by a plurality of churches, denominations,
and sects rather than the universal western Church of
mediaeval times. Divorce law reform, family limitation, abor-
tion, parents' rights and duties, even corporal punishment are
among the issues upon which Christian opinion is passionately
mobilized in contemporary western societies. And a Polish
pope from a communist country still found himself in the
1980s the arbiter of royal and princely marriages in some
western European countries.

FAMILY LIFE IN THE PRE-INDUSTRIAL ECONOMY AND SOCIETY

In this section I review the evidence of studies, mostly carried out after 1960, of what family life in western societies was like before the industrial revolution which, as noted above, was supposed in the earlier literature to have transformed it. To give a rough indication of the dates concerned, though dating a social and economic movement is always difficult, for the industrial revolution in Britain (including Scotland after 1707) a conventionally-recognized starting date is 1760. Some important inventions and new processes were first devised before that date, particularly Savery's steam engine in 1698; they came into wider use on a larger scale in the late 18th century, and the most rapid changes occurred between 1780 and 1820. By 1821, industry had decisively supplanted agriculture as the prime source of income and of employment. The great age of railway building followed in the 1830s and 1840s, and by 1851 more than half the population lived in towns – the first time in the world's history this had come about in a major country.[25] For Britain, then, anything before 1750 is safely pre-industrial, while comparisons can still usefully be drawn between life in the new industrial towns and a more traditional way of life in rural areas as late as the mid 19th century. If Britain's industrialization, by common consent the first, took place between 1760 and 1850, roughly corresponding dates for other western countries would be France 1830–1900, Germany and USA 1850–1900, Scandinavia 1860–1930.[26]

Living conditions

It need hardly be said that life in the past was hard for many people in many ways, and that family life was lived in circumstances we should now regard as adverse. Like most pre-industrial civilizations, western European societies were marked by wide disparities of wealth. Many people lived in poverty, whether in family households or perhaps even more so if they were old and alone. The houses of the poor were small, cold, insanitary, and in many cases overcrowded. They have not survived like the great houses of the rich that we see and admire today; but even the latter, though spacious, must have been cold, and they were certainly insanitary.

In an account of our ancestors' adversities, there can be little doubt that prime emphasis should be placed on disease. Thus E. A. Wrigley and R. S. Schofield in their monumental study of English population trends, based on registration data for 404 parishes, concluded that neither long-term variations nor short-term fluctuations in mortality were much affected by changes in living standards. But diseases such as plague and smallpox were endemic, and could readily become epidemic; while a hot summer would be followed by deaths from gastro-intestinal infections, particularly among children, and a cold winter would lead to deaths from bronchitis and pneumonia, particularly among the elderly.[27] Failure to combat disease was probably due more to lack of knowledge than of material resources, though the latter sometimes contributed. As more recently in countries such as Sudan, local harvest failures could result in famines even when food was available elsewhere, if transport was inadequate to move it and there was a lack of purchasing power to pay for it; the Irish famine of 1847–8 was another grim instance. Local populations whose resistance to disease was lowered by under-nourishment might then be vulnerable to epidemics which, once started, could spread to other regions not directly affected by famine. Even so, Wrigley and Schofield found that deficient harvests did not always or even generally give rise to local mortality crises, which were much more usually associated with epidemic outbreaks.

And disease was no respecter of persons or ranks. Rich and poor alike died, or lived to suffer, from many diseases that have since been eliminated altogether (such as smallpox), or that can be alleviated if not cured by modern methods of treatment (for example, schizophrenia: see chapter 6). Indeed, there are grounds for suggesting that the rich may even have suffered more, because they were more subject than the poor to pre-scientific medical advice now recognized as erroneous and in many cases actually harmful, itself the cause of needless suffering. One example was the widespread use of bleeding for all sorts of complaints. Another was the often appallingly inhuman treatment of mental illness, even when the sufferer was King George III of England. A third was the advice given by physicians before 1700 that newly-born babies should be purged and not breast-fed till about the fourth day: I return to this subject below.

Another aspect of family life affected by material conditions was privacy, or the lack of it. There can have been little enough in the often overcrowded dwellings of the poor; but for the rich too family life seems to have been lived in semi-public in houses occupied also by their servants and often thronged with visitors. In many great houses still standing there is no way into some rooms but through others. According to Michael Anderson, from the 17th century onwards 'domestic architecture changed with a segregation between rooms for sleeping, eating, and conducting business, while the introduction of corridors was particularly important in creating space where more affluent families could be secure from the intrusion of strangers and, later, of servants'.[28] This change was 'a topic of much comment in 18th-century England', and it set a pattern that latter diffused down the social scale, as will appear below.

The size and composition of households

Summarizing the findings of his analysis of the data for England, especially household listings for 100 local communities from 1574 to 1821, Peter Laslett emphasized 'how questionable it would be to assert that the transformation of English society by industrialization was accompanied by any decrease in the size of the average household until very late on in that process'. Mean household size remained fairly constant at 4.75 or a little under from the earliest date until as late as 1901. 'There is no sign of the large, extended coresidential group of the traditional peasant world giving way to the small, nuclear, conjugal household of modern industrial society'; and the large joint or extended family seemed never to have existed as a common form of the domestic group at any time covered by the records.

However, household sizes differed widely within each local community. The data for Laslett's 100 communities showed that the commonest number of persons in a household was 3, and 16.5 per cent of households were of that modal size, while single- and 2-person households together made up another 20 per cent. But some households were bigger; 33 per cent were of 6 persons or more, and over half the population lived in these larger households. Many were those of the better-off classes, including the gentry, clergy, yeomen, traders and craftsmen; and these households included unrelated servants in addition to the master's family. In an economy characterized by household production and the apprenticeship system, not all those classed as servants were domestics; country households included also agricultural workers, while town families housed apprentices and journeymen craftsmen and trade assistants. The extreme yet illustrative case, and the biggest single household in all Laslett's data, was that of the bachelor Earl of Lonsdale and 49 servants at Lowther in 1787.[29] (Perhaps such a man would have said that he 'lived alone'.) So while well-to-do households were large because they included unrelated servants, the households of the poor were correspondingly depleted especially of their young adult members who left home in adolescence to 'go into service'; and the big households of pre-industrial England mirrored its social class system rather than its kinship system.

Not that apprenticeship and service were confined to the poor. For example, all seven children of the Reverend Ralph Josselin, a 17th-century clergyman and farmer (of whom more below) left home between the ages of 10 and 16, four of them bound as apprentices or servants, three girls to school. As Laslett put it, 'service in England and the West was a stage in the life-cycle for large numbers of people';[30] and it does much to explain the late ages at which men and women married.

From the data collected by Wrigley and Schofield for thirteen English parishes between 1600 and 1799, it may be inferred that before 1750 an average couple married when he was about 27–28 and she about 25–26.[31] (After 1750 marriage ages fell; and it will be remembered that an appreciable minority of people never married.) By the time she was 40, if they both lived, she would have given birth to 7 or 8 children, of whom 5 could be expected to survive to the age of 15. By that time, though, in all probability the elder children would have left home and gone into service. As a co-resident household, then, such a family would reach its maximum size of 7 (2 parents and 5 children) only briefly if at all. Earlier in the developmental cycle the couple would not yet have had all their children; later the children would have gone away. At any one time, therefore, most households were much smaller.

Naturally, some households in the past included three

generations of the same family, especially when widowed parents lived with their married offspring and the latter's children. In England, however, the proportion of these three-generation households was remarkably low, only 5.8 per cent in all of Laslett's data for 1574–1821. Even more striking was the small number of resident mothers-in-law, only 110 in all out of a total population of some 68,000 people.

Broadly similar results were reported from similar researches and discoveries elsewhere in Europe. Thus in the village of Montplaisant in the Dordogne valley in 1644 the mean household size was 5.48, and even that is thought to have been higher than it might have been but for peasant unrest and the need for families to live together for protection. In seven French villages in 1836 the mean household sizes ranged from 3.37 to 5.08 and in four of them the mode was 3 as in England. In the Netherlands, data for four regions in the 18th century show mean household sizes ranging from 3.7 to 5.2, with households of 2, 3, and 4 persons the most frequent.[32]

In Norway, Drake's analysis of census data going back to 1735, long before the industrial revolution which started there in the 1860s, showed a clear distinction among the rural population between farmers and crofters. Farmers married later, but their wives were younger and had more children, and their households included also more servants, lodgers, and kinsfolk. Crofters married women of about their own age or even older than themselves, and had fewer children, who left home early to go into service in the farmers' households.[33]

And things were little different in colonial north America. Early censuses, such as that of 1764 in Massachusetts and that of 1790 throughout the United States, show mean family sizes of 5½ to 6, appreciably more than in England; and this was no doubt related to higher fertility among a small population facing a vast empty continent with seemingly limitless resources. According to John Demos, in Plymouth Colony 'married couples produced, ... an average of eight children apiece'; and though the mean household size was about 6 most nuclear families went through a period when, with all the children at home, they numbered many more than that. Moreover, especially in the southern states, slaves were counted with the free white households to which they belonged; and the average number of slaves per family was over

4 in South Carolina and over 3 in Maryland. However, the proportion of extended family households seems to have been
small. No doubt there were some three-generation households, but Demos emphasized that 'married siblings *never*
resided in the same household'.[34] If families in the United
States were bigger in the past than they are today, and bigger
than in Europe, it was because they had more children and
some of them had slaves, not because they practised some kind
of extended family system they have since abandoned.

Further south and cast in Europe we begin to encounter
rather more extended or compound households comprising
more than one nuclear family. This emerged from a latter-day
analysis by Christiane Klapisch of an enumeration carried out
in Tuscany in 1427. In Florence, though the ratio of nuclear
families to households as a whole was only 1.09, it was 1.32
among the most affluent, and nearly one in four of the
wealthiest households included more than one nuclear family;
while in the city of Arezzo nearly half the larger households
were multiple. These great town households of aristocrats or
would-be aristocrats tended to be vertically extended, that is,
they included three or four generations of the same family. In
the countryside, some big households were laterally extended,
that is, they included married siblings and their children,
presumably as brothers loath to divide the family land decided
to live together and merge their households.[35]

Similar considerations have clearly applied to the *zadruga* or
joint household of related males – fathers and sons, brothers,
sometimes uncles and nephews – that has been a persistent
feature of life in Serbia from the middle ages till recent times.
Where land is fertile but its availability is limited, other
economic opportunities are few, and conditions favour labour-
intensive husbandry, a peasant's sons are more likely to decide
to stay at home when they marry. A man with a wife and four
sons, their wives, and four children each, would be the head of a
household of 26 people and could be so before he was sixty.
Such indeed has commonly been the size and composition of
some households in Serbia. However, not all Serbian households were so large; as E. A. Hammel stressed, the *zadruga* is not
a thing but a process, and at any one time many households
must be of a simple nuclear family type if they are later to
develop into *zadrugas*.[36] Further, this type of household is or

was to be found in Europe only in a limited area of the Balkans, and there seems to have been nothing like it in north-western European and derived societies. However closely it may resemble the family arrangements of some non-western societies, especially perhaps the Hindu joint family, it tends if anything to emphasize by contrast the distinctiveness of family life in western societies as here defined.

The wider kindred

Outside the nuclear family, it does not seem that people's wider kinship relations were any more extensive in the pre-industrial past than they are today, and they may even have been less so. A particularly well-documented case is afforded by Alan Macfarlane's study based on the diaries of the Reverend Ralph Josselin, 1617–83, vicar of Earls Colne in Essex from 1641.[37]

Relations among near kin were evidently close. Josselin's children showed affection for one another and often visited each other in sickness and on other occasions after they left home. Earlier, he helped his three sisters through the difficult years after their father's death, and there are numerous entries recording visits and gifts and loans of money. His sister Anne died while staying with him; he records her death with fondness and sadness, and went to her funeral, though not the others'. In those days communications were slow, and people did not always hear about funerals in time; thus by the time Josselin heard of his uncle Ralph's death in London he had been four days in his grave. More surprising perhaps is that he did not attend his sisters' weddings either. When one sister lost her husband, Josselin helped by 'schooling' her children, but other-wise he does not seem to have taken much interest in his nephews and nieces.

Though most of Josselin's wider kin lived in Essex, they were widely scattered over the county, and beyond; he had uncles in Norfolk, and two cousins in New England. With some of his uncles he had quite close relations. He stayed with two of them in turn while he was searching for a living, and it was through the influence of his favourite uncle Ralph that he was appointed to his first living at Cranham. He took very little interest in his aunts, however. He had 8 or 9 on his father's side alone, but except for his uncle Ralph's wife there is scarcely a mention of them in his whole diary. His relations with his cousins were even more tenuous; he must have had at least thirty, of whom only fourteen are ever mentioned.

Josselin's wife Jane came from Buckinghamshire, and relations with her immediate family were close. Soon after they were married, her father came for a long stay that extended nearly till his death two years later, and Josselin wrote his will shortly before he died. Jane's mother too came to stay when their first child was born. There were close and friendly relations with Jane's brother Jeremy and her sister Elizabeth, sustained by visits, and by letters when Elizabeth and her husband lived in Ireland for a time. And Josselin kept up friendly contacts with Jane's uncle (mother's brother) and aunt. Beyond that, though, his interest in his in-laws was faint.

The pattern, then, was of intense and intimate relations with the inner circle of near kin, parents, children, and siblings, shading off rapidly into less close relations in the next concentric circle of uncles and aunts, nephews and nieces, and disappearing into tenuous or non-existent relations with the outer circle of first cousins. Such a kindred is, if anything, even narrower than we find today. Josselin recognized, to the extent of mentioning them in his diary, only 48 living kin at any time of his life; whereas, as noted in chapter 1, people in 20th-century England typically recognize 100 to 150 living kin, as well as others now dead. Yet the final impression is how modern it all seems, and Macfarlane concludes: 'His kinship ties were in many ways like that of a highly mobile modern family. ... Certainly the above analysis dispels any lingering illusion that the peculiar nature of modern English kinship systems is entirely a post-industrial product.'

The local community

Despite a general impression to the contrary, it seems clear that there was a good deal of mobility in pre-industrial times as people moved, singly or in family groups, from one place to another, and related family households did not necessarily live close together in the same local community. Ralph Josselin's family are a case in point, while further evidence is afforded by the parish listings for Clayworth in Nottinghamshire made by the rector, the Reverend William Sampson, in 1676 and 1688. Between those years the population grew by only 10 or 11; but only 157 of the 401 people listed in 1676 were still there in 1688, and 244 had gone. Death had claimed 92, but as many as 152 must have moved away, representing a 60 per cent turnover in 12 years or 5 per cent a year. As Laslett points out, 'we should probably overlook the replacement of one person in twenty every year in an organization which we belonged to, just as Sampson did at Clayworth. Most of the people moving, moreover, may not have moved very far.' It seems likely that most of those who moved were servants, who were engaged and re-engaged yearly at the hiring fair, and did not reckon on staying long in one place. It was a different matter with those of higher social status, especially the yeomen and other landholders, who with their families may have provided a somewhat more stable core in an otherwise shifting population. There was also an appearance of continuity in the list of craftsmen and shopkeepers always to be found in the village; but these were not necessarily the same people, only the same businesses. 'When one man got old, or went to the bad and gave up or died, he was replaced, so that there tended always to be a cooper at Clayworth, or two or three tailors, a butcher, and a blacksmith.' To one who returned to the village after an absence it must have looked like the same place, maintaining an apparent permanence that belied 'the shortness of life, the fluctuations of prosperity, the falling in of leases, the wayward habits of young folk in service and the fickleness of their employers'.[38]

Despite their shifting composition, village communities may well have exerted considerable control over individuals' actions. As already noted, there was little or no privacy for anybody; village gossip was no doubt powerful and pervasive, and those who outraged village opinion risked public humiliation. Some pre-industrial economic institutions, particularly the open field system of agriculture, heightened the extent to which everybody knew everybody else's business as decisions about the management of crops and grazing had to be made collectively. But village communities were also highly inegalitarian, with 'the parson and the squire' and the core of landholding families exercising the predominant influence. For example, at Earls Colne (later Josselin's parish) in 1598 two-thirds of the land was demesne, that is, the property of the large landlord who dominated the community. (The village land had already been enclosed, that is, the open field system had been superseded by individual farming.) The remaining third was divided among about twenty copyholders; and about three-quarters of the population had no land beyond a house and garden. As at Clayworth, some people worked as labourers on others' land, while many made a living from trades and crafts.

Another important aspect of the relation between community and family life was the provision for the aged poor through parish relief. As already noted, one of the peculiarities of western societies has been that the support of the aged has never been wholly a family responsibility. It could hardly have been in the absence of organized kin groups, when some people grew old without ever having been married, some had been married but childless, others had lost children from death or migration, or yet others had offspring unable to help them much because of their own poverty or sickness; and all that was at least as true in pre-industrial as in more recent times. But supplementing family resources through community provision or 'charity' further emphasised disparity and dependence. For example, in Kirkby Lonsdale in the north of England, according to a parish listing cited by Macfarlane, in 1695 a quarter to a third of the population were 'pensioners' receiving poor relief. Another quarter of the male population, and nearly a quarter of the females, were listed as servants. 'Thus one half of the population was supporting or paying for the labour of the other half.'[39]

Childhood in the past

In the number of studies published in the 1960s and 70s, notably including those of Ariès and Shorter, it was asserted that in earlier times childhood was not recognized, and that children were regarded as 'little adults' after about the age of 7; that there was no awareness of the stages of individual development and of children's needs for play and affection; that relations between parents and children were formal, distant, and often punitive; and that the callous neglect and abuse of children at home, school, and work was widespread, far more so than in our own gentler and more enlightened age. The evidence was drawn overwhelmingly from secondary sources:

moral and medical tracts, sermons, and early printed books dealing with children and their upbringing, supplemented by paintings, fictional literature, and travellers' impressions. Changes in the treatment of children were variously attributed to the rise of schooling, supposed changes in the family structure, the rise of capitalism, and changes in attitudes, particularly a 'surge of sentiment' in the 18th and 19th centuries.

These studies, and the 'black legend' to which they gave rise, have been strongly controverted by Linda Pollock in her study of first-hand accounts of childhood and parenthood recorded in some 350 English-language (British and American) diaries and autobiographies from 1500 to 1900.[40] Throughout that period, stages of development and children's need to play were recognized, together with their needs for care and protection, for guidance, education, and discipline, and for financial provision. Most parents, then as now, were affectionate and kind, regarding children as gifts from God and sources of happiness. They were certainly not indifferent, and they showed deep grief when a child died. Some, indeed, were evidently even more affected than most would be today by religious doctrines that compounded their natural grief with guilt at feeling such distress when they were assured that their loved ones were safe and happy in a saviour's arms. Then as now, many parents sometimes resorted to physical punishment, which was also used in schools. Then as now, there were cases of serious abuse and ill-treatment of children; then as now they aroused the same general reaction of shock and outrage, in which offending adults were themselves severely punished; there seems little reason to think such cases were more prevalent than, sadly, they are today. Most children's own diaries, and adults' recollections of childhood in their autobiographies, did not dwell much on such horrors. In so far as there were changes it seems that the early 19th century was a bad time for children. Working-class children endured great misery in the mines and factories of the industrial revolution, and there was also a greater use of corporal punishment in both home and school than in either earlier or later periods. Even so, then as now, some parents were strict, others indulgent; and Pollock's final impression was of wide individual variation in every century with no very great changes over long periods.

THE DEMOGRAPHIC REVOLUTION: 1 POPULATION GROWTH

As generally understood, the term demographic revolution (cycle, or transition) refers to successive falls, first in mortality, then in fertility, in the course of which it has been postulated that societies pass through four stages. In the first or 'high stationary' stage, high fertility maintains population numbers in the face of high and fluctuating mortality, modest growth in good years being wiped out by occasional mortality crises due to famine or disease. In the second stage mortality falls and population grows at a more rapid and accelerating rate, until in the third stage there is a corresponding fall in fertility as people adopt family limitation practices; and in the fourth or 'low stationary' stage there is slow or zero population growth. [41] It has been represented, therefore, as a transition from a state of affairs in which many children are born, few survive, and life is short to one in which few children are born, most survive, and life is long; from Malthus's 'positive' checks of poverty, disease, and war upon population growth to the 'preventive' checks of late marriage and birth control or family limitation. [42]

Though originally devised with western countries in mind, it has since been recognized that this theoretical model does not fit their population history without considerable qualifications, especially on the side of fertility. In many Third World countries in the recent past, birth-rates have been very high, typically fluctuating between 40 and 50 per 1000 population per year. As Michael Drake pointed out, it was commonly assumed that in most western countries too birth-rates and death-rates had been similarly high until the late 18th century at least, and that the increase in population then and in the 19th century was due entirely to a fall in death-rates; but this was not so. [43] Really high rates of 40 and over were not characteristic of the pre-industrial west. Thus according to Wrigley and Schofield, in England before 1750 the general level of the birth-rate for long periods was around 30 to 35, while the death-rate normally fluctuated between 25 and 30 and it was only rarely in the worst mortality crises that it exceeded 40. Similarly in pre-industrial Sweden before 1860 the birth-rate varied between 30 and 35, and the death-rate between 20 and 30.

The relationship between population trends and industrial

development, particularly in Britain, is complex, obscure, and controversial. Nevertheless, it seems both possible and important to distinguish the demographic and the industrial revolutions, and separately assess how they were related to changes in family life. One thing at least seems beyond doubt: the first industrial revolution occurred in Britain at a time of population growth. Controversy has surrounded two related sets of questions, demographic and economic. Did that population growth result from a fall in mortality? or a rise in fertility? or both, and if so in what proportions? Did the industrial revolution generate its own labour force (so to speak) by creating job opportunities that made for earlier marriages and hence, in the absence of deliberate restraint, more children? Conversely, did population growth stimulate industrial development through increased demand? Or was it just a coincidence? and did the industrial revolution happen in the nick of time to avert a Malthusian crisis of over-population, pressure on resources, and falling living standards, and make possible a combination of population growth and rising real wages unprecedented in history?[44]

It seems likely that a number of factors contributed to a fall in mortality from the 1740s onwards, and it is perhaps not entirely fanciful to trace them back to the rise of science in the 17th century, the age of Newton and the Royal Society, and the application of science to agriculture and to medicine.

Agricultural improvements in the early 18th century notably included new crops such as turnips, and new crop rotations including nitrogen-fixing plants to maintain soil fertility without the need to rest the soil for a fallow year. Associated with these developments were improvements in livestock breeding and management. Increased agricultural productivity along with improved transport no doubt reduced 'subsistence crisis mortality' from recurrent local famines, and contributed to a general fall in the death-rate, whose extreme fluctuations disappeared from then on.

In medicine, one important 18th-century advance was immunization against smallpox, first by inoculation (discovered in 1718, and denounced by the Church as unnatural and wicked), then after 1799 by vaccination.[45] A second was better advice about breast-feeding. As already noted, before 1700 physicians advised that babies should be purged and not breast-fed till about the fourth day. Presumably it was the upper classes who had the greatest if somewhat dubious benefit of this and other medical advice; and whether as a direct conse-quence or not, it has been estimated that infant mortality among the British aristocracy before 1700 was substantially higher than that of the general population. It fell to about the same as the general level between 1700 and 1750, when some medical writers began to recommend colostrum (a mother's first secretion) instead of purging; and after 1776, when it was recognized empirically that breast-feeding from the first pre-vented many infantile disorders, it fell below the general level. Indeed, according to Fildes, by far the greater part of the general fall in infant mortality from the 1680s to the 1840s was due to a big reduction in deaths in the first twenty-eight days after birth, which was more consistent with the new advice about breast-feeding than with other factors such as immuniz-ation against smallpox and the increasing use of cows' milk.[46] Thirdly, according to Wrigley and Schofield, maternal mortality fell markedly after 1700.[47]

In Sweden it had long been known that population growth after 1750 and still more after 1800 resulted from falling mortality, as the poet Tegnér succinctly put it, 'with the onset of peace, vaccine, and potatoes'. Coming as it did long before Sweden's industrial revolution, moreover, according to Alva Myrdal that increase did indeed result in Malthusian impoverishment.[48] Wrigley and Schofield suggested that the data long since available for Sweden may have been one reason why some historians thought that in England too population grew because mortality fell while fertility stayed high, as in the second stage of the paradigmatic population cycle; but that was not so (while in France, as will appear below, matters took a different course again). Though mortality did fall, the increase in England was more attributable to rising fertility; at least twice as much, or more. For centuries, indeed, before Malthus wrote his celebrated *Essay* the English had avoided pressure on resources and quietly practised a system of preventive checks mainly by marrying late or remaining single (with very low illegitimacy rates). That system was never more firmly in oper-ation than in the middle and late 17th century, especially 1650–80, when high mortality and low fertility combined to bring about an intrinsic growth rate near zero, and with quite heavy emigration the population declined. It was not entirely clear what influenced long-term changes in nuptiality (the age at marriage, and the proportion ever marrying) and fertility; they seemed to be related to living standards as indicated by real wages, though with a very long time-lag, of the order of thirty to fifty years. It was as if young adults' decisions to marry, to delay marriage, or to stay single were made by their parents, or alternatively by the couple themselves on the basis of their parents' earlier life-experience. Perhaps because labour was short in the late 17th century, real wages rose, giving rise a generation later to attitudes more favourable to marriage and family formation, a slight relaxation of the preventive check, and hence to population growth after 1750. It follows from this analysis that Wrigley and Schofield subscribed to the coincidence theory according to which the industrial revolution took place just in time to avert a fall in real wages when population was growing for quite other reasons. Wrigley concluded in brief that, 'Marriage was the hinge on which the demographic system turned.'[49]

This conclusion, clearly highly relevant to the study of family life, accorded closely with David Levine's findings on family formation in four English villages between 1550 and 1850. Allowing for adult mortality among parents, infant and child mortality, late marriage, and the 10 to 20 per cent who never married, net reproduction rates were generally close to or even below replacement level before 1750. Despite wide local variations in the nature and timing of economic changes, however, the industrial revolution as conventionally understood seemed to have been generally preceded by a period of 'proto-industrialization' based on handicrafts and market-oriented farming, during which traditional sanctions against early marriage weakened as groups who married early became more numerous while those who traditionally married late became less important. According to Levine, 'what led to earlier and more frequent marriages was the opportunity for employment offered by proto-industry and capitalist farming', though Wrigley could not accept that wage employment in general was associated with earlier marriage. Local variations served to emphasize how sensitively the age and frequency of marriage responded to diverse and changing economic circumstances. Thus at Shepshed in Leicestershire, perhaps proto-typically, early industrialization was accompanied by a fall in the age of marriage, and population growth after 1750. At Bottesford not far away, however, these changes took place only after 1800 with the rise of labour-intensive dairy farming and Stilton cheese-making for a national market. Colyton in Devon (of which more below) was badly hit by the vagaries of the wool trade early in the 17th century, and here men took to marrying women older than themselves, nearly 20 per cent remained single, and the net reproduction rate fell far below replacement. And at Terling in Essex, thirty-five miles from London, commercial farming by large tenant farmers was fully evident by 1600. Early marriage prevailed here throughout, and fewer than 10 per cent remained single; there was little chance of inheriting a holding, so no reason to delay marriage on that account, but local employment opportunities were good. Levine's conclusion, echoing Wrigley's, was that between 1700 and 1870 'for all intents and purposes, the age at first marriage of women was the main agent of demographic change'.[50]

THE INDUSTRIAL REVOLUTION

A most important factor making for change in family life at the time of the industrial revolution, and partly related to it, was the decline of the centuries-old traditions of apprenticeship and living-in service. This obviously went with late marriage, and that contemporary observer Thomas Malthus himself emphasized how strongly it dissuaded young adults from early and imprudent marriage, and so acted as a preventive check to population growth.[51] As the latter-day historian Ann Kussmaul pointed out, for centuries service in husbandry had preserved the form of the nuclear family household while enabling each family farm to meet its needs for labour at different stages in its developmental cycle and make good random losses from mortality. It allowed adolescents to leave home, and gave young adults a chance to save money or wait for an inheritance before facing the costs of setting up their own households. Kussmaul devised ingenious statistical measures to investigate the extent to which farmers met their needs for labour by employing annually-hired living-in servants as distinct from day labourers: at dates around 1700 in different parts of England from 50 to 80 per cent of all farm labour took this form. The proportion fluctuated somewhat over the centuries in response to such factors as the relative profitability of live-stock (needing constant daily attention) compared with cereals (requiring labour only intermittently at peak periods of ploughing, sowing, and harvesting). Service in husbandry was at its height during the 18th century, reaching its peak in 1750, after which it went into a decline continuing throughout the 19th century to its well-nigh total extinction in the 20th.[52]

Concurrently with the decline of service in husbandry went that of living-in apprenticeship to trades and crafts. In the new industrial towns, more and more adolescents and young adults went out to work daily and lived either in their parents' homes or in lodgings. This change was clearly documented by Michael Anderson in his studies of 19th-century Lancashire. Comparing census data for Preston in 1851 with a sample of rural areas from which people had migrated to Preston, he found that in the latter over 30 per cent of boys and girls aged 15–19 were in service, while in Preston only 3 per cent were; and the proportion of young persons living at home with their parents was markedly higher in industrial Preston than it was in rural areas. 'Children remained at home much longer in Preston than they did in the rural areas of Lancashire, and, surely also, than they had in pre-industrial England.'[53]

Most old people lived with their kin, especially when widowed. The Lancashire textile industry employed many women workers, and a grandmother living at home was about the best solution to the problem of looking after young children. Among women with children under ten, 29 per cent of those with a grandmother in the house went out to work, compared with 12 per cent of those with no non-employed person at home. 'These figures are highly suggestive of some link between grandmothers, child care, and working mothers.'[54] Other solutions included other close kin or a friendly lodger living at home, and close relatives living next door or just up the street, while the paid child-minder was a last resort in a very few cases. It seems, then, that the rise of industry led to family members living together or in close proximity, and created bigger family groups and greater cohesion than in pre-industrial times, not the other way about.

Such changes could be expected to result in a decline in the proportion of large households with living-in servants, and also perhaps a decline in the proportion of very small households (though people in lodgings were a complicating factor), along with a corresponding rise in the proportion of middling-sized households. In fact these are exactly the changes that appear from Laslett's data for England and Wales, which show falls in the proportions of households of 6 and over, and also of single-person households, while those of 2, 3, and 4-person households increased.[55]

This redistribution of people among households, however, took place at a time when mean household size was rising, presumably because of the rise in fertility which, as noted above, had started before the industrial revolution, and which culminated in the early 19th century. By all available measures, indeed, family size reached its peak at that time: the annual birth-rate in 1815, the five-year average gross reproduction rate in 1816 and net reproduction rate in 1821, the number of children aged under 15 per 1000 adults aged 25–59 in 1826, and the mean household size between 1821 and 1851.[56] Thereafter fertility fell, but not much, and large families continued to be normal until the end of the 19th century. From those awesome family groups in early photographs we can see that at least some people in the mid-19th century had big families; but we should not project the image much further back in time and suppose that they had even bigger families in the even remoter pre-industrial past. It is generally a mistake to read history backwards.

On the side of mortality, as already noted, it seems that the fall in the death-rate from the 1740s onwards began before the industrial revolution, was attributable mainly to the application of science to medicine and to agriculture along with improved transport, and had little to do with the rise of industry in the shape of steam engines, coal mining, iron smelting, and textile manufacturing. Indeed, the impact of industrialization on mortality was decidedly adverse. Towns had always been unhealthy places, and though that did not much affect the national death-rate as long as urban populations were small, the 'health of towns problem' became more severe with the rapid urban growth associated with industrial development. Outbreaks of cholera in the 1830s, 40s, and 50s in the grossly insanitary conditions of London and the new industrial towns raised the issue at the level of national politics, public health measures to install drains and safe water supplies becoming involved with a radical reorganization of local government.[57] These problems may well have checked the long slow fall in the death-rate, which went below twenty-one in 1830 but stayed at and above that level till the 1880s.

It should now be clear that latter-day western family life is not the creature of the industrial revolution. William J. Goode, one of the first to recognize this, concluded that the family itself must be judged to have had an independent effect upon industrialization; a form of the family emphasizing the husband–wife–child unit may well have been 'a facilitating factor for industrialization, rather than the other way around'.[58] The tradition of 'life-cycle service' involving migration in search of employment afforded a ready-made basis for new forms of industrial employment. In the process, the rise of industry and the growth of towns may have made it possible for individuals and couples to escape from the constant surveillance and tight social controls of village communities dominated by parson, squire, and well-to-do farmers into the relative anonymity of town life, and so accentuated a trend towards greater privacy for the nuclear family household that had already begun among the affluent. Yet for others there was not all that much privacy. According to Anderson, 'In the working classes, too, by the late 19th century there was emerging a cult of "home sweet home", though here this movement seems mainly based in a desire to preserve a little self-respect and secrecy ("keeping yourself to yourself") in what typically remained a public world of small, overcrowded houses, thin walls, public street life and precarious hold over respectability.'[59] That was the world of which Robert Roberts wrote with extraordinary vividness in *The Classic Slum*.[60]

THE DEMOGRAPHIC REVOLUTION: 2 FAMILY LIMITATION

It is a moot point whether conscious, deliberate family limitation by married couples played a part in the system of preventive checks that resulted in slow or zero population growth at times before the industrial revolution and the demographic transition, such as especially in late 17th-century England. There has been much debate about one English village, Colyton in Devon, which because of its exceptionally complete parish register – uninterrupted from 1538, when clergy were first obliged to register baptisms, weddings, and burials, to and beyond 1837 after which civil registration was introduced – was among the first to be studied by new methods of family reconstitution from registration data adopted in Cambridge in the 1960s. Analysing those results, Wrigley found that before 1770 the average age of women at first marriage was consistently high, varying from 26 to 30 and over, and that for long periods men on the average married women older than themselves. Further, Wrigley found indications of family limitation in birth spacing; in a steep fall in fertility in the later years of married women's fertile period; and in some cases a long interval between the penultimate and the last birth, suggesting that the last was either an accident or a deliberate reversal of an earlier decision to have no more. There was no direct evidence of what method might have been used, and Wrigley thought *coitus interruptus* the most likely. He called the whole system of practices 'a very flexible response to economic and social conditions'.[61] Levine's subsequent research, cited above, into Colyton's history confirmed that judgement and went into more detail about the economic depression to which those practices were a response.

Wrigley's tentative conclusion was later controverted.[62] However, evidence consistent with the deliberate control of fertility within marriage, though not conclusively demonstrating it, came to light in the analysis of short-term variations in fertility and mortality carried out as part of Wrigley and Schofield's fuller study of 404 parish registers. This revealed a close association between marriages and births up to nine months later, but not for the obvious reason; even allowing for bridal pregnancy, most of the association was *not* due to births from the new marriages. It seemed as if both nuptiality and the fertility of pre-existing marriages were responding to some other sets of factors, so that perhaps times judged favourable or unfavourable for marriage were likewise judged good or bad for already-married couples to have more children.[63]

Another case in point, involving seemingly deliberate preventive checks to population growth in an agrarian society albeit at a somewhat later period, is that of Ireland. Before 1847, according to Joel Mokyr, Irish marriage patterns were much like those elsewhere in Europe, while marital fertility was high, and population grew at about the same rather rapid rate as that in Britain. Though poorly housed and clothed, the Irish were comparatively well fed. The potato, introduced from the New World in the late 16th century, had proved a high-yielding and previously reliable basic food crop (far more reliable, indeed, than the cereals on which most of the rest of Europe depended) which when supplemented with milk and other protein sources had afforded a fully adequate diet.[64] According to older authorities including K. H. Connell and David Glass, reliance on the potato had enabled population growth to be sustained through the division of land-holdings. This process came to an abrupt end in 1845–7 when the crop was blighted, a natural disaster which changed the whole course of Irish history. In the ensuing famine, the population of the twenty-six counties of Catholic Ireland (later the Irish Republic) fell by 1.6 million as many died and many emigrated, mostly to the United States. Connell wrote that the experience of the famine years taught the Irish the wisdom of keeping the family farm whole;[65] while Glass likewise stated that

the fragmentation of holdings went no further. Instead, it became customary, as it had been before the potato era, for the farm to be passed intact to one child. A father would, during his own lifetime, arrange the marriage of the chosen son and hand the farm to him, retaining certain rights to support during old age. The dowry brought in by the bride would be used partly to compensate the father for giving up his farm, partly to satisfy the claims of other children.

The latter might be set up in business or a profession, helped to move to town or to emigrate. Daughters too went abroad to save for their own dowries in the hope of marrying and even buying a farm on their eventual return. But many remained single – as many as one woman in four, one man in three – and those who did marry tended to do so at a late age. Married fertility remained high; but the combined effect of restraints upon marriage with emigration was that the population of the twenty-six counties declined continuously from 5.1 million in 1851, shortly after the famine, to just under 3 million in 1946.[66]

Elsewhere in western Europe, however, for most of the 19th century high fertility and falling mortality resulted in rapid population growth, partly absorbed by internal migration to the new industrial towns, partly in overseas migration. This was above all the period when temperate lands in north America, Australia, New Zealand, and southern Africa were occupied by people of north-western European descent, and when many European families had cousins overseas, though with the passing of the generations the relationship became more distant.

Then, almost everywhere in Europe, fertility began to fall sharply and markedly at dates between 1880 and 1920. Even if this represented in part a return to former family limitation practices, there can be little doubt that it went far beyond them. Both quantitatively and qualitatively this was a new development resulting, not from decisions to postpone or eschew marriage, but mainly from married couples' decisions to have only a limited number of children. The centuries-old link between nuptiality and fertility was broken, and marriage ceased to be 'the hinge on which the demographic system turned'.

Far ahead of the rest of Europe, this development took place first in France, where, as Carr-Saunders pointed out as long ago as the 1930s the birth-rate followed the death-rate downwards from 1800 onwards and there was no period of rapid population increase like that in most other European countries.[67] France apart, the adoption of a small family system (in Carr-Saunders' phrase) seems to have occurred everywhere in Europe at about the same time around 1900; and according to the Princeton demographers Etienne van de Walle and John Knodel, this change took place 'under remarkably diverse socio-economic and demographic conditions'.[68] Thus in Britain the industrial revolution had well-nigh run its course, and most people lived in towns and worked in occupations other than agriculture, when fertility began to decline in about 1880 following the publicity for contraceptive methods surrounding the trials of Annie Besant and Charles Bradlaugh in 1876-7.[69] Hungary, however, was still an overwhelmingly agrarian country when fertility started to decline there, as it did about the same time. So was France when its much earlier transition began around 1800, and Bulgaria at the onset of its decline a century later. Infant mortality was still high in England and Wales, even among the middle classes, who could not realistically have expected that all their children would survive when they started to limit their families after the Bradlaugh–Besant trials. 'Literacy was also at very different levels when fertility began to fall', low in France, Hungary, and Bulgaria, for example, and high in England and Wales. Van de Walle and Knodel therefore questioned the presumption that the small family system was closely linked with, and probably the result of, the rise of industry. A different interpretation would place less emphasis on economic factors and material conditions, and lay more stress on the spread of ideas and attitudes in the cultural realm. Among them, perhaps the crucially important idea was that of having only a limited number of children, usually when quite young (women aged 20–24), and then stopping. That made all the difference between natural fertility, even when as a result of poor diet or practices such as late weaning that was quite low, and in van de Walle and Knodel's sense of the term 'family limitation'.

In retrospect, the demographic revolution in a country such as Britain seems a slow, leisurely affair, extending over two centuries from 1740 when the death-rate started to fall to 1940 when the fall in the birth-rate came to an end; and even then, there have since been 'baby-booms' with quite wide fluctuations in fertility. The sequence has since been re-enacted at high speed in Japan between 1920 and 1950, and may possibly occur in some Third World countries. Assessing its consequences for western family life: first and foremost, we now live much longer than our ancestors. We marry earlier, certainly, than our ancestors did in the 18th century. We have fewer children, and we have them while we are younger, exercising deliberate control of our fertility, and stopping when we judge we have enough. As a result, compared with past ages, those married couples who go on living together do so for longer after the marriage of their last child, and widowed persons do so independently in a single-person household after the death of one spouse (usually the husband). Mean household sizes have therefore fallen very low indeed in the 20th century compared with earlier centuries. But as people live longer to enjoy grandparenthood, three-generation family ties have become more important, and four-generation family relationships are not uncommon.

The transformation of these aspects of our family life, even over a comparatively short period of sixty years, was vividly brought out by Paul C. Glick in his estimates of the median ages at which turning-point events took place in the lives of women in the United States in 1890 and 1950. If the conditions prevailing in 1890 had persisted throughout her lifetime, a woman's typical experience would have been to marry at 22 and have her last child when she was nearly 32. When her last child married she would be 55, already a widow for two years, and have 12 years to live. By contrast, earlier marriage, fewer children, and longer life meant that in 1950 conditions a woman's typical experience was to marry at just over 20 and have her last child at 26. When her last child married she would be not yet 48 and have nearly 30 years to live, 14 of them with her husband.[70] If they stayed together, that is; the point has a bearing on divorce, to which I now turn.

THE DIVORCE REVOLUTION

This latest revolution in western family life has been brought about by a long, slow, gradual, but eventually overwhelming increase in the numbers of divorces and the availability and social acceptability of divorce that has had its full effect only since 1960.

As already noted, it was at the time of the Reformation in the 16th century that Protestant churches first conceded the principle that in some circumstances a valid marriage might be dissolved; but on the whole they did so reluctantly, deploring divorce while accepting that it might sometimes be a lesser evil. Divorce long remained the rare exception to the rule of lifelong monogamy, 'till death us do part'; it was not part of most people's ordinary experience or expectation, but shameful, stigmatised, associated with immorality and loose living. In many countries it was also very expensive, a luxury for the dissolute rich, not available to ordinary people. So while in Catholic countries no legal provision was made for divorce at all, even in countries where the Church of Rome lost its ascendancy the numbers divorcing long remained small. Thus in England and Wales before 1857 only one or two divorces a year went through the cumbersome and costly procedure culminating in a private Act of Parliament. After that date, when judicial divorce was introduced, the numbers jumped to a few hundred a year, but fewer than 1000 decrees a year were being granted on the eve of the First World War.

Divorce was less uncommon in the United States. The founding fathers' determination that there was to be no established religion ensured from the first that marriage and divorce were matters for the civil law. Later, anomalies arising from the widely diverse laws of the different states were to some extent overcome by 'migratory divorces' of the kind long popularly associated with Reno, Nevada. According to the estimate made at the time by W. F. Willcox of Cornell University, there were 72,000 divorces in the United States in 1906, 'about double the number reported for that year from all the rest of the Christian world'.[71] High and steadily rising divorce rates in the United States, along with falling mortality, had already led Willcox in 1891 to forecast that eventually the two curves would intersect, and that by 1980 as many marriages would be dissolved by divorce as by death.[72] As will appear below, that must count as one of the most accurate social science projections ever made.

Although the highest and most steadily-rising divorce rate has always been that of the United States, throughout the western world there has been a rising trend in divorce, especially since 1900. This has been associated with changes in the law, as provision has been made for divorce in some states where it was formerly unavailable, while in others the grounds for divorce have been extended, and administrative changes have made it less costly and more available to people of all classes. In addition to this generally rising trend, the enforced separations, hastily-contracted marriages, and other abnormal circumstances associated with two world wars led to big increases in the numbers of divorces. Although on both occasions the numbers fell back after reaching their peak, respectively in 1919–20 and 1947, the level was higher than before the war. Thus although the actual numbers now seem small, in England and Wales even after the post-war peak had passed the rate of petitioning more than doubled between 1913 and 1922. Many people previously unacquainted with divorce had had relatives or friends involved, and an unwillingness to condemn war-time divorces extended into the 1920s and 1930s. After the Second World War there was a similar sequence of events but at much higher levels, and in 1950 the rate of petitioning was more than four times as high as it had been in 1937.[73] Similar trends were reported in virtually every western country except Sweden, where there was no post-war peak, presumably because they had not been at war.[74]

Then, throughout the western world, divorce rates fell during the 1950s and appeared to stablilize at levels which though higher than before the war were far below the post-war peak. This contributed in no small part to a generally optimistic mood about the stability of family life at a time when there were many other reasons for optimism. The devastations of war had come to an end, Europe had made a remarkably rapid economic recovery with United States aid, there was full employment with low rates of inflation, and material conditions were better than ever before. Men were home from the war; and women too were back at home after what had been thought of as the wholly exceptional expedient, justifiable only in the desperate emergency of war, of their employment on a large scale in war production. That golden age of family life – or of a certain kind of family life – coincided with the golden age of a certain kind of sociology, namely functionalist sociology, (a point I take up in Chapter 4) at a time when it was still possible to think of lifelong monogamy as the norm and divorce as the comparatively rare exception.

But after 1960 the underlying upward trend reasserted itself, along with important shifts in public, legal, and religious opinion. In England, following the deliberations of a commission appointed by the Archbishop of Canterbury,[75] the Church of England's attitude was modified, and the way was cleared for an Act passed in 1969 (to come into effect in 1971) abandoning the old doctrine of the matrimonial offence and establishing a single ground for divorce, namely the irretrievable breakdown of the marriage. In 1969 also a new law was enacted in California with a similar effect, establishing the principle that has become known as 'no-fault divorce'; and broadly similar laws were introduced in almost all other states of the United States during the 1970s. It is hard to disentangle cause from effect in such matters; on the one hand the new laws doubtless facilitated more divorce, but on the other hand it may have been in response to a growing demand for divorce that they were enacted. Be that as it may, after 1970 the curve rose even more sharply. By the late 1970s, Willcox's forecast had been fulfilled with just a few years to spare, and in the United States more marriages were ending each year in divorce than in death.[76]

Although the trend had not gone quite so far in other western countries, that surely marked an important turning-point, indicating departures on a considerable scale from the norm of lifelong monogamy. In England and Wales, to indicate the actual numbers involved, before 1914 under 1000 divorce decrees were granted annually; by the 1930s, approximately 4000. The post-war peak in 1947 was 58,000, and by the late 1950s the numbers had dropped to around 23,000 a year. After 1960 they rose, slowly at first, jumping to over 100,000 a year in the early 1970s, and not far short of 150,000 a year in the

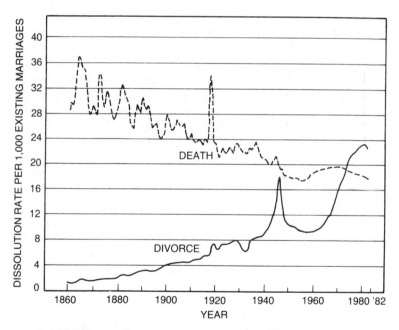

Fig. 1. Marital dissolutions per 1000 existing marriages, by divorce and death: USA, 1860–1982.
Source: Arland Thornton and Deborah Freedman, 'The Changing American Family', *Population Bulletin*, vol. 38, no. 4, Population Reference Bureau, Inc., Washington, DC, 1983.

early 1980s. Here as in the United States the numbers then appeared to level off, but it is too soon to tell at the time of writing if that will continue. In the early 1980s, too, nearly one marriage in three was a remarriage after divorce for one or both partners.[77]

Although it is difficult to assess the possible long-term consequences, already we can see the effects in a wider diversity and greater complexity in family relationships. While many if not most people still practise lifelong monogamy, for growing numbers of others being married to more than one spouse in succession ('sequential polygamy' or 'serial monogamy') has become a life-experience that has come to arouse less and less social disapproval. With an increasing readiness to end an unsatisfactory marriage, especially in the face of long expectations of life, average durations of marriage to divorce have been reduced, and average ages at divorce and remarriage have fallen; women who divorce and remarry mostly do so by the age of thirty-five. More and more children spend some of their childhood years in the care of a lone parent, usually the mother. When she remarries, they acquire a stepfather, but without necessarily losing touch with a still-living father; and if he remarries they gain a non-co-resident stepmother. 'Access' visiting leads to families of remarriage being linked in 'divorce chains', the more so if divorced ex-spouses do not sever all relations and if their new spouses form new ones. Parents who remarry while they still have custody of children from previous marriages set up complex households in which some children were formerly hers, others his, and there may be a third set of children born to the new union. In such a household the children collectively have four, not two, pairs of grandparents. I try to deal in more detail with these and other complexities in chapter 14, but I doubt if we have yet grasped the full implications of this, the latest revolution in our family life.

SUGGESTIONS FOR FURTHER READING

Jack Goody, *The Development of the Family and Marriage in Europe*, Cambridge, Cambridge University Press, 1983
Alan Macfarlane, *The Origins of English Individualism: The Family, Property, and Social Transition*, Oxford, Blackwell, 1978
Peter Laslett and Richard Wall (eds.), *Household and Family in Past Time*, Cambridge, Cambridge University Press, 1972

Peter Laslett, *Family Life and Illicit Love in Earlier Generations*, Cambridge, Cambridge University Press, 1977

Linda A. Pollock, *Forgotten Children: Parent–Child Relations from 1500 to 1900*, Cambridge, Cambridge University Press, 1983

Alan Macfarlane, *The Family Life of Ralph Josselin, a Seventeenth-Century Clergyman*, Cambridge, Cambridge University Press, 1970

Michael Anderson, *Family Structure in Nineteenth-Century Lancashire*, Cambridge, Cambridge University Press, 1971

Ferdinand Mount, *The Subversive Family: An Alternative History of Love and Marriage*, London, Unwin, 1983

J. Hajnal, 'European marriage patterns in perspective', in D. V. Glass and D. E. C. Eversley (eds.), *Population in History: Essays in Historical Demography*, London, Edward Arnold, 1965, pp. 101–43

Griselda Rowntree and Norman H. Carrier, 'The resort to divorce in England and Wales, 1858–1957', *Population Studies*, vol. 9, 1958, pp. 188–233

3

Maternal care and maternal deprivation

In the sociology of family life that developed in the 1950s, prime attention was paid to the maternal role in children's early development. In the United States this concern was central to Talcott Parsons' analysis, as detailed in the next chapter. In Britain it was most powerfully expressed in the life work of John Bowlby (b. 1907), physician, psychiatrist, and psychologist, who in the 1940s and 1950s strongly maintained that depriving children of maternal care was liable to have seriously adverse consequences for their physical health and mental development. The evidence he amassed included studies of children in old-fashioned 'institutions' such as orphanages, where, like patients in hospital, they were housed in wards and looked after by nurses working shifts, so could not attach themselves to one mother-substitute. Bowlby also reviewed studies of the children of women in prisons; children deprived of maternal care temporarily because of their own or their mothers' illness in hospital; children evacuated from British cities under threat of air attack at the start of the Second World War; and his own study of forty-four juvenile thieves. Temporary deprivation, as in hospital, was found to result in loss of sleep, appetite, and weight; listless, quiet, unhappy, withdrawn behaviour; regression, such as bed-wetting; and susceptibility to minor infections. On return to a normal family life, children who had been temporarily separated went through a long period of demanding, attention-seeking behaviour, as if testing their mothers' affection to breaking-point. Permanent deprivation, as in the old-fashioned orphanage, was associated with physical and mental retardation in which the normal development of speech, intelligence, and school performance were impaired. There was an inability to make and keep friends, relationships were shallow, and Bowlby found an 'affectionless' personality in some of his young thieves.

Bowlby summarized these studies in a monograph published in 1951 by the World Health Organization, and republished in 1953 and 1965 in a slightly simplified version as a popular paperback.[1] These publications became highly influential, not only as a scientific thesis embodying a theory or set of propositions and the evidence upon which they were founded, but also in their implications for social policy. Under their influence, old-fashioned orphanages and children's homes were reorganized into small groups, with children of different ages under the care of 'houseparents' in a setting more like that of conventional family life. Legal and social-work policies concerning adoption and fostering were profoundly affected, with a greater emphasis on keeping children with their mothers and avoiding traumatic separations wherever possible. It became almost a dogma in the training of social workers, indeed, that only the most extreme considerations would justify parting a child from his or her natural mother, a dogma called in question in some notorious and much-publicised cases of child abuse in more recent years. There has been public and official pressure on hospitals to allow unrestricted visiting of children by their mothers, and even to make it possible for them to stay overnight; pressure that has had some effect, despite the traditional attitude of some nurses that parental visits only unsettle the young patients in their care. Most widely of all, Bowlby's work raised serious doubts about the propriety of mothers of young children going out to work or, indeed, leaving them for any other reason.

In his later work,[2] Bowlby drew support from the findings of research on behaviour in animals other than human, including studies of maternal deprivation among (for instance) monkeys, with findings remarkably like his own.[3] Though he may have been influenced to some extent by the psychoanalytical school of Sigmund Freud and his followers, Bowlby's work lacked the heavy Freudian apparatus of ego, super-ego, id, infantile sexuality and its repression, the unconscious and the subconscious. There was little more than a general presumption that what happens to people when they are very young greatly, and perhaps permanently and irrevocably, shapes their adult personality and behaviour. Such a view certainly did not originate with Freud; on the contrary, it has been the taken-for-granted common sense of western thought ever since Plato.[4]

For the sociology of the family, Bowlby's thesis entails concentrating attention on the mother–child unit as primary, while the husband/father is seen as having a mainly supportive role, including emotional as well as economic support, assuring the wife/mother of long-term security during the children's dependence. Implicitly it is congruent with a division of labour between the sexes in which the father goes out to work while the mother stays at home to look after the children. Such a model, assailed by latter-day feminists, is very like that of Talcott Parsons to which I turn in the next chapter; Parsons, indeed, might well have based his work on Bowlby's at this point, though he did not do so, and relied rather on the classical psychoanalytical work of Freud.

Bowlby encapsulated his thesis in a statement, usually taken as definitive:

> What is believed to be essential for mental health is that the infant and young child should experience a warm, intimate, and continuous relationship with his mother (or permanent mother-substitute; one who steadily 'mothers' him) in which both find satisfaction and enjoyment.[5]

It will be noted that Bowlby expressly accepted the possibility of a mother-substitute. He clearly saw the relationship in terms of interaction, not in biological or genetic terms; and he does not seem to have said, or implied, that the person who 'mothers' need be the woman who bore the child. He did not even say that that person need be female, though his use of the feminine word 'mother' as both noun and verb might seem to imply as much. On these points, it seems possible that ideas may have been mistakenly attributed to Bowlby in subsequent controversies which he did not hold, or express.

As the English social scientist and magistrate Barbara Wootton remarked in 1959, however, engaging with Bowlby's thesis is not made any easier by a certain elusiveness, and by the way he kept expressing it in different terms.[6] Sometimes he emphasized actual physical separation:

> The actual physical separation from the mother in early childhood, to the extent that it involves privation or deprivation of a relationship of

dependence with a mother-figure, will have an adverse effect on personality development, particularly with respect to the capacity for forming and maintaining satisfactory object relations.[7]

The words 'will have' may be noted in that passage. Elsewhere, though, Bowlby tended more cautiously to say 'may have'; and he was indeed always 'puzzled as to why some children succumb to deprivation while others appear to be unaffected', although, as he pointed out, the fact that not all children exposed to tuberculosis or polio actually contract those diseases does not mean that we should dream of intentionally submitting children to such hazards.[8]

Moreover, though perhaps less in Bowlby's own work than in that of others derived from it, more emphasis may be placed on rejection that on actual physical separation, though to be sure one outcome of rejection may be separation. Actual separation, moreover, may be interpreted by the child as rejection, in some cases in fulfilment of a threat of 'Be good or I'll send you away.' As Wootton pointed out, it may actually strengthen the case for the break-up of a family if in consequence the children come into the care of someone from whom warm continuous affection is forthcoming, more so than from their own mother. It can equally well be argued that children may be deprived of maternal care, though physically not separated, if the quality of their mother's care or their relations with her are poor.

Wootton remarked that when the great English social reformer Elizabeth Fry exposed the insanitary conditions in 19th-century prisons, 'no one applauded her for the discovery that good sanitary conditions were to be desired; the merit of her work was its demonstration that such conditions were not to be found in prisons'. In just the same way, Bowlby's readers needed no convincing of the importance of maternal care: 'even the best work on maternal deprivation [had] obscured its own genuine discoveries by highlighting what are little more than platitudes'. Its chief value was 'its incidental exposure of the prevalence of deplorable patterns of institutional upbringing, and of the crass indifference of certain hospitals to childish sensitivities'. This research had excellent practical effects in reforming children's homes and hospitals. Where the bad old methods survived, children would suffer in various ways and to various degrees, in some cases 'in a well-marked pattern of indifference to everybody except themselves, of which one of the expressions is repeated stealing'. But 'that the damage is life-long or irreversible, that maternal deprivation is a major factor in criminal behaviour, or that the younger the child the greater the risk, all these must be regarded as quite unproven hypotheses'.[9]

On institutional care, Bowlby did state in his 1951 monograph that 'children thrive better in bad homes than in good institutions', and added that 'the attachment of children to parents who by all ordinary standards are very bad is a never-ceasing source of wonder to those who seek to help them'.[10] According to Michael Rutter:

his early dictum was widely accepted and led to a very marked reluctance by some Children's Officers to remove children from even appalling home circumstances ... Actually, there is no satisfactory evidence in support of the dictum 'better a bad family than a good institution'. Taken at its face value it seems to imply some mystical quality present in the family and suggests that the quality of mothering provided is irrelevant. This is such obvious nonsense (and certainly not intended by Bowlby) that it scarcely warrants serious consideration.

The development of children in the worst families, including those where baby-battering occurs, is so bad, that even an institution may be preferable. Children reared in institutions certainly do worse than the general population, but the outcome for many children from the best institutions is reasonably satisfactory; and the frequency of deviant behaviour in institutional children, though above average for the population as a whole, is below that of children from the most disturbed and loveless homes.[11]

Twenty years after the publication of Bowlby's monograph, Rutter, in reviewing the vast array of research it had stimulated was concerned to disaggregate the central concept of maternal deprivation. Do we mean deprivation or privation, loss or lack? Are we, in particular cases, concerned with the effects upon children of having some form of care and then being deprived of it, or of never having had it at all? And of what forms of care? Diet? Could the retardation of children in orphanages, in those early studies cited by Bowlby, be attributed to poor diet? – unfortunately it does not seem to have been recorded. What are the effects of, respectively, lack and loss of sensory stimulation? – for example, when young children are left for long periods lying on their backs seeing nothing but the ceiling of a hospital ward. Lack or loss of social stimulation could be difficult to distinguish from lack or loss of sensory stimulation, but their effects could extend to the development or impairment of language skills and, among older children, of wider mental horizons; and Rutter cited studies suggesting that children brought up in very small isolated communities might be somewhat adversely affected in these respects. Likewise, and perhaps even more important, the effects of failure to form bonds should be distinguished from those of the disruption of bonds once formed. Rutter re-examined Bowlby's forty-four case-histories of juvenile thieves, and found that the 'affectionless' characters among them were strongly associated, not so much with prolonged separation, as with multiple changes of mother-figure in infancy or early childhood. And do the bonds have to be with the mother, or can bonds with others serve the same purpose? Bowlby evidently thought that relationships with playmates, for instance, were quite different from those with the mother, and reserved the term attachment for the bond with the mother alone. However as already noted, he saw mothering purely in terms of social interaction, and argued for instance that feeding was not an essential part of it. That being so, while it was true that another child of the same age could hardly provide what was necessary for a strong stable attachment, there did not seem any reason why any adult or even an older child could not do so. Rutter further distinguished bonding, caretaking, and play as different aspects of 'mothering' which might or might not be performed by the same person. It might be hypothesized that so long as all three were available, the ill effects of 'affectionless psychopathy' might be prevented, no matter who provided them, and whether or not the mother did so. Indeed, although Bowlby used the term 'monotropy' and argued that the primary bond had to be with one person, Rutter concluded that the admittedly sparse evidence suggested otherwise.

The father, the mother, brothers and sisters, friends, school-teachers and others all have an impact on development, but their influence and importance differs for different aspects of development. A less exclusive focus on the mother is required. Children also have fathers![12]

Another aspect of Bowlby's thesis was criticised by the psychologists Alan and Ann Clarke, namely the supposed irreversibility and permanence of the ill effects of maternal deprivation – an implied assumption that had already been questioned by Barbara Wootton. The Clarkes set out to show that, on the contrary, the harm is remediable. They did not deny that the experience in question is harmful; indeed, the case-studies they reviewed included some quite horrifying accounts of maltreatment. Perhaps the most striking occurred in Czechoslovakia, where according to Jarmila Koluchová the authorities gradually became aware of the plight of twin boys who were isolated, kept indoors, underfed, and cruelly chastised. On their removal into care at the age of seven, they could hardly walk, and their mental ages were about three. Their speech was retarded, they were unfamiliar with and afraid of such things as traffic in the street, and they were terrified of the dark. After some months in a children's home, they were placed in a foster home, yet it was no conventional family but two unmarried sisters, one of whom had previously adopted a child. In fifteen months their mental ages advanced by three years, and they were able to leave the special school for the mentally retarded and enter an ordinary primary school where they made good progress. By the time they were fourteen their intelligence was normal. Deep emotional bonds formed between the boys and their foster family, and many of the consequences of deprivation – such as a narrow outlook, and a small range of emotional expression – which persisted while they were in the children's home, gradually diminished.[13] So far from proving irremediable, then, the harm done to those two boys in their first seven years was in fact remedied by loving care in their later childhood and early adolescence.

As the Clarkes insisted, it is important to be clear what is *not* being said by way of criticism of Bowlby's thesis:

The swing of the pendulum which resulted from Bowlby's 1951 monograph had many humane effects, sensitising the public to the needs of children. It would be more than unfortunate if [there were to be] a reaction against the new humanism, on the mistaken grounds that 'it doesn't matter what happens early in life'. Thus while the evidence does suggest that no mother of a very young child should feel bound to remain at home (provided satisfactory alternative caretaking arrangements can be made), equally no mother should feel that her responsibilities diminish after her child becomes older . . . There is absolutely no implication that infancy and early childhood are unimportant, only that their long-term role is *by itself* very limited . . . The whole of development is important, not merely the early years.[14]

However, there has been a reassertion of Bowlby's central theme in the work of Mia Kellmer Pringle and the UK National Children's Bureau. Kellmer Pringle accepted Rutter's disaggregation of the concepts of maternal care and deprivation, and considered in detail the needs of children and how they are to be met. She gave some prominence to the father's role, and wrote of 'parenting – a shared task' rather than 'mothering'. She was concerned to dispel myths, such as that it is necessarily best if the biological mother cares for a child, or that having a child is important for a woman's self-fulfilment. The second, indeed, she repudiated with particular vigour, because it involves putting another's interest before that of the child; it 'sacrifices the child's welfare to that of the adult'. Being able to care for children well is 'neither dependent on, nor necessarily consequent upon, biological parenthood'. Yet it seems clearly to be her unstated major premise throughout that children are normally looked after by their mothers, with some help from their fathers; so the very next question she asked was 'How are women – and men for that matter too – to decide whether they are really cut out for parenthood? whether they possess the unselfishness, patience, sensitivity and physical stamina to cope with all its demands?' In a world where women now have the choice, motherhood should be a well-informed choice, not swayed by any glamourized mother-and-baby image; and women who choose motherhood should devote themselves to it full-time during their children's infancy.

Women should no longer be subjected to the twin pressures to marry and have children, yet to feel that they are 'wasting their education' or are otherwise 'unfulfilled' if they devote themselves full-time to childcare. While it was the destiny of yesterday's woman to raise a family, today it can be her choice. Henceforth only those willing to devote some years to this task should contemplate it; and they should then receive recognition for undertaking one of the most crucial tasks for society's future.

Arguably, that should include pay; and as a corollary, Kellmer Pringle asked whether there should not be 'sufficiently generous allowances to enable one parent (including a single parent) to look after young children full time . . . in preference to an outside paid job?'[15]

More than thirty years after the publication of his WHO monograph, then, Bowlby's views continued to be the subject of lively controversy. Yet, viewed in a historical perspective, it might be argued that he said nothing new. The evidence from the studies whose findings he drew together did no more than afford scientific warrant for what people in western societies had always known and practised. As Pollock emphasized, children's needs for affection and for play to further their normal development have been recognized for centuries, while parents generally have always cared for their children and taken pleasure and satisfaction from seeing them grow in health and happiness.[16] If the image of loving motherhood needed any reinforcement, it was surely to be found in Christian representations of the Nativity. Bowlby's 'warm, intimate, and continuous relationship' between mother and child 'in which both find satisfaction and enjoyment' can hardly be reckoned as a major scientific discovery of the mid 20th century.

However, Bowlby wrote at a time when large numbers of children had recently been taken from their familiar surroundings in the war-time evacuation of British cities, with undoubtedly traumatic effects in many cases; and when large numbers of women, including mothers of young children, worked in war factories and did other kinds of war work. There may well have been a feeling at that time that the harm done to children must be counted as part of the untold cost of war, and that such measures could be justified only as a last resort in that extreme emergency. The favourable public attention paid to Bowlby's report, if not the report itself, can be seen in retrospect as manifesting that mood of the 1950s in which things were regarded as returning to normal, family life was regaining its stability, and women were free once more to devote themselves to home-making and child-care.

Thirty years on, such memories had faded, and as detailed in chapter 9 large numbers of married women had again entered employment outside the home, this time not in response to emergency conditions but on a regular basis. Meanwhile, many women had come to experience the idealized mother–child relationship, not as freedom, but rather as a form of servitude, that of the housebound mother, Hannah Gavron's 'captive wife', imprisoned daily within the confines of the home and enslaved to the clamant needs of young children. [17]

Further, while no one seriously denies that children need loving care and suffer terribly for lack or loss of it, some of Bowlby's incidental contentions have been questioned. It is seriously doubted whether he was right about 'monotropy', or the need for a child to form a particularly strong attachment to one mother-figure; and a soberly responsible case can be made out for the view that a child's experience may even be enriched and its development enhanced by regular interaction with a limited number of other adults – father, grandparents, aunts, friends and neighbours – each making their own different contribution to the child's needs. Thus, as noted above, neither Rutter nor the Clarkes saw any reason why the mother of young children should not go out to work, provided satisfactory arrangements were made for them to be cared for in her absence by others with whom they had good relationships. Such arrangements have no doubt liberated many who would otherwise have been involuntarily 'captive wives'. Others, however, accept Kellmer Pringle's view that no one should undertake motherhood unless she is prepared to devote herself to it full-time during the infancy of her children. The continuing controversy about working mothers and children's needs has obviously important implications for women's employment, women's careers, and family life, which I take up in later chapters.

SUGGESTIONS FOR FURTHER READING

John Bowlby, *Maternal Care and Mental Health*, Geneva, World Health Organization, 1951

Barbara Wootton, *Social Science and Social Pathology*, London, Allen and Unwin, 1959, ch. 4, 'Theories of the effects of maternal separation or deprivation'

Michael Rutter, *Maternal Deprivation Reassessed*, Harmondsworth, Penguin, 1972

Ann M. Clarke and A. D. B. Clarke, *Early Experience: Myth and Evidence*, London, Open Books, 1976

Doria Pilling and Mia Kellmer Pringle, *Controversial Issues in Child Development*, London, Elek, 1978

4

Sociological models of western family
life in the 1950s

The title of this chapter refers back to my contention in
chapter 2 that in the 1950s the golden age of the autonomous
nuclear family coincided with that of a kind of sociological
analysis, loosely termed functionalist, that flourished especially
in the United States. The analytical models then developed
were highly influential, partly because most of the sociology
ever done in the world has been done in the United States, and
partly because of what anthropologists used to call cultural lag:
ideas originating in the 1950s became the received wisdom in
the textbooks of the 1960s, and then in the 1970s served as
objects for rebuttal in the critical temper of the time. If we are
to make sense of recent controversies, then, it is well to begin
with those analytical models, the most influential of which
were those of Talcott Parsons and William J. Goode.

TALCOTT PARSONS AND THE NUCLEAR FAMILY

Talcott Parsons (1902–79) was by far the most eminent
American sociologist of his time, though paradoxically his
work stemmed almost entirely from European traditions of
social thought and owed little to the already established
schools of sociology in the United States.[1]

In his general theoretical approach, an important unit for
analysis was the social system, representing all the patterned,
institutionalized modes of interaction among the actors
(individual or corporate) who composed a group and occupied
roles within it. It was a concept equally applicable at all levels of
scale from the whole society of a nation-state down to a small
group such as a committee; and he said of the analysis of social
systems that 'it is expedient that it should be structural-

functional'.[2] By structure he meant 'those relations or aspects of the system which are sufficiently stable to enable us to treat them as constant', and the concept of role was crucial. The concept of function he derived at least in part from the social anthropologist Bronislaw Malinowski (1884–1942), who asked (in effect) of each of a society's institutions what contribution it made to meeting human needs and enabling the group to survive.[3] In Parsons' analysis, however, the emphasis shifted away from the flesh-and-blood survival of human populations to the maintenance of that abstraction, the social system itself.

Applying his general theoretical approach to the study of the family, Parsons concentrated on the nuclear family in contemporary United States society.[4] At the same time, however, he had strong grounds for regarding the nuclear family as a universal human grouping. In a study of 250 representative human societies, the anthropologist George P. Murdock had found that without exception the nuclear family was either the prevailing form of the family or the basic unit from which more complex forms were compounded;[5] while Parsons' colleague, Morris Zelditch Jr, found only one or two exceptions reported in the entire anthropological literature.[6] Though it has sometimes been questioned, indeed, there has continued to be general support among anthropologists for this thesis of the universality or near-universality of the nuclear or elementary family.[7]

In his analysis of the nuclear family as a social system, Parsons was much influenced by the work of another colleague, Robert F. Bales, in the experimental study of small groups in laboratory conditions.[8] Bales found leadership to be no simple matter, and distinguished two kinds. A group's instrumental leader, or task specialist, was the one who both initiated and received most communications, and most effectively organized the co-operative performance of requisite tasks. Such a one was not generally the best liked, however, and Bales identified also an expressive leader or social–emotional specialist whose prime concern was the others' feelings and the quality of group relations. Generally these were two different people; to be able to exercise both kinds of leadership was a gift rarely to be found in one person, and characterized perhaps the great leaders of history.

Viewed in this light, the social system of the nuclear family could be regarded as comprising just four roles:

Husband/father	Wife/mother
Son/brother	Daughter/sister

In this scheme, the generations were separated vertically along a hierarchy or power axis into leaders and followers, reflecting children's dependence on adults particularly in the early years. Instrumental leadership, which Parsons identified as the husband/father's role, was differentiated horizontally from expressive leadership, the role of the wife/mother. 'The universal fact that women are more intimately connected with early child-care than are men (with lactation playing a very fundamental part) is the primary reason why the feminine role, in the family as well as outside, tends to be more expressive in this sense than the masculine.'[9]

To carry out the family's functions of 'maintaining the emotional balances of all members of the family including the adults, and its paramount role as an agency for the socialization of children', there should be a strong coalition between two parents of opposite sex, with marriage as an important structural bond of solidarity transcending the parental functions. Each nuclear family group had to have a fairly long duration of a considerable span of years, but not an indefinite duration. 'One of its most important characteristics is that the family is a self-liquidating group', since as children grow up they marry, leave home, and establish new nuclear families of their own. Launching them into independence, indeed, was one of the family's functions. The family 'must be a group which permits and requires a high level of diffuse affective involvement of its members'; clearly living together for a long time was important. In the family more than in any other social group, the expression of affection should be amply provided for, yet carefully regulated. Sexual love ('genital eroticism') between spouses was their monopoly, institutionalized in marriage. It had to be distinguished from loving attachments ('pre-genital eroticism') between children and parents, especially the child's attachment to the mother, 'the "rope" by which she pulls him up from a lower to a higher level in the hard climb of "growing up"'.

Here Parsons drew heavily on Freud's account of the stages of development of the individual personality, in which eroticism was held to play a very important part. In the early stages, which Freud identified as oral, anal, and phallic, the mother was the object of the child's primary attachment. In the next stage, the child's overt erotic attachment to the mother had to be blocked and its drives redirected. Had to, in the case of boys, because its continuance would become incestuous; and as a matter of observation all societies prohibit mother–son incest, and hold it in particular horror, for reasons upon which Parsons attempted to throw some light. Since the nuclear family is centred on a sexual relationship between a woman and an unrelated man, at some stage boys' interests have to be directed outside the family. With girls the case is somewhat different; forced to abandon her primary attachment to her mother, it might seem that a girl's next object might be her father. But if that were allowed to happen, it would seriously weaken the leadership coalition of husband/father and wife/mother. Furthermore, if boys are to be encouraged to look for partners outside the family, this is only possible if girls do too. It follows that 'not only is the original object denied, but those "next in line", that is all other members of the original nuclear family, are tabooed' in the process of self-liquidation of each nuclear family. It should be added here that the Freudian theory of the incest taboo is not the only one, and I go into the question in more detail in chapter 7.

According to that theory, however, since the attachments formed in infancy were strong and 'addictive', they had to be even more strongly blocked. Hence the special intensity of the emotions aroused by the very thought of mother–son incest. By a typical Freudian inversion, what we most abominate is what we secretly most desire; prohibition, guilt, and desire are all 'really' the same.

Further, 'what Freud called the period of "latency" . . . seems to be the period in which the individual is above all learning to perform extrafamilial roles'. To some extent, children at this stage identify themselves with and model themselves on the parent of the same sex, and are so introduced to the men's world and the women's world respectively. But this still leaves unresolved the leader–follower relations of the nuclear family, which have to be broken if the latter is eventually to be self-liquidating. More important, in Parsons' view, was the one-sex peer group.

It seems to be significant that just at this period children begin to be much more independent of their families and to associate particularly with other children ... The phenomenon so familiar in Western society of the one-sex peer group seems to have a nearly universal counterpart to some extent elsewhere. [10]

Friendships with children of the same sex and about the same age 'reinforced the individual's self-categorization by sex', and furthered the child's independence of the authority and help of the parental generation.

'Adolescence comes only after a considerable period of this latency-level peer group activity', when the erotic drives had been redirected in such a way that they could now be channelled towards a person of opposite sex of about the same age, and one perceived as an equal, not a generation-superior. 'When all this has taken place the circle is closed by the individual's marriage and parenthood.' [11]

Parsons' theory represented, therefore, an ambitious attempt to integrate three sets of phenomena: the group dynamics of the nuclear family, and its developmental cycle through time; the age-old puzzle of the incest prohibition; and the one-sex peer group. On the last point at least he showed considerable prescience, for the tendency of the peer group to take on a life of its own, outside parental control and that of other agencies such as schools and youth organizations, became very marked in the United States and other western countries in the 1960s; I take up the question in chapter 8.

Parsons wrote of 'the isolation of the nuclear family' as characterizing the contemporary United States scene. By that he meant that adults' ties with their families of origin were weak, in contrast to the kinship systems of other societies where solidarity with wider kin was more pronounced. Consequently there was a sharper distinction between family members and others; and the former, particularly the marriage pair, were in a 'structurally unsupported situation', unable to lean for support on other adult kin. [12] However, 'isolation' was no doubt too strong a word, for Parsons consistently made it clear that the nuclear family cannot be a closed system. One reason for this has already been seen: it was essential for the developmental cycle that young people should find age-mates, and later marriage partners outside their families of origin.

Moreover, family members occupied other roles in other social systems in addition to their family roles. Of particular importance was the occupational role of the husband/father, which linked the family with the economy and determined the family's socio-economic status in the social stratification system.[13] Parsons made his view quite explicit that the solidarity of the conjugal unit was 'facilitated by the prevalence of the pattern that normally only *one* of its members has an occupational role which is of determinate significance for the status of the family as a whole', and that it was important that the wife and mother was either exclusively a housewife or at most had a 'job' rather than a 'career'.

By confining the number of status-giving occupational roles of the members of the effective conjugal unit to one, it eliminates any com-petition for status, especially as between husband and wife, which might be disruptive of the solidarity of marriage. So long as lines of achievement are segregated and not directly comparable, there is less opportunity for jealousy, a sense of inferiority, etc., to develop.[14]

It need hardly be said that that view gave rise to controversies, to which I refer in chapters 10 and 11.

Like Ferdinand Tönnies before him, Parsons saw the prevail-ing trend in advanced industrial societies as one towards a calculating impersonality that made for efficiency yet left many sides of human nature unsatisfied. Elaborating Tönnies' con-cepts of *Gemeinschaft* and *Gesellschaft* and Max Weber's four types of action, Parsons wrote of 'pattern variables' represent-ing contemporary trends from ascription to achievement, from diffuseness to specificity, from particularism to universalism, and from affectivity to affective neutrality.[15] Increasingly in such societies the family is the one remaining stronghold of warm, diffuse, affective relations. It is where we are valued for who we are rather than what we do (ascription rather than achievement); and where it is legitimate to favour family members above others (applying particular rather than univer-sal criteria), which outside the family would be stigmatised as 'nepotism' and run counter to all the principles of an open, universalistic, achievement-oriented society. In such a society

Parsons saw the family's indispensable functions as those of maintaining the emotional balance of its members, and above all of socializing children, for which indeed it seemed virtually inconceivable that it could ever be superseded. Without actually using the phrases himself, therefore, Parsons gave powerful support to a view of the family as an island of security, a 'haven in a heartless world',[16] that prevailed among many sociologists especially in the United States.

WILLIAM J. GOODE AND THE CONJUGAL FAMILY

William J. Goode, to whose work I make a number of references in this book, compiled during the 1950s a mass of data on family patterns in western and many non-western societies; organized this material around a central concept, the conjugal family; and advanced two theses, those of fit and convergence.[17]

For Goode, the conjugal family was 'an ideal type, and also an ideal'. It was an ideal type in Max Weber's sense of the term: a mental construct or 'model' in the mind of the social scientist, representing a simplified theoretical approximation to a more complex reality, rather as a map is a simplified representation of a portion of the earth's surface. And it was also an ideal in that it appeared to be present in the minds of the participants; they referred to it in justification of their actions, and represented it as proper and legitimate, even though their actual behaviour might observably depart from it. Thus for instance, 'although parents in the USA agree that they should not play an important role in their children's choice of spouse, they actually do'.

Goode set out the distinctive characteristics of family life in western societies much as, following him among others, I have already done in chapter 1. Among them was the relative exclusion of a wide range of kin and affines from the everyday affairs of the couple and their children, which I have called the autonomy of the nuclear family household. Relations between a married couple and their respective kin were not perceived in terms of rights and obligations, and there were few moral controls. Kinship was bilateral, there was no lineage system, and each individual was related to a different set of kindred. Marriage was neolocal, that is, a newly married couple if possible set up a new household and did not reside with either family of origin, so reinforcing their relative independence. Marital relations therefore primarily involved adjustment between the couple themselves, rather than that of an incoming spouse to his or her in-laws. Compared with other family systems, there was a freer choice of mate. Courtship and marriage were based on mutual attraction, and parental controls operated only to determine who was allowed to meet whom. The age at marriage, therefore, was not very young; marriage took place when the couple were in a position to exercise choice, both in the sense of knowing what they were doing, and in that of being self-supporting economically. Further, a married couple looked to each other for an 'emotional input–output balance' based on affection. If that failed, a couple must part; so there had to be provision for divorce, and there was likely to be a good deal of it, and also of remarriage. Another guiding principle was egalitarianism. Goode did not of course maintain that there was actual equality between the sexes, but he considered that it was regarded as an ideal and that there was an observable trend towards it. And family limitation, though not integral to the conjugal family, was generally congruent with it, involving as it did rational joint decisions by the couple about how many children they should have.

Goode emphasized that 'the conjugal family is not equivalent to a nuclear family composed only of parents and children'. Both on theoretical grounds and as a matter of observation, it seemed impossible to cut down the family to its nuclear core; siblings were involved with their siblings-in-law, spouses were tied to their in-laws, grandparents were emotionally attached to their grandchildren, and so on. He could well have added that the conjugal family is an abstraction of an altogether different kind; whereas the nuclear family is a group of people, the conjugal family is a set of ideas. Rather as in medicine a syndrome is regarded as a set of symptoms which appear together and are systematically related to a single underlying condition, therefore no one symptom is diagnostic by itself and a confident diagnosis is made only when all or most of them are present, so it was the whole complex pattern of related traits sketched in the last paragraph to which Goode applied the term conjugal family.

His first thesis was that the conjugal family, so characterized, fits an industrial economy. Not that it had arisen in response to the rise of industry; on the contrary, as already noted, even the scanty historical studies available to Goode in the 1950s quickly convinced him that 'the classical family of western nostalgia' was a myth ('It is a pretty picture of life down on grandma's farm...'), and that a form of the family emphasizing the husband–wife–child unit may very well have been 'a facilitating factor for industrialization, rather than the other way around'. Among the reasons he gave for this were that it made mobility easier, both geographically and up and down the social scale. It favoured achievement orientation, the idea of making one's own way without owing much to family influence; and it offered fewer opportunities for nepotism.

Goode's second thesis was that as other societies industrialize their family systems may be expected to converge on the western conjugal model; and he supported it with an impressive array of evidence from major areas including Arabic Islam, Africa south of the Sahara, India, China, and Japan. Consideration of this subject would take us outside the scope of this book, and I have given some attention to it elsewhere.[18] Goode clearly hoped and intended that his analysis should be objective and non-evaluative in the best traditions of a scientific sociology. However, in a final comment, he acknowledged that he personally welcomed the newly emerging family patterns, seeing in them the hope of greater freedom from the domination of elders, from caste and racial restrictions, and from class rigidities; the right to choose; and the potentiality of greater fulfilment, 'even if most do not seek it or achieve it'.

It will have become clear that Parsons' and Goode's analyses had much in common. Recognizably they were looking at the same reality, though they saw it from different theoretical viewpoints. As already pointed out, the nuclear family is not the same as the conjugal family, and they are not even the same *kinds* of thing (or, to be more precise, the same kinds of abstraction from reality); one is a social group, the other is a set of ideas. Further, Parsons and Goode differed on some points of substance. Although Parsons' nuclear family was not in truth isolated, its principal links with the outer world were through the one-sex peer group and the occupational roles of its adult members (especially the husband/father) in the world of work.

They were not the links of kinship and affinity, whose importance in contemporary United States society Parsons explicitly discounted. As already noted, Goode differed from Parsons on that point and emphasized the importance of the wider kin.

Parsons certainly saw the formation and dissolution of each particular nuclear family as processes in time, and related them to the upbringing of children and the processes of individual development. However, since he had been convinced by the anthropological evidence of the universality of the nuclear family, the latter seemed to become for him as it were an eternal object, and his analysis of the way it worked as a social system took on a universal timeless quality. Though not lacking altogether, then, both his sense of history and his comparative perspective were weak. Further, his choice of the nuclear family in the contemporary United States to exemplify his analysis, natural though it was for a distinguished American scholar, unfortunately seemed to imply a view of American family life as prototypical of family life generally, everywhere and at all historical periods.

Goode's work, on the other hand, was strong where Parsons' was weak. As has been seen, he put the western family firmly into a comparative setting with his massive compilation of data on family life in many other societies. He was equally aware of the processes of social change, both in the history of family life in the west and, with his convergence thesis, in the industrialization of contemporary societies. However, his analysis was also weak where Parsons' was strong. His concentration on the conjugal family as a set of ideas – an ideal type, an ideal, or a syndrome – led him to pay less attention than Parsons to the group dynamics of the family and the formation and dissolution of particular families viewed as processes in time. Clearly what we need is an approach combining both perspectives, in which an individual's lifetime experience is seen also as a part of a wider process of social change. If we now find it more feasible to adopt such an approach, no doubt that is partly because our understanding of the history of family life in western societies has been greatly deepened by research published in the 1960s and 1970s, which I have attempted to review in chapter 2; and partly because of the changes which, as we cannot fail to be aware, have taken place in our family life since the 1950s.

SUGGESTIONS FOR FURTHER READING

Talcott Parsons and Robert F. Bales, *Family Socialization and Interaction Process*, London, Routledge and Kegan Paul, 1956

William J. Goode, *World Revolution and Family Patterns*, New York, Free Press, 1963; revised edition, with a new preface, 1970

5

Criticisms and critics of the 1950s models

The 1950s models, especially Talcott Parsons', were the objects in the 1960s and 1970s of critical rebuttal from widely different viewpoints, so many and so various, indeed, as to defy classification. A broad initial distinction may be made, however, between those critics who shared a commitment to the idea of a social science and those who were hostile to it. For the former, the appropriate test of a scientific theory was that of the correspondence theory of truth; the more closely a theoretical representation corresponds to observable reality, the better the theory. For the latter, there was not one truth but many, and no one's account of his or her experience was intrinsically to be preferred to any other's. There could be no such thing as a value-free social science, therefore – fortunately, perhaps, for if there were it could be the instrument of a tyrannous total social control. What purported to be a neutral, value-free, objective analysis of a social institution constituted in fact a conservative endorsement of the *status quo*, since analysing an institution while refraining from adversely criticising it amounted to a tacit acceptance. Among sociological theories, a functionalist analysis was particularly suspect from this point of view, for it tended not only to represent the way an institution actually worked, but also to advance cogent reasons for thinking that that was the way it must necessarily work.

It will be noted in what follows, therefore, that most critics of the second kind did not support their arguments by reference to objectively verifiable observations, which on the whole they scorned. Characteristically, they relied rather on a polemical assertion of their own subjective insights and convictions.

As a result of this deep cleavage in social thought, it could be said that Parsons (personifying his theory of the family) was put in a double bind. On the one hand, if he was 'wrong' – that is, if his representation of western family life did not correspond to observable reality – then he would of course be faulted. On the other hand, however, if he was 'right' and what he said about family life was broadly true and correct, then he would get into even more trouble from those who said, in effect, that he was lending the weight of his scholarly authority to endorsing a social reality which in their various ways its critics found repugnant. Among the latter, indeed, it was not always clear whether the object of their attack was Parsons' analysis or western family life itself.

THE NUCLEAR FAMILY IS NOT ISOLATED

From the first point of view, the main thing wrong with Parsons' analysis was its concentration upon the nuclear family to the exclusion of wider kinship relations. As already noted, Goode differed from Parsons on this point; and there was a wealth of evidence from field studies showing the importance in industrial societies of at least three-generational family ties.

The importance of the wider kin

Notable among the field studies was that of the New Zealand anthropologist Sir Raymond Firth on kinship in London, which I cited in chapter 1. Other studies in London, though widely different from Firth's in style and content, included those of Michael Young and Peter Willmott in the working-class district of Bethnal Green. They indicated a particularly close relation between young married women and their mothers, who in many cases lived nearby though not generally in the same house. The relationship was one of mutual support, including the care of children, who were as much at home in their grandmother's house as in their own, if not more so, and who enjoyed a closely affectionate relationship with their 'Nana'. When such ties were broken, as they had been in some cases at the time of Young and Willmott's fieldwork by re-housing schemes, families were found to go to considerable trouble and expense to maintain three-generation links by visiting at week-ends.[1] Turning next to Woodford, an affluent middle-class suburb, Young and Willmott found that though related three-generation family households lived further apart in geographical terms, motor vehicle ownership and the telephone enabled them to keep in as close effective touch and be available to help in emergency as was the case among working-class people. Compared with the East End, 'kinship may mean less in the suburb at other stages in life, but in old age, when the need arises, the family is once more the main source of support... This sense of filial duty is as strong in one district as another.'[2] Confirming these observations, Peter Townsend, a colleague of Young and Willmott in Bethnal Green, found that the great majority of old people were looked after by their middle-aged offspring.[3]

Following his work in London, Michael Young collaborated with Hildred Geertz in a comparison of the family life of older people there with that of older people in California. While there was wide individual diversity in both areas, they found that in general there were two similarities and one difference. First, most parents in their old age maintained close touch with their adult children – ' "close" both in geography and in frequency of contact' – and had warmly affectionate relations with their grandchildren. The three-generation family was an important reality in both communities. As people lived longer, indeed, the four-generation family was becoming a reality for some; thus an elderly lady in their California sample was being looked after by her married granddaughter and enjoyed a loving relationship with her infant great-granddaughter. Secondly, of the adult children, daughters consistently played more important parts in their parents' lives than did sons. The difference was that whereas few people in Britain know anything about their forebears beyond their grandparents, many Americans had extensive knowledge of their remote ancestry and traced it back to such people and events as the families who sailed aboard the *Mayflower*.[4]

The T-core

In their study of family and kinship in Swansea, Colin Rosser and Christopher Harris were equally concerned to stress the importance of what, following Firth,[5] they rather confusingly termed 'extra-familial kinship' and 'the extended family'.

Besides kinship in the narrow sense, affinity was important, and Rosser and Harris considered that people's relations with their 'in-laws' had been underestimated in many earlier studies. 'The kinship structure is essentially made up of families interlocked through a succession of marriages.' Its irreducible basic unit was not the nuclear family, but what they called the 'core family' of 'two sets of grandparents linked through the marriage of a son or daughter to a common set of grandchildren', giving rise to a characteristic T shape when presented graphically as in fig. 2.[6]

Burgesses and spiralists

Where Rosser and Harris had interviewed a representative 2 per cent sample of all the households in the borough, Colin Bell concentrated his fieldwork in two private housing estates on the outskirts of Swansea.[7] These were inhabited mainly by young middle-class families going through the home-making and child-rearing stages of the family cycle and, as Bell soon became aware, getting substantial help from their parents in the process. Bell considered that while earlier studies had brought out the way old people were helped by their middle-aged offspring, they had underestimated the extent to which resources also flowed the other way, from the older to the

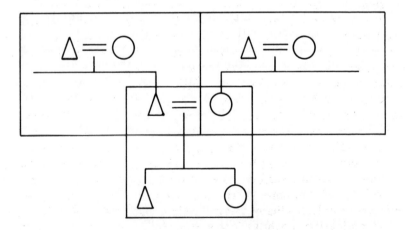

Fig. 2. The T-core (after Colin Rosser and Christopher Harris, *The Family and Social Change: A Study of Family and Kinship in a South Wales Town*, London, Routledge and Kegan Paul, 1965).

younger generation, at another stage in the family cycle. He also thought that although such studies as those of Willmott and Young had emphasized the link between mothers and their married daughters among the working class, even more important for the middle class were links among male kin, especially in matters of money and business.

These links were most obviously important for the 'burgesses' (as Bell called them, following William Watson), who were rooted in the locality, in many cases by family businesses built up over two and three generations. These he contrasted with 'spiralist' families who had moved there in pursuit of the husband/father's career, for which mobility was a prerequisite (a point I take up in chapter 10). Many had been sent there by the husband's firm, with or without promotion, and fully expected to have to move again unless he was nearing retirement. But though family business influence and help in getting a job were less important to spiralist families than to burgesses, for them too there was no lack of family help, financial and otherwise, at times such as the birth of a child.

Roles and networks

In an intensive study of twenty London families, all in the child-rearing stage, Elizabeth Bott found marked variations in the division of labour between husbands and wives.[8] Some couples organized their lives so that their activities were different and separate, but complemented each other to form a whole; and some carried out their activities independently of and without reference to each other. Complementary and independent organizations Bott classified together and termed a 'segregated' conjugal role-relationship. This she contrasted with the 'joint' conjugal role-relationship of couples who carried out many activities together, exchanging many household tasks and spending much of their leisure time together. Secondly, Bott found wide variation in the extent to which families were, in Parsons' term, isolated. The external social relationships of all families took the form, not of an organized group, but of a network including neighbours and friends as well as relatives; and there was considerable variation in the 'connectedness' of these networks, that is, the extent to which the people known by a family know and meet each other independently of that family. She used the term 'close-knit' to describe a network with many relationships among its component units, and 'loose-knit' for one with few. Bott proceeded to the important discovery that the two variables were related: the more close-knit the networks in which a family was involved, the more segregated tended to be the role-relationships between the spouses.

Close-knit networks characteristically developed where husband and wife had grown up in the same area and continued to live there after marriage. Then only minor changes occurred. The wife tended to see less of her former girl-friends and more of her mother and other female relatives, and the birth of her children forged an even closer bond with her mother, the children's grandmother. The husband's life continued to be centred on work and some form of recreation away from home, usually in the company of male colleagues and friends rather than kin. Their marriage having been superimposed upon these pre-existing relationships, each partner was sensitive to the opinions and values of the people in their respective networks, in which women tended to associate with women and men with men. With men and women pursuing their separate activities, these norms tended to reinforce role segregation between husband and wife. While his life was centred on work and recreation, hers was centred on her home, her children, and her relatives.

When a person was involved in a loose-knit network, however, there was more likely to be a variety of norms within the network, and social control and mutual assistance would be more fragmented and less consistent.

If husband and wife come to marriage with such loose-knit networks, or if conditions are such that their networks become loose-knit after marriage, they must seek in each other some of the emotional satisfactions and help with familial tasks that couples in close-knit networks can get from outsiders. Joint organization becomes more necessary for the success of the family as an enterprise.

Bott emphasised that the connectedness of the family's network was not the only factor affecting the segregation of conjugal roles; among other things, the spouses' personalities were of crucial importance. Nor were the two types to be thought of as polar opposites. Between the two extremes there were 'medium-knit networks'; and there were also transitional families, changing from one type of network to another. Networks became loose-knit when people moved from one place to another, or when they formed new relationships not connected with their old ones, and were thrust anew into a joint conjugal role-relationship. Conversely, in families changing from a loose-knit to a more close-knit network, the first reaction was likely to be one of defensiveness against a perceived threat to their privacy; but in time they tended to develop an intermediate degree of network-connectedness and conjugal segregation.

Although Bott's findings bore only obliquely on Parsons' theory, they could hardly be said to afford it direct support. Parsons envisaged a role-relationship between husband and wife of a kind that in Bott's terms might well have been called segregated, with the husband going out to work and exercising instrumental leadership at home, while the wife 'more intimately connected with early child care' concerned herself with expressive leadership. Yet this seemed more likely to be found in just those families which, in Parsons' term, were least isolated. Conversely, the relative isolation of some other nuclear families seemed to have the effect of lessening the distinction within them between the husband's and the wife's roles.

The 'modified extended' family

A more direct criticism of Parsons' model from within the United States functionalist tradition came from Eugene Litwak, whose work with Ivan Szelenyi on primary groups I cited in chapter 1. Litwak distinguished four models or generic types according to which family life had been represented in the sociological literature. First there was the traditional or classical extended family attributed to the peasant societies of countries such as Poland, Italy, and China, consisting of related nuclear subfamilies living close together in mutual dependence with a hierarchical authority structure. Secondly, at the other extreme there was the dissolving or weak family, a concept based on the view that in advanced industrial societies most of the family's functions have been taken over by large-scale formal organizations, leaving the family with little to do: 'all that is left are very tenuous husband and wife relations'. Thirdly, there was the isolated nuclear family model of husband, wife, and small child, with certain essential functions – early socialization of the child and tension management for the adults – concentrated sufficiently in the family to ensure its stability, even if rather precariously so. And fourthly, Litwak coined the term 'modified extended family' for a coalition of partially interdependent nuclear families bound together on an egalitarian basis, and maintaining those extended family bonds as an end in themselves. Such families 'exchange significant services with each other, thus differing from the isolated nuclear family, as well as retaining considerable autonomy, . . . therefore differing from the classical extended family'.

Citing social survey findings in support of his contentions, Litwak directly controverted Parsons' thesis that there was a basic disharmony between extended family relations and a modern democratic industrial society, for which the isolated nuclear family was especially functional. Thus it had been said that extended family relations hindered both occupational and geographical mobility, and that such mobility when it took place tended to break up extended families. Litwak contended that, on the contrary, the extended family played an important role for the upwardly mobile, as parents saw to it that their children learned a trade or profession with more prestige than their own, and helped them in the initial stages of a career. Radical shifts in socialization were not needed by the upwardly or downwardly mobile, while the modified extended family could provide help for the latter, and neither upward nor downward mobility created any real barrier to family communication. Turning to geographical mobility, Litwak pointed out that the modified extended family often helped people to move by providing them with material and moral support; such had indeed been the experience of those who had migrated to the United States in the past from the Irish potato famine and Russian pogroms. The first to move relayed information back to their kinsfolk at home about opportunities in the new land, and helped related families over crucial hurdles when they decided to follow, while money borrowed to finance the move was paid back in remittances home. As for losing touch with kin, modern communications on the contrary enabled extended family relations to be maintained. Moreover, related families who separated in search of work opportunities could and did come together again later. Thus a man near the end of his career and at the peak of his earning capacity could either look for a job near his extended family, or encourage his retired parents to come and settle near him.

Litwak did not suggest that the modified extended family was the sole, nor even the predominant family form in the United States, and he urged that a variety of types of family structure should be recognized. Clearly, however, the modified extended family was a reality for large numbers of people; and, considered strictly from a functionalist point of view, it was more consonant with an industrial democratic society and more functional than the isolated nuclear family.[9]

Norbert Elias and the civilizing process

One of the most fundamental and searching criticisms of Parsons' functional theory was that of Norbert Elias. Most of Parsons' works were published between the first printing of Elias' book *Uber den Prozess der Zivilisation* in Switzerland in 1939 (not the best of times for a work on such a subject by a liberal German scholar, especially one of Jewish descent) and its re-publication in 1968 with a new introduction including Elias' critique of Parsons.[10]

All that we are concerned with in sociology are processes in time. Social change is a process in time, but so also is what Parsons called 'the social system', consisting as it does of regular, repeated patterns of interaction, for example between mothers and babies. In Parsons' scheme, these patterned interactions are aggregated into role-relationships, structures, and systems, and so falsified by being made to seem more static than they really are. To oppose the social system or social structure on the one hand to social change on the other is to perpetrate a false dichotomy. Further, by reducing processes to states Parsons introduced other unnecessary and misleading dichotomies, as in the pattern variables, and even more fundamentally in the separation of 'the individual' from 'society'; these 'do not relate to two objects existing separately but to different yet inseparable aspects of the same human beings... Both have the character of processes.'

Though actions and interactions are to some extent patterned and predictable, no action is ever repeated exactly. Family life in European history affords apt examples. According to Elias, civilizing processes (for 'civilization' itself is also a process in time, a becoming-more-civilized) are to be seen as *both* long slow sequences of historical change *and* processes in individual development, particularly in the upbringing of children. Elias illustrated with a wealth of detail how manners and habits, learned by children in family interaction, changed gradually but consistently over the centuries, always exemplifying greater and more exacting self-restraint. For instance, people learned to use forks and separate plates at meals, instead of eating with fingers out of a common dish; they took to using handkerchieves to wipe their mouths and blow their noses; they learned to relieve themselves in private rather than in full view of others, and eventually to accept the hygienic necessity of special rooms and equipment for excretion. All of those changes involved re-directing natural, spontaneous drives into more elaborate, skilled performances. They were the subject of internal self-control rather than external constraint, hence more 'repression' in the Freudian sense, the Freud of *Civilization and its Discontents*.[11]

Though doubtless well grounded in general, however, Elias' criticisms may have been too sweeping as applied to Parsons' analysis of the family in particular. In terms analogous to the distinction between anatomy and physiology, Parsons thought of structure as consisting of the relatively – but only relatively – enduring relations among the components of a system, like the organs of an animal, its skeleton, heart, liver, lungs, etc. Even though none of these are permanent and all are subject to long-term change and decay, in the short term they are sufficiently enduring to enable us to treat them as constant compared with the functions such as digestion, the circulation of the blood, respiration, and the animal's search for food. Further, as I have already suggested and contrary to Elias' strictures, precisely the strength of Parsons' analysis lay in the way he conceived of each particular family's life as a process in time from pairing through parenthood and the development of the children to the dissolution of the family and the formation of new ones, over a twenty to thirty years' period.

AGAINST FAMILY LIFE

During the 1960s and 1970s hostile criticisms were directed not only against the analytical models of the 1950s but also against contemporary western family life itself. Edmund Leach in his 1967 Reith lectures exactly caught the mood of the time: 'Far from being the basis of the good society, the family, with its narrow privacy and tawdry secrets, is the source of all our discontents.'[12] The criticisms were based on widely different grounds, and as David Morgan observed it was not simply a matter of distinguishing between functionalist and anti-functionalist, between abolitionist and retentionist, or between optimist and pessimist, but rather a question of identifying points of view arising out of various combinations and intersections of these opposing positions.[13]

As has been seen, a functionalist analysis tended to present matters benignly. The institutions and values of an industrial democratic society, like that of the United States, were taken as given facts and not subjected to adverse criticism in an analysis that was intended to be objective and value-free. Family life was found on the whole to be functional for that society, adequately socializing children and affording home comforts for adults; there was, however, debate about what particular form or forms of family life prevailed, and whether the 'isolated nuclear', 'modified extended', 'T-core', or other model most closely accorded with reality and was best fitted to such a society's other institutions.

Pessimism

Opposed to this may be set a long tradition of pessimism: the family is in decline, alas! As long ago as the 1870s Frederic Le Play, founding father of social science, traced a sequence from the patriarchal family in stable societies through the 'stem family' – still an 'extended' family of three or more generations, but with more freedom for its branch families – to the unstable two-generation family of modern disorganized society.[14]

Our most fatal error is through the State's encroachments to disorganize the authority of the father of the family, the most natural and fertile of autonomous groups, one which best conserves the social bond by repressing original corruption and training the young generations in respect and obedience.[15]

In direct succession to Le Play, Carle Zimmerman wrote in 1936 that 'Until 1855 a simple, happy state of affairs was common in eastern and northern Europe... Under this simple regime the father of the family [was] the main agent of social peace';[16] while as recently as 1972 he stated that 'When the ideological structure of the family system loses its virility and strength the social system generally gets into trouble.'[17] A conviction that the family was weak or dissolving, and so failing alike its members and the wider society, was eloquently expressed by the American philosopher Ruth Nanda Anshen in 1959:

The moral ambivalence of our society has penetrated to the very heart of the problem of our time – the family and the home in which our children must receive their precepts and guidance. The failure of society is reflected in the failure of parenthood... Ethical imperatives are lacking ... We live in a climate of moral amnesia and physical violence and our children reflect the world of which they are a part... The false standards of an adult society which exalt material achievements at the expense of spiritual worth are embraced by the youth... Man has lost himself as a living center because the family has lost itself as a living center ... The family in its present state of dissolution reflects the spiritual poverty of modern man.[18]

It was to controvert such moralizing that the English sociologist Ronald Fletcher wrote in 1962:

To unfortunate sociological generalizations to the effect that the family has been stripped of its functions and is diminishing in importance as a social institution has come to be attached what can only be called a moral wailing and gnashing of teeth ... This moral denigration will do no good whatever if only because it is based upon a completely false diagnosis. The family has *not* declined. The family is *not* less stable than before. The standards of parenthood and parental responsibility have *not* deteriorated.[19]

The effect of his reaction, therefore, was to propel Fletcher back into the optimistic company of the functionalists in his 'defence of the modern family and, implicitly, of modern parents'.

An optimistic abolitionist

One critic who might be classed in Morgan's terms an optimistic abolitionist was the American political scientist Barrington

Moore, Jr. According to Moore, the family was ill adapted to modern industrial society, of which he took a generally favourable view, and was deservedly in decline. For one thing, it was the last stronghold of ascription in societies otherwise organized on the basis of achievement. Just as the recent development of western societies had rendered quite obsolete some earlier elements of their culture and society, such as slavery, so there was at least *prima facie* evidence for a similar argument concerning the family. 'One of the most obviously obsolete features of the family is the obligation to give affection as a duty to a particular set of persons on account of the accident of birth. This is a true relic of barbarism. It is a survival from human prehistory, when kinship was the basic form of social organization.' For another, though sociologists credited the family with performing the function of 'making human beings out of babies and small children', in countries such as the United States it did so either badly or not at all. It had been supplanted by adolescent neighbourhood gangs and by the mass media, which had 'largely succeeded in battering down the walls of the social cell the family once constituted'. And it put impossible demands on wives, particularly middle-class wives. To some extent the burdens of housework, once borne by slaves and later by servants, could be relieved by machines. Those associated with the care of children presented more difficult problems, but perhaps not quite insuperable. The 'part-time family' was already a prominent feature of the cultural landscape, and might yet be further transformed if specialized agencies, 'developing from such contemporary human forms as the crèche, play school, and boarding school', assumed a larger share of the burden of child-rearing without becoming coldly impersonal and in the derogatory sense bureaucratic.[20]

Pessimistic abolitionists

For many pessimistic abolitionists, however, the trouble was quite the contrary; not that the family was weak or dissolving but that it was still strong and resistant to change; that it was 'too well adjusted to a destructive culture'.[21] and carried out all too effectively its functions, particularly that of socializing children to take their places in a wider society from which its

critics recoiled in horror. Thus it was a rhetorical commonplace in the 1960s that normal, healthy American boys reared
in normal, healthy American families were prepared to go on
bombing missions dropping napalm on North Vietnamese
villages. What was held to be wrong with the family, though,
naturally varied according to each writer's view of what was
chiefly wrong with western society. For example, Morgan
wrote of those 'who locate the source of authoritarianism and a
willingness to accept facism in the family structure ...
espeically the lower middle-class family', and he quoted
Wilhelm Reich to the effect that 'the authoritarian state gains
an enormous interest in the authoritarian family; it becomes
the factory in which the state's structure and ideology are
moulded'.[22] Herbert Marcuse wrote in similar terms about how
Luther and even more Calvin, saw parental (=paternal)
authority as habituating 'man' to subjection, and of 'the social
function of the family in the bourgeois authority-system',
though unlike the more pessimistic abolitionists he thought
that that function was in decline. He followed Freud in
associating civilization with the repression of sexual and
aggressive drives and the formation of the superego, originally
in the Oedipus situation by the father; but 'the progressive
father is a most unsuitable enemy and a most unsuitable
"ideal" ' for the young to rebel against. He went on to advocate
a 'non-repressive reality principle' according to which the
taboo on the reification of the body would be lessened, with an
'erotization of the entire personality' in which the body would
be re-sexualized, an object of cathexis, an instrument of
pleasure. This would lead to 'a disintegration of the institutions
in which the private interpersonal relations have been organized,
particularly the monogamic and patriarchal family'.[23]

Force and violence in family life

From the view that the family embodies authority and repression it seems natural to pass to the contention that all
social systems depend in the last resort on force or the threat of
force, and the family is no exception. Somewhat surprisingly,
this was the view of William J. Goode, whose general approval
of western conjugal family patterns and their 'fit' with industrial society put his *World Revolution and Family Patterns*

clearly into the functionalist category, but whose contribution on force and violence in the family has to be seen in a rather different light.[24] Functionalist explanations characteristically emphasize consensus, shared values, and reciprocal role expectations in accounting for human interaction and the maintenance of social systems. In family life in particular, as Goode put it,

Typically, family members want spontaneous affection from each other, not calculated obedience or compliance. If a family member conforms to rules because of. . . force. . . while resenting it, others are both hurt and angry. Each wants the others to *want* to offer services, pay respect, cooperate and help, give loyalty or obedience. If members discharge their role obligations because that is the best bargain they can get in the face of superior force, the foundations of the family are fragile.

Yet

not only do we use force and threat in order to socialize our children, we also teach them thereby that force is useful, and we do in fact train them in the use of force and violence . . . No very sharp eye is needed to know that American parents typically use force on their children from the earliest ages on . . . Within the family itself, the harsh fact must be faced that the member with the greater strength and willingness to use it commands more force than others do. This is usually the father, and in most cases it will also be the parents as compared with the children.[25]

A great deal of family life has to do with inducing others to act differently. Whether for the best or the worst of reasons – to dissuade another from a potentially disastrous course of action, to claim fulfilment of a legitimate expectation wrongfully withheld, or merely to demand one's own convenience and comfort – urgent representations may become heated, and may be backed with threats or show of force, or actual blows. The physical punishment of children is well-nigh universal, but also very variable, some parents using it oftener and more severely while others resort rarely to a light slap. Goode reviewed numerous surveys correlating this with other variables: boys more than girls were so punished, by fathers more than mothers, in working-class families, by parents more inclined to believe in divine wrath and to try to exercise authoritarian control over their children.[26]

A second issue, even more emotionally fraught, is that of extreme violence in the forms of assault, murder, and child abuse. Much family violence does not come to the notice of the police or other official authorities, yet a high proportion of all murders – 40 to 50 per cent in Goode's estimation – are committed within the family. Other studies have reached similar conclusions. In Britain a Home Office survey of murders in 1957–68 showed that while most male victims were acquaintances of or strangers to their killers, most women victims were the wives, girl-friends, or relatives of those convicted or suspected of their murder. A separate analysis of murders followed by the suicide of the suspect, and by those found to be insane, showed an even more marked concentration of them to be within families. 'The principal victims of the mentally abnormal were their own wives and children. This was particularly so for suicide-murder, in which members of the immediate family accounted for about 80% of the victims . . . Motives could not be assessed for insane murder or suicide murder, although it was apparent that family stress, depression, and despair played a large part.'[27]

Child abuse, non-accidental injury, or 'baby-battering' likewise generally comes to official notice only after parents' attempts to conceal it have failed, and presumably not in all cases. This large and grievous subject has its own considerable literature, which I can only indicate here.[28] 'Wife-battering' too has aroused public concern.[29] And one writer has suggested that 'husband-battering' may be more prevalent than is generally recognized, perhaps surpassing wife-battering as the most hidden crime.[30] Some women even commit murder; and when they do (according to Wolfgang's findings, quoted by Goode) it is most often in the kitchen, secondly in the bedroom in order of frequency.[31] The upshot surely is that so far from the family being an 'island of security', for some people – children, women, and even men – it is an island of terror.

Feminist criticisms

According to some feminist writers, family life enshrined and perpetuated all the sex-role stereotyping and what they regarded as 'the oppression of women' that they most vehemently opposed. They took a dim view of sociology, too, for representing the reality of family life without adversely criticising it.

Kate Millett's prime concern was with literacy criticism, and with appraising sexual themes in the works of D. H. Lawrence, Henry Miller, and Norman Mailer. She also had sharp things to say about sociology in general: 'Were such a thing as a value-free social science even possible, it would very likely be monstrous; one which disguises its values is insidious,' and about functionalism in particular: 'Moreover, functionalist description inevitably becomes prescription.' Talcott Parsons' characterization of the male role as instrumental, the female as expressive, she saw as a mere camouflage for misogyny. Moreover, although the list of characteristics which lesser functionalists, following Parsons, attributed to the female included such genial traits as sympathy, kindness, and cheerfulness, it expressed a male-supremacist mentality and recalled the language in which superior classes always characterized their inferiors, as aristocrats spoke of peasants or whites of blacks. She concluded:

Thus sociology examines the status quo, calls it phenomena, and pretends to take no stand on it, thereby avoiding the necessity to comment on the invidious character of the relationship between the sex groups it studies. Yet by slow degrees of converting statistic to fact, function to prescription, bias to biology (or some other indeterminate), it comes to ratify and rationalize what has been socially enjoined or imposed into what is and ought to be. And through its pose of objectivity, it gains a special efficacy in reinforcing stereotypes ... Functionalists, like other reactionaries, are out to save the family.'[32]

Juliet Mitchell was similarly convinced that women were an oppressed under-class:

Women in today's family are the main repositories for . . . the screaming illusions of our society: freedom, equality, individuality. 'My wife and I are equals' is the correlate of 'the two sides of industry'. 'Equality' and 'sides' suggest a faint line drawn down the *middle*. In both cases there is a topside and a bottom side, an unequal division of labour and an unequal division of profits – to put it mildly.

Her prime concern was to bring feminism into relation with other radical movements aiming at social change, including the more revolutionary versions of socialism. Thus where feminists declared that men were the oppressors, socialists saw men and women alike as oppressed by 'capitalism'. Was women's oppression the result of a psychological power struggle, which men won, or was it economic, to do with private property? In countries that had undergone communist revolutions and called themselves socialist, women had not fared particularly well, and could still be regarded as oppressed. But if men, rather than 'capitalism', were the enemy, what of relations between the sexes? Even more important, perhaps, what of the children?

Mitchell thought that the sexual liberation urged by some other radical writers such as Marcuse could help women to gain greater freedom; but it could equally presage new forms of exploitation and oppression. As for the care of infants, the work of psychologists including Freud had placed its importance beyond dispute, while Parsons' analysis, too, had valuably made clear the importance of socialization and the exact role of the maternal socializer. However, 'These undoubted advances in the scientific understanding of childhood have been widely used as an argument to reassert women's quintessential maternal function, at a time when the traditional family has seemed increasingly eroded.' John Bowlby had something to answer for on that count, and the wide acceptance of his findings showed how readily the family could be made the subject of a backward-looking ideology.

The family, thus, embodies the most conservative concepts available: it rigidifies the past ideals and presents them as the present pleasures. By its very nature, it is there to prevent the future. No wonder revolutionaries come up with the vulgar desperation: abolish the family.

It was not entirely clear, though, how wholeheartedly Mitchell identified herself with so desperate a measure. No doubt profound changes were needed in the relations of women, children, and men: 'The liberation of women can only be achieved if *all four* structures in which they are integrated are transformed – Production, Reproduction, Sexuality, and Socialization.' Nevertheless, in the end she acknowledged that 'the germ of the family . . . has certain universal characteristics – heterosexual parents and offspring'.[33]

Heterosexual relationships, however, were repudiated by some more extreme feminists who appeared to base their argument on two premises. First, truth was a matter not of objective verification but of subjective experience: there could be more than one truth. Jessie Bernard's dictum was cited with approval, to the effect that in every marital union there are two marriages, his and hers.[34] Women's experience was so different from men's that only a woman could really understand another woman and truly share her feelings. Secondly, men were the enemy. Therefore, loving relationships between women and men were impossible. To be completely free of men, women had to have as little to do with them as possible, and create and inhabit an exclusively female world. Taken to its logical conclusion, this meant that the only true feminists were lesbians.

But for some women to go into a self-imposed *apartheid* seemed to yet other feminists a wholly mistaken approach, and one not likely to further the women's cause. Not all women could be lesbians. It was not men as such who were the enemy, but male dominance, and men imbued with 'patriarchal' attitudes. The essential claim was that women and men should be equal. That meant minimizing, not maximizing, the social attention paid to the irreducible biological differences between females and males, and abolishing altogether the social differentiation between feminine and masculine genders. In so far as they lived according to these androgynous ideals, persons would value and love one another as persons rather than as women and men. Marriage as a union specifically between a man and a woman would presumably be inconsistent with those ideals. Domestic groups might rather take the form of communes which adults could enter and leave at will, and in which they would live in intimate relationships irrespective of their biological sex and social gender. Heterosexual relationships and freely-chosen parenthood would not be ruled out, therefore, though the care of children would be the equal responsibility and concern of all adults and not be assigned mainly to women as mothers.[35] Such utopian visions may have partly inspired some experiments in alternatives to conventional family life, to which I turn in the last chapter.

Madness and family life

And finally, criticism of family life came from those who blamed it for mental illness in general and schizophrenia in particular. The best-known though not the only exponent of this view was the Scottish psychiatrist R. D. Laing, who studied interaction patterns among the families of those diagnosed (some would say labelled) as suffering from schizophrenia. Laing maintained that members of such families frequently tied each other, and parents in particular tied their children, in 'knots', chiefly the 'double-bind', an expression originated by the English anthropologist Gregory Bateson. This occurred when one person simultaneously transmitted contradictory messages, making it impossible for the other to do right. In an oft-cited example Bateson described how a mother invited her son to kiss her, 'but her posture, freezing, tension simultaneously tell him not to'.[36] Or one person, such as a child, might receive incompatible messages from two different people, such as quarrelling parents (a situation which the older functionalist theory would have called role conflict). Family members tried to invalidate each other's experience: 'It's all in your imagination', 'It never happened that way', 'How can you think such a thing?' And they practised mystification, denying what they were doing, and invalidating any perception that it was being done. Such interpersonal interactions were, in Laing's judgement, enough to provoke much of the behaviour that others saw as deranged. Far from demonstrating mental illness or 'madness', such behaviour was the suffering victim's intelligible reaction: '*without exception* the experience and behaviour that gets labelled schizophrenic is *a special strategy that a person invents in order to live in an unlivable situation*' (italics in original).[37]

Laing made it clear that his studies did not involve a comparison between families with a member diagnosed as schizophrenic and those without, presumably 'normal' families.[38] In scientific terms, he made no use of 'controls'; indeed, he rejected scientific objectivity, which he regarded as 'depersonalizing'[39] and setting a barrier between himself and his patients, in favour of a subjective understanding of their experience (a key word in much of his writing). Moreover, he does not appear to have regarded the disturbing knots he found in the interaction patterns of the families he studied as specific to the family life of those suffering from schizophrenia. In his more polemical writings, indeed, he was sweeping in his denunciation of family life in general, which he saw as perpetuating the alienated condition that passed for 'normal' in our society, subjecting each baby to the 'forces of violence, called love' and producing by the age of fifteen or so 'a half-crazed creature, more or less adjusted to a mad world'.[40] Thus at several points he seemed to imply that the mentally ill were no more mad than the rest of us, or many of us, in 'a mad world'.[41] though later he appears to have withdrawn from that position.[42] So if family life as he vividly described it from his case-notes was recognizably, even horribly, like that which many of his readers had experienced without themselves becoming mentally ill, that only strengthened the impact of his hostile, pessimistic criticism of the family as a powerfully harmful influence on people's lives. Family life drives people mad; that, in effect, was his message. It is important enough to deserve consideration in a separate chapter.

SUGGESTIONS FOR FURTHER READING

Norbert Elias, *The Civilizing Process: The History of Manners*. trans. Edmund Jephcott, Oxford, Blackwell, 1978

Elizabeth Bott, *Family and Social Network*, second edition, London, Tavistock, 1971

Colin Rosser and Christopher Harris, *The Family and Social Change: A Study of Family and Kinship in a South Wales Town*, London, Routledge and Kegan Paul, 1965

Colin Bell, *Middle Class Families: Social and Geographical Mobility*, London, Routledge and Kegan Paul, 1968

Eugene Litwak, 'Occupational mobility and extended family cohesion' and 'Geographic mobility and extended family cohesion', *American Sociological Review*, vol. 25, 1960, pp. 9–21 and 385–94

D. H. J. Morgan, *Social Theory and the Family*, London, Routledge and Kegan Paul, 1975

6

Family life and mental illness, especially schizophrenia

According to one school of thought, then, family life drives people mad, and the mentally ill are to be seen as victims of disordered communications among family members. Figures such as 'the authoritarian father' and 'the schizophrenogenic mother' found their way into the mythology of the 1960s and 1970s, as part of the hostile criticism of family life that was widely current at that time.

ANTI-FAMILY, ANTI-PSYCHIATRY

Associated with this was an anti-psychiatry movement according to which the mentally ill were equally to be seen as victims of orthodox medical psychiatric practice and of their treatment in mental hospitals. Thus the Canadian sociologist Erving Goffman's influential study of life in a large mental hospital in the United States in the mid-1950s compared it with other 'total institutions' in which people were confined, such as prisons, warships, monasteries, and boarding schools.[1] Just as Laing had suggested that the actions of those labelled as mentally ill were their intelligible reactions to their situation in the family, so Goffman interpreted some of the devious actions he observed among mental patients as intelligently directed towards safeguarding their personal property and maintaining an area of privacy, however small, in which they could take their own decisions in a total institution in which their lives were controlled by the staff. Some of the things that were done to patients in the name of treatment were seen as punishments with which staff could threaten patients in order to assert control. These included, in particular, electro-convulsive therapy

(ECT), a form of treatment around which intensely emotional controversies have centred. And in what he called the moral career of a mental patient, Goffman identified the key role played by the 'next-of-relation', usually though not necessarily of patient's next-of-kin. This person was regarded, and trusted, by the patient as the one on whom the latter could most depend, and who should be the last to doubt his or her sanity. To be delivered by that person into the hands of the mental hospital was likely to be bitterly resented as a betrayal. The patient's emotional reaction to that betrayal, however, along with many other aspects of the patient's intelligible behaviour in the hospital situation, was likely to be regarded by staff as confirmatory evidence of the disturbed state of mind that had justified admission to hospital in the first place.

Goffman showed some sympathy with hospital staff and some insight into their difficulties. However, he explicitly dissociated himself from 'the medical model' and put words like 'mental disorder', 'treatment', and 'cure' firmly in quotation marks throughout. While he rejected the crudely cynical notion that mental hospitals exist primarily to provide jobs for their staff, he did not think they were run for the benefit of patients either. Emphasizing almost exclusively their custodial function, Goffman argued that they existed mainly to make life easier for the rest of us, their true clients notably including the relatives of the mentally ill.

Goffman's ideas, like Laing's, were reflected in popular versions in novels, films, and the mass media generally. Mental hospitals were presented as dreadful places in which sadistic staff subjected hapless patients to humiliating, frightening, and harmful maltreatment including unnecessary ECTs and even brain surgery, and those patients who were not mad when they were admitted quickly became so. Although views such as these are widely at variance with our present understanding of mental illness and its treatment, they received extensive publicity in the 1960s and 1970s. They also gained wide credence among social scientists, many of whom accepted them quite uncritically; and they were influential therefore in the training of a whole generation of social workers. They were, however, seriously misleading, and may well have done more harm than good.

MENTAL ILLNESS

If illness causes suffering and disability in varying degrees of severity, then mental illness is rightly so called. In what follows I adopt the usage of the National Schizophrenia Fellowship in writing of sufferers and their relatives. The latter, like Goffman's 'next-of-relation', are those with a concern for the sufferer that leads to their becoming (in the jargon of medical social work) 'primary care agents'. Usually they are close kin or spouses, sometimes intimate friends; those who assume this role are mostly women, most commonly of all the sufferer's mother.

I write of mental illness rather than of madness, sanity, or insanity. Madness is an imprecise term with other connotations in ordinary speech ('hopping mad', 'mad about music'). Sanity and insanity generally refer to the degree of responsibility which people are deemed to have for their actions, and their capacity to look after their own affairs. Certainly, these are adversely affected in many cases by mental illness. However, as will perhaps become clear below, it would seem that a person can be mentally ill yet sane, leading a normal life outside hospital, acting sensibly, looking after him- or herself, and enjoying normal social relations, especially if as a result of appropriate treatment the sufferer recognizes the symptoms of mental illness, such as hallucinations, for what they are and discounts them accordingly. Further, all the foregoing need to be distinguished from mental deficiency, mental defect, or subnormal intelligence. Some of the severest forms of mental illness, including schizophrenia, afflict people of every IQ level indiscriminately and leave their intelligence unimpaired. It is a popular fallacy to regard the mentally ill as necessarily stupid. On the other hand, it is also a romantic fallacy to attribute to the mentally ill specially acute powers of insight, sensibility, or even creativity. To be sure, some creative geniuses have been afflicted by mental illness, but the evidence suggests that it crippled, not inspired them.

Schizophrenia: its nature

There are of course many forms of mental illness, and in place of the former distinction between psychoses (schizophrenic, paranoid, manic, etc.) and neuroses (depressive, obsessional, hysterical, phobic, etc.) a hierarchy of psychiatric disorders is now recognized. Of these by common consent the severest is schizophrenia.[2]

It is clear from the accounts of many sufferers and ex-sufferers[3] that the central schizophrenic experience is of thought control: of their thoughts, emotions, and actions as being under the control of some outside force or agency. Varieties of this experience include thought insertion; the sufferer's thoughts are not his or her own, but are put there by someone or something else. Or thought withdrawal; the sufferer's thoughts are taken out of his or her mind under external control. Or thought broadcasting; what goes on inside the sufferer's head (so to speak) is becoming known to others without having been expressed. Associated with this central experience are hallucinations. The inserted thoughts may be so definite as to take the form of voices 'inside the head'. These may be heard by the sufferer discussing his or her thoughts or behaviour in the third person, often in a derogatory way. Other auditory hallucinations beside voices take the form of bells ringing, loud bangs, etc.; and there are also sometimes visual hallucinations. Many such experiences are extremely distressing, and even literally maddening, provoking the sufferer to outbursts of verbal hostility and even physical violence quite inexplicable to others, notably his or her relatives, who of course do not hear the voices or share in the other experiences and have no idea what is going on.

As the sufferer attempts to account for the central experience of thought control, explanatory delusions may develop to the effect that natural or supernatural forces are at work. Sinister conspiracies are attributed to persons known or unknown, or the voices may be perceived as coming from a divine source and conveying divine commands. There are also primary delusions about the meaning of perceptions which are in themselves normal; irrelevant features may become all-important, and everyday objects and situations come to possess a special, usually sinister meaning.[4] The sufferer's self-perception may therefore be of a specially important person, or as one singled out as a victim, or both.

As seen from the outside, the sufferer may appear to others to undergo a change of personality, especially when a previously sunny, equable person becomes inexplicably capricious and given to outbursts of unprovoked rage. A common manifestation is of 'inappropriate affect' when the sufferer's emotional reactions appear to be strangely unrelated to what is going on. Silly giggling when there is nothing to laugh at has given the name 'hebephrenia' to one form of this disease. Often angry without cause, a sufferer may nevertheless react with indifference to really bad news such as the death of a close relative. Patterns of waking and sleeping may be disturbed. Many sufferers become wildly irresponsible about money. Their performance at work or study is generally seriously affected, so they become dependent on family support, if it is forthcoming. At home, however, there is often a partial or complete social withdrawal in which the sufferer retires to his or her room (if any) and spends much time sitting or standing doing nothing at all. It need hardly be added that living with such a person is a distressing, even harrowing experience for the relatives;[5] I return to this subject below.

Schizophrenia: diagnosis

The definition and diagnosis of schizophrenia has in the past been a difficult and controversial matter for more than one reason. The condition itself is disconcertingly various; unlike the well-defined syndrome associated with many organic diseases, no two cases seem quite alike, and it is still not clear whether schizophrenia is one disease or several. Secondly, in the nature of 'functional' mental disorders (as distinct, that is, from those obviously related to 'organic' conditions such as head injuries or brain tumours) it was long the case that others had to rely mainly on sufferers' own accounts of their experiences: and, to put it crudely, if we knew that they heard voices it was because they told us so, and they might all have been lying. This lack of externally observable and verifiable signs enabled some of the anti-psychiatry school (though themselves practising psychiatrists), notably Thomas Szasz, to support their assertion that there was no such thing as mental illness at all.[6] Laing too, inclined as he was to see the psychiatric patient as the victim of a pathogenic family's interaction patterns, expressed strong reservations about whether schizophrenia could be reliably identified as a clinical syndrome.[7] Thirdly, attempts at international standardization and comparison have been hampered by the circumstance that, for quite different and unrelated reasons, psychiatrists in the two biggest industrial countries, the United States and the Soviet Union, have defined and diagnosed schizophrenia far more widely than their colleagues in other countries.[8]

Nevertheless, despite these difficulties, during the 1970s two international studies identified a group of symptoms that were highly discriminating for a diagnosis of schizophrenia; when they were present, there was a more than 90 per cent probability of this diagnosis being given in nine different parts of the world by psychiatrists speaking languages as diverse as Chinese, Hindi, Russian, Yoruba, and English. These central symptoms, as already indicated, included thought insertion, thought broadcasting, certain kinds of auditory hallucinations, and delusions of control. Other delusional and hallucinatory syndromes, such as delusions of persecution or grandeur or religion, were less reliable indicators in themselves; less reliable still were disturbances of behaviour such as persistently talking to oneself. It was patients who showed only these less reliable symptoms who were more likely to be diagnosed as schizophrenic in the United States and the Soviet Union, in addition to those exhibiting the core symptoms.[9]

A clearer understanding and a more reliable diagnosis have enabled statistical estimates to be made of the annual incidence of new cases, the prevalence at any one time, and the lifetime risk of schizophrenia. Studies in different countries have found prevalence rates of 2 to 4 per 1000 people currently suffering from the disease, and lifetime risks averaging 8 or 9 per 1000, or just under 1 per cent. The risk is much higher for the near kin of sufferers; among their parents and siblings between 4 and 14 per cent, for sufferers' children 12 per cent, and when both parents are sufferers the risk increases to about 40 per cent. The available evidence suggests that an hereditary liability is a factor as well as environmental influences.

Men and women are about equally affected. The onset of schizophrenia is characteristically slow and insidious, and difficult to identify precisely; and there are also great individual variations. However, the most usual ages of onset appear to be the late teens and early twenties for men, slightly later for women. The course of the disease is also very variable; some suffer for the rest of their lives, others experience a spontaneous remission, sometimes around the age of forty, while in yet other cases an apparent recovery is followed by a relapse. [10]

Schizophrenia: treatment

The treatment of schizophrenia was revolutionized from the late 1950s onwards by the almost accidental discovery and largely empirical use of new drugs, variously called major tranquillizers, anti-psychotics, and neuroleptics. With their use, some sufferers need not enter hospital at all; while for the majority who do, as Wender and Klein well put it, the revolution in psychiatric practice they have wrought has transformed the back wards of public mental hospitals from snake pits into fourth-class residential hotels. [11] The new drugs have proved quite dramatically effective in relieving even severe symptoms including hallucinations, and even if these do not disappear altogether the sufferer is generally able to recognize and discount them, or as psychiatrists say to gain 'insight'. With treatment, many sufferers can lead a more or less normal life out of hospital; many too can resume employment, though most have to learn to accept a lower level of achievement and to avoid stresses which quickly give rise to a return of the symptoms.

Following diagnosis, then, many psychiatrists now see their art as primarily that of finding the right combination of drugs in the right quantities for the individual patient, controlling the side-effects (which can be tiresome, though trivial compared with the major symptoms the drugs relieve), and adjusting the medication periodically to suit the patient's changing condition. Electro-convulsive therapy is no longer considered appropriate for schizophrenia, though it is for severe depression; while 'psycho-surgery' (that is, brain surgery to modify behaviour or relieve emotional disorders, as distinct from brain tumours etc.) has been largely abandoned. [12]

At the same time, that form of treatment once popularly thought of as lying on a couch and uncovering the source of one's troubles by pouring out one's innermost soul to a wise analyst, the psycho-analytic method originally associated with Sigmund Freud and his famous couch, has been in decline.

According to some psychiatric opinion, indeed, psycho-analysis is actually contra-indicated in severe illnesses including schizophrenia, because the intensely emotional personal relationship it sets up between patient and analyst creates just the kind of stress with which the sufferer is least able to deal. It is also inordinately costly, alike in money and in the time and attention of highly-qualified practitioners. Available and appropriate mainly for articulate, well-to-do patients not ill enough to need hospital care, it long contributed, especially in the USA, to a state of affairs in which the majority of psychiatrists were psycho-analysts in lucrative private practice attending, without stirring from their consulting rooms, to the less severe illnesses of the wealthy minority, while the great majority of the mentally ill, including virtually all the severely disturbed, were treated in overcrowded public mental hospitals by a desperately overworked minority of the psychiatric profession.[13] It should be added, though, that according to the latest reports much has been done in the United States in recent years to rectify that state of affairs.

Without going into deep Freudian analysis, however, talking through one's problems with a detached yet sympathetic professional outsider is no doubt a helpful thing for anyone in trouble to do, including mental patients and their relatives. But this has come to be regarded as an adjunct to the treatment of mental illness, not as the treatment itself; and opinions differ about whether a medical training is necessary or even particularly appropriate for this 'generalized' or 'non-directive psychotherapy', or whether it could not be done as well or better by psychologists or psychiatric social workers, perhaps under the name of 'counselling'.

So a diagnosis of schizophrenia, once virtually a sentence of life imprisonment, now typically entails a few months' stay in an open if not particularly attractive residential institution while the psychiatrists get the medication right, exposed to nothing worse than tablets, injections, and occupational therapy, before being discharged – in many cases quite unwillingly – to what, with a vagueness infuriating to a sociologist, is termed 'the community'. Usually, as noted above, that means in practice the care of some long-suffering female relative, most commonly the patient's mother.

Swinging the balance heavily from the hospital's custodial

function to that of treatment and discharge, the new regime has not only been arguably far better for the patients, but has also enabled great savings to be made on costly in-patient care. However, governments have not generally appeared willing to perform the other half of the trick, and invest enough of the savings in suitable housing and in services such as day centres, counselling, and community mental nursing to support the discharged sufferers and their relatives, upon whom falls an increased burden of their primary care. This is a false economy if, as Wing has indicated, discharged sufferers denied adequate community care are more likely to end up in prisons or other residential institutions such as homes for the aged. [14]

In the United States in the 1950s, when Goffman carried out his study, most mental hospital patients were compulsorily detained. It may well have been the case then, as his and other studies suggested, that the crucial decision to be made by the psychiatrist was whether or not to commit the sufferer to hospital; diagnosis may have been a secondary consideration, especially if it made little difference in practice to the way the patient was treated in hospital. [15] In such circumstances, the severer the illness from which the patient could be said to be suffering, the stronger the justification for committing him or her to hospital; and that may have had something to do with the tendency to over-diagnose schizophrenia in the United States in the past.

However, matters are now very different. The legal position in the United States has changed, while in Britain the great majority of the inmates of mental hospitals have long been voluntary patients. Although there are a few locked wards, most patients are free and even encouraged by staff to enter and leave the hospital grounds for purposes such as shopping, recreation, and visits to relatives and friends; the walls and gates that once made the mental hospital a 'total institution' like a prison are largely things of the past. Powers exist for sufferers to be treated without their consent, but they are very narrowly circumscribed; and those who exercise them as psychiatrists and social workers are generally very reluctant to exercise even the limited powers they possess, especially at the relatives' request.

In this respect too, current reality is at the opposite extreme from that portrayed by the anti-family, anti-psychiatry school, of relatives and psychiatrists in collusion to have a troublesome individual 'put away'. Under the influence of that school, indeed, many social workers are more likely systematically to disbelieve relatives, whom they suspect of being responsible for the sufferer's condition; I return to this point below. And matters are not helped by some pressure groups who often appear more zealous in a legalistic way for the rights of the mentally ill than concerned that they should be treated and their sufferings relieved, and whose activities may induce extreme caution in psychiatrists, nurses, and social workers about doing anything that might involve them in subsequent litigation. All this places an added burden upon relatives, who over and above their distress at the sufferer's plight may find themselves engaged in a desperate struggle to persuade the appropriate authorities to take action even when the sufferer's need for treatment is obvious and urgent.

It will have become apparent that there is at present no cure for schizophrenia; rather, with medication, the symptoms can be greatly relieved and the sufferer can lead a fairly normal life, albeit in most cases with some degree of disability. Nor is the cause known. Evidence is accumulating for a theory attributing the symptoms to an excess, or an over-stimulation, of certain neuro-transmitter substances in the brain, particularly dopamine.[16] If proved, that would mean that there is after all an 'organic' basis for the disease; yet it would in a sense only push the explanation one stage back, leading us to ask why that particular derangement of the brain's biochemistry occurs in some people and not in others. That in turn prompts the questions, most relevant here, of whether family life in general, or particular patterns of family interaction, are 'pathogenic' and give rise to schizophrenia or other forms of severe mental illness.

FAMILY INTERACTION PATTERNS AND MENTAL ILLNESS

One study addressed to these questions was that of Henry L. Lennard and Arnold Bernstein in New York in the late 1960s. Using an elaborated version of Bales' interaction categories (see chapter 4), they compared the interaction patterns of severely disturbed boys and their parents with those in 'control' families free of any apparent psychiatric disturbance.[17] As expected, they found some differences. In particular, the concordance ratio (agreement/disagreement) tended to be lower in the 'schizophrenic' families' interactions; but the average difference was not great, and the overlap was wide. Moreover, as they pointed out, while some investigators had advanced the theory that family interaction patterns were involved in the development of schizophrenia, others had assumed an almost reverse process and suggested that the patterns currently identified in 'schizophrenic' families represented reactions to the illness or deviance of the child. Even a clear-cut finding of distinctive interaction patterns in 'schizophrenic' families, therefore, could have been interpreted in more than one way, and would not necessarily have proved the first theory. And in fact the differences between 'schizophrenic' families and controls were 'not as substantial as clinical reports would lead one to assume'. Surprisingly, they wrote, when their data were compared with those from other contexts, including therapy and discussion groups,

a much more significant finding emerged. Family contexts as a whole, whether or not they involve families with a mentally ill member, exhibit lower concordance ratios than any other form of social context on which we had data available. Moreover, family interaction process, as mirrored in the findings yielded by our research, does not meet the criteria set forth by Bales for a viable, task-oriented system . . . The family interactional environment then must be considered as a difficult context for interaction – an observation that is, needless to say, not inconsistent with common experience.[18]

Somewhat similar thoughts were expressed by Jules Henry, an anthropologist who carried out intensive 'naturalistic' studies of five families each including at least one mentally ill member, without controls. Despite his general conviction that psychopathology was a consequence of disturbed interpersonal relations, he acknowledged the great difficulty in separating cause from effect. Of 'the new group of family therapists' he wrote:

One cannot help feeling that they often conceptualize as specifically pathological what is really common to many families and perhaps emerges as a necessary consequence of living together . . . in families never considered or labelled 'sick'. I wonder where the family therapists would find *any* family lacking all the following 'pathogenic' features: a mother's great emotional dependence on her daughter, the need of mothers to feel superior . . . parents keep much of what goes on and their own motivations secret from the children, two members of the family form an alignment, etc., etc., etc. I worry that we have here, perhaps, a sudden discovery of the contemporary *family* rather than the pathologic family, unless, of course, we urge that in our culture most families are pathogenic, in some sense – a position I take.[19] (italics in the original)

But if most families are in some sense pathogenic, why do no more than 1 in 100 of us suffer from schizophrenia? We have to distinguish, it seems, between a general pessimism and a particular theory. It may well be the case that family inter-action even in most 'normal' families in western societies leaves much to be desired. Moreover, recognition that family life is a difficult interactional environment has no doubt been a salutary corrective to the kind of blandly optimistic func-tionalism that prevailed in the sociology of the 1950s, especially in the United States. Yet most of us cope with our family life, however difficult, most of the time without becom-ing mentally ill. What the anti-family, anti-psychiatry school seem to have done was to buttress their general pessimism with a particular theory, namely that there were identifiable patterns of interaction (such as double-binding) specific to the family life of schizophrenics that played a causative role in the onset of their illness, and of which they were the victims. That theory has not been borne out.

In their comprehensive review of the literature on this subject to 1975, the London psychiatrists Steven Hirsch and Julian Leff came to a number of conclusions.[20] The mothers of schizophrenics seemed to be more concerned, protective, and possibly intrusive than normal, control mothers; but that might well be their response to an abnormal child, rather than the reverse, as children who later suffered from schizophrenia were more often ill or experienced mild disabilities early in life. Indeed, one of the first studies in this field as long ago as 1934 had noted the circularity of cause and effect on this point in a way often lost sight of in later studies. There was no evidence for the 'cold, aloof schizophrenogenic mother' (a phrase coined by Fromm-Reichman in 1948). The fathers of schizo-phrenics did not differ from other fathers in their interaction roles, and there was no difference in parental dominance patterns between schizophrenics and controls. The evidence about marital disharmony in the parents of schizophrenics was unclear; some studies had failed to show a significant difference from controls, others had found such a difference. There was more psychiatric disturbance among the parents of schizophrenics than among those of normal children, but at least part of that disturbance might be ascribed to the effect of bringing up a child suffering from schizophrenia. 'The double-bind hypothesis has not been adequately tested experimentally, but what tentative results there are suggest that double-bind messages are not specific to the parents of schizophrenics.' A study by Wynne and Singer in the United States had identified other kinds of disordered communication patterns, and Hirsch and Leff attempted to replicate their findings in Britain; but 'we failed to find the same degree of gross communication disorder in an unbiased sample of parents of schizophrenics'. However, sufferers involved in over-intense relations with relatives were more likely to relapse (a finding to which I return below). Discussing various possible explanations of the known facts, including child-to-parent, early environment, and recent environment models, Hirsch and Leff concluded that the theory most consistent with all the observed data was a genetic model.

Summing up current knowledge in 1982, the psychiatrist Ming Tsuang came to many of the same conclusions. He too stated quite categorically that 'there is no evidence supporting the schizophrenogenic mother hypothesis', and that 'there is neither uniform agreement on what constitutes double-bind messages nor convincing evidence to support the double-bind theory of schizophrenia'. Disordered family communication could be a factor in chronic personality disorganization, which in the United States had often been classed with schizophrenia; in studies using the stricter British definition in terms of hallucinations and delusions, however, it was found not to be a factor. And adoption studies had likewise discounted family interaction patterns. As already noted, sufferers' near kin were more likely than others to become sufferers in their turn; but this was due more to genetic than to environmental transmission. 'No convincing evidence exists to support a direct link between parental rearing factors and the development of schizophrenia. On the contrary, evidence that there is no causal relationship between rearing factors and schizophrenia abounds.'[21]

But although it seems clear that the *cause* of schizophrenia does not lie in family interaction patterns, they do affect its *course*. Just as discharged sufferers are vulnerable to stress at work, so they are at home. George Brown, a sociologist of Bedford College, London, in collaboration with the leading British psychiatrist John Wing and others, found that 'schizophrenic patients who returned home after an acute attack to live with a critical, hostile, or domineering relative had a much higher risk of relapse during the ensuing nine months. The more the face-to-face contact with such a relative, the greater the chance of further breakdown.'[22] Their results were confirmed by Christine Vaughn and Julian Leff, who identified three factors in the relapse rate of schizophrenic patients: the level of expressed emotion (EE) among their relatives, the time spent in face-to-face contact with them, and medication. Of these the most important was EE. Among patients not on drugs who spent more than thirty-five hours a week in face-to-face contact with high EE relatives the relapse rate was as high as 92 per cent. Medication and reducing the time spent in face-to-face contact, however, reduced the risk, and among patients doubly protected the relapse rate was 15 per cent, about the same as that of patients in low EE homes.[23] These and other studies have indicated that there is a narrowly critical relation between social interaction and the course of a schizophrenic illness. Too little social stimulation, and the sufferer can relapse into withdrawal, isolation, and even a catatonic stupor; too much can bring about a recurrence of severe symptoms, especially if it is exacerbated by anxiety, high arousal, or intrusions however well-meant upon the sufferer's privacy. In this as in many other ways, sufferers and their relatives have to learn to walk a tight-rope. Fortunately, however, many sufferers are themselves the best judges of how much social interaction they need, and what is required of relatives and others generally is a quietly tolerant understanding when, having had enough, they withdraw.

MENTAL ILLNESS: THE FAMILY BURDEN

So while the theory attributing (specifically) schizophrenia to family interaction patterns must be regarded as generally discredited, there has been a growing recognition that to be properly understood mental illness has to be seen in its setting in family life. But whereas the anti-family, anti-psychiatry school tended to portray the mentally ill as victims of their families, in a truer and fairer view sufferers and their relatives alike are to be seen as victims of shared misfortune.

The effects of mental illness on family life were particularly clearly shown in studies by Jacqueline Grad and Peter Sainsbury during the 1960s in south-western England, where they followed up the families of 410 patients referred to psychiatric centres in Salisbury and Chichester. Many relatives had been apprehensive about the danger that sufferers posed to themselves from suicide or accident. Disturbing too were sufferers' frequent complaints about bodily symptoms, and behaviour variously described as importunate and demanding; odd, with peculiar ideas; unco-operative; restless and over-talkative by day, and troublesome at night. In a few cases they threatened the safety of others, acted in objectionable, rude, or embarrassing ways, and caused trouble with neighbours. Social and leisure activities, children's lives, and domestic routines had been disrupted. Some families' incomes had been reduced, in some cases because the employment of others besides the sufferer had been affected. The mental health of 20 per cent of the patients' nearest relatives had been severely disturbed before the patient was referred, and a further 40 per cent had shown some disturbance.

At that time of transition to new ways of treating the mentally ill, Grad and Sainsbury were able to compare the traditional, hospital-centred regime in Salisbury, where 52 per cent of all new patients referred were admitted to hospital, with the new community psychiatric service in Chichester where only 14 per cent were. As they expected, 'community care as practised in Chichester left families with more problems to contend with than the more conservative type of psychiatric service offered in Salisbury did'. However, in spite of admitting fewer patients, the community service equalled the hospital-oriented one in the help it gave to the severely burdened families. The families to whom it provided less social support were a less severely burdened group consisting mainly of the families of younger psycho-neurotic patients.[24]

As has been seen, then, living with mental illness is a harrowing experience that can in itself give rise to conditions such as anxiety which need treatment. Moreover, the new methods of treatment of the seriously mentally ill place new and heavy burdens on their relatives, who need help and support in learning how to carry out the responsibilities that now rest on them for the primary care of the discharged sufferer. If they do not always get that support, it is not only because of mistaken policies about public expenditure, but also as a result of an uncritical acceptance of the teachings of the anti-family, anti-psychiatry school.

For though the exponents of that school of thought were doubtless sensitive, compassionate, and high-minded people, it may be contended that their ideas have done more harm than good. Although the impressions they gave of psychiatric practice and life in mental hospitals had no doubt considerable basis in fact at the time, they were being overtaken by events even as they were being extensively publicised in the 1960s and 1970s, and by the 1980s they were long out-dated. Meanwhile, though, and especially in some of the more lurid popular versions, they did not exactly encourage sufferers to seek or accept the treatment that would have brought relief, and so they may have been responsible for much unnecessarily prolonged suffering. Equally, their influence was such as to deter the relatives of the mentally ill from recommending sufferers to seek or accept psychiatric help, especially if it involved hospital treatment; and to impose a quite needless burden of guilt upon relatives who in the end, and in the face of pressing necessity, had to acquiesce in sufferers' entering hospital ('being put away') if only for a time.

And when they did seek help relatives, whose prime concern was for their afflicted kin, were liable to find themselves under suspicion of having been responsible for the sufferer's condition in the first place. Many relatives have complained bitterly that their accounts of sufferers' behaviour, based as it was on close personal observation over long periods, have been systematically disbelieved by briefly visiting professionals, especially social workers influenced in their training by the teachings of the anti-family, anti-psychiatry school. It is indeed ironic that the latter, who dismissed psychiatric diagnosis as mere 'labelling' and deplored the 'stigma' of mental illness, should have themselves succeeded in labelling and stigmatizing relatives 'in a particularly insulting way as incompetent and "schizophrenogenic" '. Insulting – the word is John Wing's – and also groundless, as has been seen. Wing continued:

Relatives and patients can often themselves acquire a detailed knowledge of how to minimize chronic disabilities. Relatives are highly motivated to help. In administrative jargon, they are 'primary care' agents. But, far from getting the help they need, they have often been vilified as the major causal agents.[25]

The burden of mental illness upon the family is quite heavy enough without that additional and gratuitous source of distress. And some relatives even come to believe or half believe themselves that they are to blame, and suffer needless agonies of guilt and remorse; or, unable to face that agony, try to avert their own guilt by denying that the sufferer is ill, disputing the diagnosis and the whole concept of mental illness, and withholding co-operation in the sufferer's treatment. Where some of the sufferer's near kin take one view and others another, the potential for family conflict is high; where spouses disagree over so emotionally fraught a matter, there is a serious risk of the breakdown of the marriage. I quote in conclusion from a pamphlet of the National Schizophrenia Fellowship that represents, to my mind truly, the realities of the matter.

The impact of schizophrenia on the most ordinary family can be .. shattering .. and many extreme reactions are probably normal and even to be expected. In the schizophrenias of slow onset particularly, families may be living with schizophrenia and making innumerable adaptations to it – good or bad, but all modifying any ordinary family pattern – before they or anybody else knows that they are, in fact, living with schizophrenia. It is difficult to imagine what this means. Suppose that one of your adolescent children begins to behave oddly. At first he just moons about. But many adolescents moon about. He or she becomes moody, bad tempered, slovenly, 'difficult'. But many adolescents day-dream and are moody or difficult.

To you, as a sensible parent, such behaviour is well within the limits of the normal growing-up process and no attention is paid to it. He or she will 'grow out of it', you say. But time goes on and he or she does not grow out of it. A crisis occurs when some wild display of aggression, truancy, or merely bizarre behaviour, drives you to seek expert help.

Blessed are you if, at this point, you get a firm diagnosis: twice blessed (one is almost tempted to say) if there is an acute and unmistakable schizophrenic episode and rapid hospitalisation.

But often you will get no firm opinion . . . Meanwhile your home, in an atmosphere of simulated normality, a determined show of ordinary living, is rapidly becoming preoccupied by the sick member: the ups and downs of his moods, his unpredictable vagaries of behaviour.

Reactions of brothers and sisters may differ widely and their resentment may be deep if the sick one is not handled according to the ideas of each: affectionate concern; or, alternatively jealousy over the attention he is getting; irritation at the sufferer's 'laziness' or 'selfishness'; rejection; guilt for past teasing or bullying (shadowing the omnipresent and inescapable parental guilts); refusal to accept that he is ill at all, but only 'being himself', 'doing his own thing', that it is not he or she but 'society' which is 'all wrong'. . . .

Do not be surprised . . if your family, with the abnormalities of its home-life, shrinks from introducing too many fresh outsiders into the home. To be thereupon typecast by the investigator with the clipboard as: 'introverted family which finds social contacts difficult'.

Some members of your family may never accept the diagnosis and will quarrel with the parent who tries to implement it. You then have a divided and part alienated family on your hands, if you haven't one already – to say nothing of the cases where once happily married parents are themselves driven apart because one rejects or partially rejects, which the other cannot forgive.

The sheer disruptive power of schizophrenia over a family is fully intelligible only to those who have been through it.[26]

SUGGESTIONS FOR FURTHER READING

Agnes Miles, *The Mentally Ill in Contemporary Society: A Sociological Introduction*, Oxford, Martin Robertson, 1981

Ming T. Tsuang, *Schizophrenia: The Facts*, Oxford, Oxford University Press, 1982

J. K. Wing, *Reasoning about Madness*, Oxford, Oxford University Press, 1978

Anthony Clare, *Psychiatry in Dissent: Controversial Issues in Thought and Practice*, 2nd edition, London, Tavistock, 1980

David Taylor, *Schizophrenia: Biochemical Impairments, Social Handicaps?* London, Office of Health Economics, 1979

Paul H. Wender and Donald F. Klein, *Mind, Mood, and Medicine: A Guide to the New Biopsychiatry*, New York, Farrar Straus Giroux, 1981

7

Exogamy and the avoidance of incest

In this chapter and the next I take up two related subjects introduced in chapter 4, both concerned with ways in which individuals in the course of their development enter into interaction and form relationships with people outside their nuclear families of origin.

Exogamy means marrying out, and the term refers to those 'prohibited degrees of kindred and affinity' who may not marry. Incest as generally understood refers to sexual intercourse between near kin. Clearly the two are related, for if a couple were too close kin for sexual intercourse between them to be permissible or acceptable, there would not be much point in their marrying, nor would theirs be a marriage in any ordinary sense. The converse is not true, however, and in some societies a couple (e.g. in England an uncle and niece) may not marry although illicit sex relations between them would not amount to the crime of incest. In brief: incest is about sex, exogamy is about marriage. While we have little difficulty nowadays in recognizing the distinction, failure to do so in the past has led to much confusion.

Further, I would suggest that while exogamy is a matter of rules, incest is rather the subject of feelings or attitudes of aversion, distaste, or – a word much used in the older literature – horror; sentiments which in some societies, though not all, find expression in formal prohibitions and penalties. Some such rules, and some such attitudes, have been found in almost all human societies, past and present, but there have been great variations both in the categories of kin concerned and in the intensity of the feelings aroused. In some societies the lines excluding couples from marriage and from sex relations coincide, in others not. In some they are widely drawn, in others more narrowly.

Despite variations, however, in most known societies sex and marriage alike have been proscribed, at a minimum, between the closest kin: mother and son, father and daughter, brother and sister. Exceptions and borderline cases have been rare enough for the incest prohibition to be widely seen as a universal human characteristic. More, it has been identified as *the* universal and distinctively human characteristic, which marked off in a quite crucial way our species from other animals, and whose development in human evolution constituted the great transition from the biological to the social, from 'nature' to 'culture'. This view, of which the French anthropologist Claude Lévi-Strauss was a notable exponent, was based on the widely-held belief that in other animals the mating of near kin was a natural and common phenomenon. [1] That has proved to be a misapprehension, [2] and I return to the point below.

Why should all this be so? Why do we have rules and feelings of this kind? What purpose do they serve? How have they developed in the course of human evolution? How do we, or most of us, come to accept the rules and share the feelings the subject arouses? For a long time, certainly since the 1880s, these questions have puzzled eminent anthropologists and sociologists, giving rise to scholarly debates to which voluminous literature bears witness. As long as the subject was treated primarily as an intellectual puzzle to which there seemed no satisfactory solution, it prompted the further questions: can the rules and feelings be rationally justified? Do restrictions on the marriage and mating of near kin serve any useful purpose in modern society? If not, why retain them? To a 'liberated' school of thought who asked 'why not?' there came a vehement response, very different in tone from the earlier literature, from those for whom incest represented not an intellectual puzzle but a pressing social problem, an evil causing much distress and misery in contemporary society.

THE OCCURRENCE OF INCEST

As to the actual occurrence and nature of incest in industrial societies in recent times, Christopher Bagley of the Institute of Psychiatry, London collated 50 published reports from a number of western countries and Japan. These covered 1025 cases of incest, 425 of them in enough detail to justify analysis, to which he added a further 52 from psychiatric and prison sources. Though most of these cases involved either social disorganization, especially in overcrowded urban areas (20 per cent), or some degree of mental defect or disturbance in one or both partners (57 per cent), in 23 per cent incest could be regarded as 'functional'. Many of these involved isolated patriarchal families, either on a remote farm in the country or an urban family turned in on themselves, in which the wife, unable or unwilling to fulfil her household or sex roles, or both, allowed or even positively encouraged a daughter to do so. Singled out as she was for favoured treatment, the daughter was generally happy with her role, while the whole family approved of an arrangement that met their needs and operated smoothly over a long period.[3]

From a subsequent review of the literature, including Bagley's work, the Israeli anthropologist Joseph Shepher concluded that incest is comparatively rare. (Not everybody would agree, and it is largely a question of definition, to which I turn below. Some would argue that the rarity of incest is attested by the great difficulty Bagley and others have experienced in assembling enough data for a worth-while sample; others might say that this does not show that incest is uncommon, only that it is uncommonly well hidden.) However, though rare, incest does not occur with equal frequency in all three core pairs, but most frequently between father and daughter (about 80 per cent of all cases), next between brother and sister, and very rarely indeed between mother and son. It is nearly always initiated by the male, while the female usually refuses, resists or tries to resist, or complains to an outside party. As will be noted, this finding was somewhat at variance with Bagley's of female compliance in his 'functional' cases. However, Shepher fully endorsed Bagley's finding that isolation is highly conducive to incest.[4]

According to Shepher, behaviour may be rare because it is *prevented* by circumstances such as lack of opportunity, or *inhibited* by internal psychological mechanisms, or *prohibited* by rules and norms, socially enforced. Prevention and inhibition operate among all animals, prohibition only among humans. These three mechanisms are not mutually exclusive, and in particular inhibition and prohibition may be mutually reinforcing.[5] If there are things we do not much want to do ourselves, find distasteful, and cannot imagine ourselves doing, we may well think there must be something wrong with others who do behave in that way, react punitively towards them, and say such things ought not to be allowed. Thus although incest in human societies is clearly not prevented (in the sense used here), and indeed the intimacy of life in nuclear family households affords ample opportunity for it, both inhibition and prohibition may play their part in making it a relatively rare occurrence. In other words, we have to account for both the feelings and the rules that make for the general avoidance of sexual intercourse between near kin, least completely so between fathers and daughters, more effectively between brothers and sisters, and most of all between mothers and sons.

In attempting to explain the facts, it may be useful to follow the ethologist Norbert Bischof and distinguish final from efficient causes.[6] Final causes (which might in other contexts be termed functions or origins) refer to the advantages to a human population or group of having such rules and feelings, and conversely to the disadvantages of not having them, or of flouting them. Efficient causes are the ways in which the feelings and rules are implanted in our individual development, so that most of us share the feelings and observe the rules most of the time.

In the long debates about the final causes, the advantages of avoiding incest have been seen as either biological or social, though the two types of explanation are not necessarily mutually exclusive.

FINAL CAUSES: BIOLOGICAL

Much argument has centred on the allegedly harmful effects of close inbreeding. In genetic terms, it was argued, such inbreeding increases the probability that recessive characteristics, usually overlain by the corresponding dominant genes, will 'surface' and become manifest in individuals. Although recessive characteristics are not necessarily harmful (undesirable, having negative survival value), there is good reason to think that many of them will be, for example, haemophilia; indeed, through the phenomenon known as the evolution of dominance, there will be a positive survival value in the emergence of genes dominant to these characteristics, which accordingly have become recessive precisely because they are harmful.

Against this it was argued in the older debates that the disadvantages of inbreeding were not obviously apparent. Some distinguished families in England, for example the Darwins, the Galtons, and the Wedgwoods, had gone on producing generation after generation of people of the highest ability in their various fields despite cousin marriages, and perhaps even because of them.[7] Not all recessive genes were harmful; and they might even include characteristics highly desirable in human terms though devoid of survival value, such as artistic creativity and emotional sensitivity. Further, it was argued, the deliberate mating of close kin was the means by which humans as stockbreeders developed lines of domestic animals that bred true and reliably reproduced desired characteristics. The allegedly harmful effects of close inbreeding, therefore, cannot have been blindingly apparent to early humans at the dawn of history who were supposed to have made such a point of avoiding it in themselves by banning incest, contrary to their animal nature.

For a time, then, the genetic arguments for incest avoidance were regarded with some reserve as not fully proven.[8] More recently, however, they have gained ground. In part this has been because of direct evidence of high rates of congenital defect in the children of incestuous unions. One such study was that by Morton S. Adams and James V. Neel, who compared 18 women pregnant as a result of incest (12 with their brothers and 6 with their fathers) with 18 other unmarried mothers matched for age, ethnic group, body build, intelligence, and socio-economic status under the care of the same agencies in the same state of Michigan. Six months after birth, only 7 'children of incest' were normal and could be recommended for adoption, while 11 had either died or were suffering some degree of defect or morbidity, including the three least severely mentally retarded whose IQs were around 70. By contrast, none of the comparison children died, none had an IQ of less than 80, and though the adoptions of 3 were deferred the IQs of the remaining 15 ranged from 91 to 133 with an average of 105.[9]

In part, too, the genetic argument has been extended as biologists have also stressed the positive advantages of exogamic mating in order to 'stir up the gene pool' (so to speak) and increase the possible combinations and recombinations of hereditary characteristics, the main source of variety in a species that has to adapt continually to different and changing environments. A species in which mating was mainly between near kin would lose many of the advantages of sexual reproduction. In fact, and contrary to what was once generally believed, not many animal species are known in which under natural conditions inbreeding occurs to any considerable degree. The exceptions are mainly lower animals, particularly parasites, closely adapted to living in stable environments in conditions unfavourable to exogamic mating.[10] Genetic stability in such species is clearly an asset, whereas in most wild species including ourselves it would be a distinct liability. The older theorists were misled, no doubt, by their observations of farm, domestic, and zoo animals into thinking that those species had no inhibitions about mating with their near kin. The point is, though, that human stockbreeders generally give domesticated animals little choice, and enforce close inbreeding by withholding other mates, while in zoos too the choice of mates is usually limited by circumstances if not by design.

On the other hand, although some degree of outbreeding is no doubt advantageous, some degree of inbreeding is inevitable since all human beings are to some extent interrelated, and it is probably desirable if we are not all to marry complete strangers.[11] Assortative mating, which sociologists term endogamy or homogamy, generally limits the effective breeding population or intermarrying community in humans mainly to those of the same language and nationality, region, social class, and religion, and greatly increases the probability that if a couple trace their genealogies far enough back they will find common ancestors. Between inbreeding and outbreeding there may well be a long range of degrees of relatedness at which the balance of biological advantage can be struck; and at the inbreeding end of the scale the question, how close is too close? may be one admitting of no very clear-cut answer. However, the genetic hazards of very close inbreeding seem clear; and we may conclude with some confidence that the biological function of incest avoidance is to minimize its occurrence.

FINAL CAUSES: SOCIAL

It has long been argued that avoiding incest and limiting sex relations within the nuclear family to the married couple is necessary to protect the family from internal strife. As noted in chapter 4, those arguments were echoed in Talcott Parsons' view that incestuous relations between parents and children would seriously weaken the leadership coalition of the married pair. However, such arguments were always vulnerable to the criticism that sexual jealousy is (so far as we know) a learned response, not an innate or necessarily inevitable aspect of human behaviour. Thus jealousy between mothers and daughters seems to have been successfully overcome in some of Bagley's 'functional' cases.

Another time-honoured argument is that marrying out creates a wider society with bonds extending beyond the selfish particularism of family groups. As the royal families and landed gentry of Europe have always recognized, marriages create alliances. Particularly in stateless societies in which people rely on their kin groups for protection and support, and political relations take the form of feuds between lineages and clans, exogamy is an important – perhaps the most important – way of keeping the peace. In a society composed of exogamous lineages, many a man would have a sister literally in the enemy camp, so that if there were a fight he might kill his brother-in-law, widow his sister, and orphan his nephews and nieces; while even a serious quarrel and lasting bitterness would make social visits and family reunions difficult. In such a society, neighbouring lineages would have reason to patch up disputes as quickly and amicably as possible, and stop well short of fighting and bloodshed.

Such an argument is unexceptionable and indeed cogent as far as it goes. However, it leads to further puzzles. It makes it seem as though we prohibit incest because we practise exogamy: a chicken-and-egg puzzle, no doubt, but one that leaves unsolved the question of the peculiar emotions aroused by the subject of incest and its prohibition, which is predominantly one of feeling rather than of rational calculation. And it applies to conditions of life which, though no doubt they prevailed in some societies in the past have long been superseded in western societies by the rise of other forms

of social organization through which people enter into interactions outside the family. Obviously we in western societies
do not rely on alliances between exogamous lineages to keep
the peace. Are we then to regard exogamy and the incest prohibition as social fossils, vestigial remains of an earlier stage of
human evolution? If so, can we rationally justify retaining them
in a modern industrial society?

Turning to the question of how an aversion to incest is engendered and sustained in our individual development, I
mentioned in chapter 4 one major theory, that of Sigmund
Freud, which Talcott Parsons incorporated at the centre of his
analysis of the nuclear family. That theory, it will be recalled,
focussed on mother-son incest and its prohibition, and
postulated that because the desire was so strong it had to be
even more strongly blocked.

A rival theory was put forward as long ago as 1891 by Edward
Westermarck, the Finnish anthropologist, sociologist, and
philosopher, who maintained that though there was no innate
aversion to marriage with near relations, 'there is an innate
aversion to sexual intercourse between persons living closely
together from early youth, and that, as such persons are in most
cases related, this feeling displays itself chiefly as a horror of
intercourse between near kin'. [12]

This theory was long criticised as inadequate. [13] Freud himself
explicitly rebutted it, along with genetic theories, saying that
they failed to explain the need for stern prohibitions, which
would point rather to strong desires. [14] Why should we be so
strongly forbidden to do something we don't particularly want
to do anyway? More recently, however, it has come back into
favour as evidence for it has been found in observations both of
human societies and of the social behaviour of other animals.

For, as already noted, detailed studies of animal behaviour in
the wild in the 1960s and 1970s seem to have established that
close inbreeding is the exception rather than the rule in the
animal kingdom. In many lower species such as fishes it is prevented by dispersion; although near kin do not necessarily
recognize one another as such, they seldom meet so seldom
mate. In some higher species in which there is individual

recognition, however, it seems to be inhibited by an actual aversion to mating with near kin. Particularly impressive in this respect were the observations of Jane Goodall among wild chimpanzees. Females on heat eagerly solicited sexual advances and mated in quick succession with any males who happened to be around – but not their sons, and only rarely and reluctantly with their brothers.[15] Somewhat similar observations among other primate species begin to make it look as if an aversion to incest, so far from being distinctively human, is actually common to us and other related animal species, and marks a continuity rather than a disjunction between 'nature' and 'culture'.

Observations in human societies notably include those of the American anthropologist Arthur Wolf in rural Taiwan in the 1960s. There, one of five forms of marriage involved infant betrothal and the removal of the bride-to-be, *sim-pua*, to her future husband's family's home when she was no more than three years old, to be brought up there like his sister until the couple were old enough to complete and consummate the marriage. This arrangement minimized the archetypal Chinese conflict between mother-in-law and daughter-in-law by ensuring that the latter was no intruder but already one of the family. It did so, however, at the cost of a sexual aversion so strong that some couples eventually consummated their marriage only under duress. *Sim-pua* marriages were clearly unsatisfactory, as evidenced by much more resort to prostitutes on the part of men married in this way compared with others, and a much greater tendency of *sim-pua* wives to take lovers. And in response to Wolf's questions, people said they found the prospect of such a marriage 'shameful', 'uninteresting', or 'meaningless', or by their embarrassed silence left him to deduce a lack of sexual arousal. After carefully considering other possible explanations, Wolf was in no doubt that his observations supported Westermarck's theory.[16]

Exactly similar effects have been noted by several observers among children brought up together in kibbutzim (collective farm settlements) in Israel. I have more to say in chapter 14 about the rejection of traditional Jewish family patterns in search of a radically different way of life that formed part of the whole ideology of the kibbutz movement; suffice it to say here that it led parents as a matter of principled conviction to hand over their infants when no more than a few days old to be looked after and brought up in communal nurseries under the care of a professionally trained child nurse, the metapelet, night and day apart from two hours every evening spent in their parents' company, a recreation time valued by parents and children alike. In Westermarck's terms, therefore, these unrelated children of similar age in the same peer-group 'lived very closely together from childhood' like brothers and sisters. It was Melford Spiro, a United States sociologist, in the 1950s who first recorded their behavioural development.[17] Under the age of about twelve years, children romped and played happily together, including some quite uninhibited sex play. In their early teens, however, sexual shame increased very markedly, as girls became very hostile towards boys, would not talk to them, and refused to go in to the shower bath with them though they had previously done so all their lives. Spiro added that in the kibbutz he studied there had been no marriage, nor to the best of his knowledge sexual intercourse, between age-mates. Explicitly they viewed each other as siblings; and when they became interested in heterosexual relationships, it was with others outside their group.

Spiro's observations were confirmed in the 1960s by the psychoanalyst Bruno Bettelheim, though he accounted for them in Freudian rather than Westermarckian terms;[18] by the Israeli sociologist Yonina Talmon-Garber, who found no case of the marriage of members of the same peer-group in three kibbutzim, and no record of any love affairs either; and most conclusively by Joseph Shepher, who searched the records of 2,769 kibbutz marriages. Only 14 of them were of couples who had ever belonged to the same peer-group. Most even of these had joined the same group after the age of 6; only 5 had been in the same peer-group at any time before that age, and none had been socialized together during the whole of their first 6 years. As for premarital sex, Shepher was able to make detailed inquiries in only one kibbutz. There he found not a single case between children brought up together, in complete contrast to the intense sexual attraction between boys and girls joining a peer-group at later ages.[19]

The anthropologist Robin Fox put forward a refined version of Westermarck's theory after examining in detail the data from seven well-documented and widely diverse cultures about their patterns of child rearing and the nature and intensity of their incest prohibitions. Emphatic incest prohibitions, drastic penalties, and strongly internalized guilt feelings occurred in those societies in which young brothers and sisters, though members of the same household, were not allowed to engage in playful bodily contact, see each other unclad, bath together, be alone in each other's company, etc. Indeed, if such practices were intended as precautions against the arousal of incestuous desires, they were self-defeating. The more freely brothers and sisters are allowed to romp and play together before sexual maturity, the less likely it is that they will want to have sex relations with each other after puberty. Like Westermarck, Fox focussed on sibling incest, partly as a corrective to the undue emphasis he considered had been placed on parent–child incest in psychoanalytical writings. However, he was concerned to reconcile the apparently opposed theories of Freud and Westermarck, and as a first step set them out schematically:

Westermarck
childhood propinquity   positive aversion   ( ) prohibitions

Freud
(   )   strong desire   stern prohibitions

If we filled in the blanks, the arguments might prove to be complementary:

Childhood propinquity   positive aversion   (lax) prohibitions
(childhood separation)   strong desire   stern prohibitions

In more elaborate schemes, mere 'propinquity' might be distinguished from intimacy and bodily contact, for as noted above the one without the other in early childhood seemed to be tantalizing, reinforcing rather than preventing the arousal in adolescence of desires that had to be even more strongly repressed. And in some societies the 'stern prohibitions' took the form of external sanctions, ferocious penalties for incest, whereas in others the sanctions were internalized and took the form of self-punishment through guilt. As for the aversion to parent–child incest, perhaps the same effect of close bodily contact in infancy leading to sexual indifference or aversion later in life would apply with even more force to mothers and their infants than it did to siblings. That would explain why mother–son incest seemed to be the most 'unthinkable', while the father–daughter relation was less strongly inhibited and occurred more often.[20] Indeed, intimate propinquity and bodily contact between a father and his infant daughter would, according to this theory, make her averse to him as a sex partner in later life without doing anything to inhibit his possible desire for her. That certainly seems to fit the facts, especially if it is the case that when father–daughter incest occurs it is almost always initiated by the father and resisted by the daughter.

So the Westermarckian theory that incest is avoided mainly through an inhibition engendered by close physical contact in early childhood, though focussed initially on sibling incest, seems also to account for the facts about parent–child incest. On the other hand, the Freudian argument that stern prohibitions are needed to block strong desires is flawed; inhibitions and prohibitions are not mutually exclusive, and can be mutually reinforcing. Indeed, Shepher speculated that throughout human development incest has always been rare, because, in us as in other primates, it is inhibited. Being rare, it came to be regarded as strange and unnatural. 'Because people could not tolerate even a few exceptional cases – precisely because they were so monstrously exceptional – they prohibited them.'[21]

These are, however, only general tendencies permitting of many exceptions. According to this theory, brothers and sisters separated in infancy, for instance following their parents' death or some other calamity, might later meet and fall in love. There are even occasional newspaper reports of siblings and half-siblings, ignorant of their true parentage, innocently and inadvertently marrying, only to find the marriage null and themselves open to criminal charges for consummating it.

EXCEPTIONS

And the prohibition of incest is not total in all societies. According to Robin Fox, 'At the last count, there were at least ninety-six societies with some evidence of permitted sexual relations among family members, including full marriage.'[22] In most of them, it seems, incest was tolerated or indulged only in special circumstances or for exceptional people: in the strictly literal sense they were the exceptions that proved the rule. Thus in traditional African beliefs a man who would dare to commit incest set himself apart from ordinary men as a sorcerer,[23] a mighty hunter,[24] or a great chief: 'Royal incest, instead of threatening the security of the society, strengthens the divine right to rule.'[25]

Incestuous unions in some royal families in the past, such as those of ancient Egypt, may also be seen under another light as a special case of isolation. 'What is a poor princess to do? She had almost no way to go but down.'[26] Especially in a family at the apex of an imperial system, almost the only possible mate of equal rank might be her father or brother. And if the arrangements for the care of infant princes and princesses in royal households were such that they did not have much to do with each other, or with their father, they may not have had much Westermarckian aversion to such a union, quite apart from any pressure of dynastic considerations to overcome it.

In the most striking case, that of ancient Egypt where over periods of thousands of years many kings married their sisters and some their daughters, it was long thought that such considerations applied, and that they were maintaining the ritual purity of a line of divine rulers and asserting their power to do what ordinary mortals could not. Now, however, it has become known that though that may possibly have been true of the Pharaohs and the Ptolemies, there were many brother–sister marriages among commoners too at least under Roman rule. According to the United States sociologist Russell Middleton, although evidence about the Pharaonic period was scanty, there were records of just one fairly certain and several possible cases of brother–sister marriage among commoners; while for the period of Roman rule from 30 BC onwards there was much more abundant evidence from papyrus documents and records indicating that 20 per cent or more of all marriages were of siblings or half-siblings. One papyrus set out the genealogy of a woman named Demetria whose parents, grandparents and great-grandparents were all full brothers and sisters.[27]

The English sociologist Keith Hopkins was equally convinced by the evidence from Roman Egypt that 'We are dealing here not with occasional premarital sex between siblings, abnormal but condoned, but with lawful, publicly celebrated marriage between full brother and sister, replete with wedding invitations, marriage contracts, dowries, children, and divorce.' Householders' census returns showed that between 15 and 21 per cent of all current marriages were of full or half-brothers and sisters, the majority being of full siblings. Some returns used the unambiguous phrase 'his wife who is his sister of the same father and of the same mother'. With the high mortality then prevailing, only about 40 per cent of families could have had both a son and a daughter or both sons and daughters surviving to marriageable age; so at least one-third, and perhaps more, of all men with marriageable sisters must have married them in preference to someone outside the family. Judging from letters, such unions were just as loving as those of unrelated spouses. Hopkins was sceptical of the explanation put forward by Middleton and later by Goody, that such a marriage conserved family property in a society in which women had full rights of ownership and inheritance. A family with both a son and a daughter might expect to gain when a daughter-in-law brought property in about as much as they would lose when the daughter took property out, and there would be little advantage in marrying the daughter to the son for that reason. Moreover, there was a well-developed market in land in ancient Egypt, and families could and did reconsolidate their holdings, so there was no need for brothers and sisters to marry to keep the family land as an undivided workable farm. As for the genetic disadvantages, Hopkins speculated that while occasional inbreeding in a population with a lot of harmful recessives in its gene pool would be likely to have visibly adverse effects, after regular inbreeding over several generations most of the harmful recessives would have 'surfaced' and been eliminated. Meanwhile, in a population such as that of ancient Egypt in which infant and general mortality alike were extremely high, the extra mortality due to inbreeding would pass more or less unnoticed. Be that as it may, it seems clear that brother–sister marriages were quite usual for over two centuries till they were prohibited when Roman law was extended to Egypt in AD 212, a ban strongly reinforced by the growing influence of the Christian Church after AD 300.[28]

INCEST AND THE PROHIBITED DEGREES IN WESTERN SOCIETIES

It was noted in chapter 2 that the mediaeval Church extended the prohibited degrees to second and even more distant cousins, and identified affines with kin for this purpose according to the doctrine that husband and wife became 'one flesh'. Marriage within the wide circle of the prohibited degrees was condemned as incestuous, contrary to an older folk-tradition that rather favoured the marriages of fairly close kin and the remarriage of widowed persons to affines in order to conserve family property, form alliances, and consolidate land-holdings. Since the Reformation the circle has narrowed again. Roman Catholic canon law itself has fallen back somewhat in the 20th century from the severity of its mediaeval position. The canon law promulgated in 1917 extended the prohibited degrees only as far as the third collateral degree, that of second cousins, whose consanguinity moreover constituted only a minor impediment to marriage, though there were greater difficulties about the marriage of first cousins.[29] In England, however, as noted in chapter 2, Henry VIII's Parliament legalized the marriage of first cousins; and in 1907 after more than fifty years of controversy Parliament finally decided that a man should be allowed to marry his deceased wife's sister. In the United States cousin marriage is lawful in some states, not in others.

As with divorce, then, the glacial retreat of the Church's ascendancy has left moraine heaps of confusion and inconsistency. Thus according to the English lawyer Anthony Manchester, in most western countries incest is specified as a criminal offence; in some, however, including France, Belgium, and the Netherlands, incestuous acts are punishable even though there is no law specifically against incest. In France, for example, indecent assault by an ascendant upon a minor is punishable with life imprisonment if violence is involved. In some countries illicit sex within the prohibited degrees counts as incest, so that the categories of kin between whom sex and marriage are prohibited are the same; in other countries they are different, and incest is defined as sex within a narrower circle than those who may not marry. It is even the case that some states' laws permit people to marry between whom sex relations are forbidden in other states where incest is widely defined, including Scotland and some states of the United

States. How rigorously the law is enforced in the latter, however, is another question.[30]

In Scotland, the law both civil and criminal long rested on an Act of 1567 which in effect incorporated into Scots law the provisions of the 18th chapter of the Book of Leviticus, 'uncover the nakedness of' being taken as a euphemism for sexual intercourse.[31] In England and Wales, however, incest became a crime only in 1908. Before that it had been dealt with, rather ineffectively according to Manchester, by the ecclesiastical courts. The 1908 Act was passed, partly to end the anomaly that incest was a crime in Scotland but not in England, partly in an atmosphere of moral panic and acute concern about the welfare of women and girls; it defined incest far more narrowly than in Scotland, and more narrowly than the prohibited degrees in England. Thus for example though a man could not marry his niece, sexual intercourse between them was not a crime. Similarly, the law in England and Wales protected a man's illegitimate daughter but not his adopted or step-daughter.

Opinions could not be more sharply divided than they are about this subject. On the one hand, a liberal (not to say 'liberated' or 'progressive') attitude questions the need for laws prohibiting incest and preventing near kin from marrying in modern societies. Whether they are seen as representing a continuity between humans and other animal species, or as having been socially advantageous in keeping the peace between exogamous lineages before the rise of the state, these prohibitions are relics of the past; they should be re-examined, and if they are found to serve no useful purpose should be discarded. In some, admittedly rare, cases they cause hardship, such as those mentioned above in which brothers and sisters parted in infancy meet later in life and fall in love. To avoid bringing such cases to court, the Criminal Law Revision Committee in England recommended in 1984 that sex relations between a brother and sister both over twenty-one should no longer be an offence.[32] In Sweden a more far-reaching proposal put forward by an official commission in 1976, but not implemented, was to abolish the penal provisions dealing with incest altogether. Sexual relations between parent and child would have been punishable only if the child was under eighteen, and would have come under a more general prohibition of sexual relations with children of dependent status in the adult's care. Similarly, sexual relations between brothers and sisters would have been an offence only if one or both were under the age of consent, which the commission proposed should be lowered to fourteen.[33] In the Swedish debate the argument was put forward that, though there are genetic disadvantages and dangers in the unions of close kin, they are considerably less than those arising from the unions of unrelated persons affected by hereditary diseases. We do not in general prohibit sexual liaisons between such persons, nor forbid them to bring children into the world. Is it not inequitable to single out the unions of close kin for prohibition on genetic grounds while permitting those about whose genetic hazards there can be no doubt, such as deaf-mutes or haemophiliacs and haemophilia-carriers, or those possibly at risk, such as schizophrenics?

Needless to say – so the liberal argument continues – if a father by violence or threat forces his daughter to have sex with him, that is an offence and should rightly be penalized. But the offence lies in the force or threat of force. There is indeed a liberal case also for ceasing to regard rape as a separate criminal offence, and considering forced sex with an unwilling partner as assault; and doubtless any court would take into account any sexual overtones in assessing the severity of the assault and the appropriate sentence. Similarly, it is readily accepted that children cannot give informed consent, and this is generally recognized in laws against under-age sex. But whether girls need special additional protection from the advances of their fathers and brothers in particular, or whether such cases could be dealt with as they are in Belgium under the general law protecting minors, is questioned in current debates.

On the other hand, according to a considerable body of opinion among professionals such as physicians and social workers, incest is unequivocally an evil. It involves an incestuous aggressor, usually male, and a victim, usually female. It can hardly be distinguished in practice from other forms of abuse including rape and generally violent assault, and it is often associated with other problems such as alcoholism. The question of force is meaningless in practice; the father is generally the biggest and strongest person in the family, and his position of authority is said to be buttressed by a whole tradition of male dominance, so that it is extremely hard for a daughter to resist his advances even if they are not backed by an immediate show of force.

Legal definitions of incest have been regarded as too narrow, first in the circle of kin they delineate. Thus sexual advances by a girl's step-father, adoptive father, or uncle should, it is held, be regarded as incestuous though hitherto not so defined in English law. The Criminal Law Revision Committee in England (cited above) in 1984 went some way to meet this point, recommending that 'the protection of the young and vulnerable against sexual exploitation within the family' should be extended to adopted daughters and step-daughters. Adopted children (sons too, for consistency's sake) should be included in the law on incest, while a separate new offence should be created of unlawful sexual intercourse with a step-child under twenty-one. However, it seemed that such extensions might collide with another trend, that of narrowing the prohibited degrees and allowing more closely-related people to marry. There had been 'a measure of support' in the House of Lords for a bill which would have enabled step-parents to marry their step-children over the age of twenty-one, and a private Act had been passed in 1980 enabling one such couple to marry.[34]

Secondly, in some writers' opinion to limit the definition of incest to heterosexual intercourse is also too narrow. This is a matter not only of legal definition; clearly, only heterosexual intercourse with the possibility of pregnancy and childbirth is relevant to discussions such as those I have reviewed above of the genetic hazards of inbreeding and the biological function of incest avoidance. On the other hand, however, a wider concept of incestuous behaviour may be more appropriate to a consideration of the quality of inter-personal relationships in family life. Thus it is a moot point whether homosexual relations between near kin should be included. Similarly, the Canadian forensic psychiatrist Ingrid Cooper had stated that a clinical definition, wider than that of the law, would include sexual play, fondling, fellatio, and masturbation.[35] This question too was considered by the English Criminal Law Revision Committee, who, however, decided against recommending that the definition of incest should be widened to include indecent sexual acts other than sexual intercourse.

Other writers have drawn fine and elusive lines between

nurturing and exploitative touching, distinguishing for example a father's friendly and protective hugging of his daughter from erotic fondling. A relationship between a mother and her adult daughter has even been described as incestuous although it involved no genital touching and was characterized mainly as flirtatious. Widely understood in this way, incestuous behaviour has been experienced as traumatic and associated with later difficulties in forming heterosexual relationships and satisfactory marriages. From the point of view of this body of opinion, the liberal school of thought is seen as a 'pro-incest lobby', turning a blind eye to a prevalent social evil. For, widely so defined, incestuous behaviour is certainly not regarded as a rare occurrence, but one which according to some estimates affects possibly one woman in ten at some time during her childhood and adolescence.[36]

However, there may be a middle ground between these two extremes. Thus although Bagley classified 23 per cent of incest cases as 'functional', more than 50 per cent fell into his categories 'pathological', 'object fixation', or 'psychopathic'; so his finding afforded some support for both points of view. And those who, like Ingrid Cooper, urge the 'decriminalization of incest' do not necessarily advocate repealing laws that prohibit it, but rather, recognizing that more often than not it indicates that a family has severe problems, recommend handling them outside the judicial process if possible.

SUGGESTIONS FOR FURTHER READING

Robin Fox, *The Red Lamp of Incest*, London, Hutchinson, 1980
Norbert Bischof, 'Comparative ethology of incest avoidance', in Robin Fox (ed.), *Biosocial Anthropology*, London, Malaby Press, 1975
Joseph Shepher, *Incest: A Biosocial View*, New York, Academic Press, 1983

8

Age-mates and adolescent socialization

Family life is not the only influence in individual development, and among the many other socializing agents the peer-group of age-mates plays an important part. In the language of social anthropology, age-grades are the stages through which an individual passes, like Shakespeare's seven ages, while age-sets are the groups of age-mates who pass through those stages together. In demography, sets of people born at about the same time – in the same year, or five-year period – are termed age-cohorts; in politics, people of similar age who shared important formative experiences are sometimes called generations; in social psychology, an individual's age-mates are referred to as peers, who may or may not form peer-groups.

The widening world of which a child becomes aware, and the influences shaping a child's development, may be listed in some such sequence as follows.[1] At first, as Bowlby emphasised, the baby's world consists of mother and very little else. Very soon, however, the infant begins to respond to father, siblings if any, and other co-resident kin. Soon the world of the growing child extends to neighbours and to non-co-resident kin: grandparents, uncles and aunts. Among neighbours there are generally children, so that a peer-group of age-mates begins to form before they all go to school together. Needless to say, schooling is a powerful socializing force; it is intended to be, and it is. But its influence goes far beyond that of classroom instruction. The school class as a peer-group in involuntary daily interaction, with the friendships and enmities that form among its members, set patterns that persist for life. At a fairly early age, too, in modern western societies the child's world begins to include the mass media of communication. Children not allowed to watch a particular TV programme at home at apt to slip away, to be discovered after a short search in front of the small screen in a neighbour's home. Peer-groups and mass media influences interact over programme choice and evaluation, and parents find it difficult to control their children's exposure to television and the other media. Short of bringing up their children in well-nigh total seclusion, a way of life many would regard as indefensibly restrictive, parents cannot wholly shield their children from knowledge of the wider world reaching them through the media, ranging all the way from news of grave international tensions and major domestic political issues to currents of artistic expression and fashions in dress, music, dancing, and the like. Awareness of these trends, dawning in adolescence, may give each generation its own distinctive character according to the events that were prominent when they were in their teens, as the Vietnam war and the rise of the Beatles did to those born around 1945–50 who were adolescent in the 1960s. Adolescence, too, is a time of decision in individual development when political and religious convictions are formed that generally last for life. This came out very clearly in studies of young people in British politics by Philip Abrams and Alan Little,[2] and of religious behaviour by Michael Argyle.[3] True, as both studies found, most young people followed their parents' lead in these matters; but a substantial minority did not, and rejected their parents' beliefs in a mood of adolescent rebellion in which they were more open to the influence of friends. In countries with conscription, military service is another important socializing influence; and while that has not much affected most western countries since 1945, it has been shown to be an extremely powerful influence on the lives and attitudes of men in the Soviet Union,[4] following as it does on years of indoctrination in the official communist youth movement, of which more below. And finally there is the world of work.

In a society with a marked division of labour between the sexes, and in which women and men inhabit separate social worlds (Bott's segregated roles), babies of both sexes will be born into the women's world and looked after in infancy by their mothers; but while the girls stay in the women's world as they grow up, boys at some stage in their development must cross over into the world of men. The point has a bearing on the views of some feminists who, as noted in chapter 5, have envisaged a society in which women have as little to do with men as possible. It is related also to the wealth of examples in the literature of social anthropology of the initiation rituals in which boys were turned into men in some traditional non-western societies, in many cases involving painful mutilations and traumatic ordeals that tested young males to their limit. In some societies there were *rites de passage* for young women too. Especially severe were those involving clitoridectomy;[5] but the prime object even of those that did not, like the *chisungu*, female initiation ceremonies, minutely observed and analysed by Audrey Richards among the Bemba of Zambia, was quite clearly to turn girls into submissive wives.[6]

A full consideration of the anthropological detail would lie outside the scope of this book; but it may be contended that there are echoes of the underlying theme particularly of male initiation, even if they are not explicitly recognized as such, in widely diverse social and occupational milieux in western societies past and present. Examples include the Spartan regimes of some boys' boarding schools, military academies, and colleges connected with the armed services, especially where stringent discipline is enforced in part by senior pupils who are thereby licensed to bully their juniors. At less exalted socio-economic levels there are the ordeals of young entrants to industrial occupations, for example, the 'deckie-learner' fishermen in Hull trawlers portrayed in Jeremy Tunstall's study.[7]

Totalitarian regimes both fascist and communist have exploited to the full the socializing influence of adolescent peer-groups. Organizations such as the Hitler Youth were set up to mobilize the energies of young people, to imbue them at an impressionable age with the values of the regime and to enlist their loyalty to it. Such organisations have also served as the means to counter dissident influences reaching young people from their families, even to the extent of encouraging children to denounce their parents to the authorities for what are judged to be subversive or anti-social activities. Membership of the official youth movements in such regimes is virtually universal, at least in the younger age-grades, and independent youth organizations are usually discouraged if not banned outright.

By contrast, the voluntary youth movements in our pluralistic western democracies appear fragmented and diverse, and not all adolescents belong to any youth organization at all. Organizations such as the Scout movement, youth groups connected with religious dominations, and the youth wings of political parties, do not in general set out to counteract parental influence and are much more likely to reinforce it since parents generally have some part in choosing which if any youth organization their children join. However, there is generally little or no adult influence upon the spontaneous group activities of neighbourhood peers or school classmates. That unorganized or only very informally organized group life is often in conflict with parental norms, and perceived by adults as anti-social and threatening, giving rise to expressions of concern about a 'generation gap' and 'the disintegration of family life'.

Demographic and economic trends combined to bring these tendencies to the fore in the 1950s. Birth-rates in western countries had been low in the 1930s and early forties, so that the age-cohort who were in their teens in the 1950s was a small one. Moreover, a rising proportion of them stayed on at school, and the numbers of school-leavers entering jobs in industry were therefore small at a time of general prosperity, high employment, and low unemployment. The scarcity of young workers enabled them to earn high wages at an age when they could still live inexpensively in their parents' households. They had plenty of money to spend on consumer goods, and in response to that unprecedented demand there was a rapid growth of a new market for goods and services with a distinctive appeal to adolescents or young adults: new fashions in dress and hair-styles, motor-cycles, electronic audio equipment, dance halls catering for a young public, and so on.[8] At that time, too, young working-class adults had money and freedom denied their middle-class age-mates, who stayed on at school, still economically dependent on their parents, their juvenile status symbolized by the school uniforms still insisted on by many schools, their leisure time curtailed by study for important examinations. Paradoxically therefore it was those who in a life-time perspective were relatively privileged who in the short term experienced relative deprivation and tried, as far as their limited resources of time and money allowed, to join in the exuberant world of the discos and the groups. High-lighted by an incident when Eton boys were said to have queued for tickets for a Beatles concert, these trends led some observers to see the new generation as harbingers of a classless society. For reasons already indicated, however, I think that was a superficial view.

Whether their activities were seen as hopefully forward-looking or threateningly out of control, then, adolescent peer-groups were the subject of a good deal of earnest adult discussion in western societies in the 1950s and 1960s. It was against that background that the United States social psychologist Urie Bronfenbrenner carried out his comparative study of child-rearing and peer-group life in the United States and the Soviet Union.

Bronfenbrenner pointed out that the prevailing view in western countries had been that environmental influences on children's psychological development were determined almost entirely by their parents, and within the first six years of life at that. As noted in chapter 3, Bowlby's work affords a leading example. 'Western studies of influence on personality development in childhood overwhelmingly take the form of research on parent–child relations, with the peer group, or other extra-parental influences, scarcely being considered.' By contrast, such studies in the Soviet Union and other East European countries had 'focused equally exclusively on the influence of the peer group, that is, the children's collective'.[9]

In the Soviet Union, children were cared for and brought up from their earliest years in collective nurseries and crèches for at least part of the time, especially when their mothers were out at work. At school, each class was also a unit of the communist youth organization for the appropriate age-grade. Membership of the Octobrists (for ages 7–9) and the Pioneers (10–15) was virtually universal. The Komsomol or Young Communist League (16–28) was more selective, but enrolled more than half of those eligible by age. The aims and values of these organizations were fully consistent with those of the school system, both having been derived from the same source in the official principles of Soviet pedagogy especially on the side of character training or communist morality. In many ways too they resembled those of the independent youth movements like the Scouts in western countries: be prepared, truthful, thrifty, diligent, helpful, friendly, etc.[10]

But there were profound and subtle differences. Each pupil's standing was periodically evaluated by the peer-group, following standards and procedures taught by responsible adults such as teachers. Pupils were encouraged to watch over their comrades, praise their good performance and behaviour, and help them when in difficulties. Helping one's comrades, however, included criticizing them for falling short of the standards of communist morality. So the children's collective became the agent of 'adult society' as a source of reward and punishment, the latter taking the form of public criticism and ultimately the threat of expulsion from the youth organization with all its rewards and benefits. Similarly, being truthful included, in the words of one Soviet educator, 'expressing one's opinion publicly about a comrade's misconduct'. Thus among posters illustrating the laws of the Pioneers, one showed a boy denouncing a class-mate for carving his name on his desk.[11] But there was a poster within the poster; on the clasroom wall was one depicting a young Pioneer named Pavlik Morozov who, during the forced collectivization of agriculture in the 1920s and 1930s, had denounced his own father as a collaborator with the Kulaks who were resisting that measure, and testified against him in court. Killed by the village people in revenge, Pavlik had been identified as a martyr in the cause of communism. 'A statue of him in Moscow is constantly visited by children, who keep it bedecked with fresh flowers, and many collective farms, Pioneer palaces, and libraries bear his name.' So although Bronfenbrenner wrote of the children's collective as the agent of a generalized 'adult society' in the Soviet Union, it seems important to ask: which adults? He quoted a leading Soviet writer on child-rearing:

We cannot risk our children's future by allowing their upbringing to be determined by spontaneous drift. The school and the parents [note the order: U.B.] must hold the reins of upbringing in their own hands and take all measures necessary to insure that children obey their elders.[12]

Similarly, an eminent Soviet educationist had written:

The very concept of 'children's collective' is to some degree qualified, since in the life and activity of any children's collective one always assumes the participation of adults. A collective which forms without adult involvement is not likely to endure . . . The life experience of its leaders turns out to be inadequate to hold the collective to a right course even if the goal which the children have set themselves is a proper one.[13]

By contrast, 'allowing children's upbringing to be determined by spontaneous drift' was just what Bronfenbrenner thought was happening in the United States. Some studies there and in other western countries had drawn attention to peer-group influences in relation to, and often in conflict with, those of parents. Thus children in families with absent fathers, such as American soldiers in the Second World War and Norwegian seamen, were found to be low on such qualities as achievement motivation, self-esteem, responsibility, and leadership, and more susceptible to peer-group influence.[14] A study in Seattle by Charles E. Bowerman and John W. Kinch found that up to and including the seventh grade children looked more to their families for company and as a source of identity and values; in the eight and higher grades, more to their peers. However, a lowered orientation to the family in adolescence was not inevitable, but took place only when a poor adjustment was made to other family members; and that in turn seemed to be 'a function of the way the family reacts to the child during the period of increasing peer-orientation.'[15] Bronfenbrenner and his colleagues found that sixth grade children (age 13) chose to spend twice as much time at week-ends with peers, singly or in groups, as with their parents; boys more than girls, and boys more with groups, girls with a single friend. Some children were more peer-oriented than others, apparently responding to a lack of attention and concern at home rather than the positive attractions of the peer-group. They showed a greater tendency to engage in illegal or otherwise anti-social activities such as lying and teasing other children, and their parents were rated low on both expressed affection and the exercise of discipline and control.[16]

Similarly, a study by James S. Coleman had shown that the aspirations and actions of American teen-agers were primarily influenced by the 'leading crowd' in school. For boys, athletics; for girls, the 'popular date' represented the glory of success, to which educational achievement came a poor second. In another study, Coleman had found that schoolmates' social background came second only to children's own family background as a factor in their intellectual development, and ahead of their school's resources (class size, laboratories, libraries, etc.) and the characteristics of their teachers. Lower-class children with schoolmates from advantaged homes did reasonably well, while those whose classmates also came from deprived backgrounds did poorly. Coleman reported that the converse was not true, and that children from middle-class homes were not 'pulled down' or held back by schoolmates from less advantaged homes.[17] Others disputed this in a debate about 'compensatory education' which raised the question whether concepts such as educational deprivation and disadvantage were not inadmissibly evaluative and class-biased,[18] and I return in chapter 11 to a discussion of social class and educational opportunity in relation to family life. For present purposes, however, the point is that these studies left no doubt of the importance of peer-group influences upon adolescents' performance and behaviour in school.

Out of school, these influences were most vividly illustrated in a study by the American social psychologist Muzafer Sherif that became known as the Robber's Cave experiment. Eleven-year-old boys attending a summer camp were first organized into two groups competing in sports, a treasure hunt, and so on. The two groups soon became hostile and contemptuous towards each other; 'name-calling, scuffles and raids were the rule of the day'. Bringing the two groups together for social events such as going to the movies and eating in the same dining hall, far from reducing conflict, 'only served as opportunities for the rival groups to berate and attack each other'. Conflict was dispelled, however, by a series of stratagems in which the boys were called upon to co-operate in pursuit of 'superordinate goals', real and compelling for all concerned, such as restoring the camp's interrupted water supply.[19]

Bronfenbrenner's balanced conclusion was that if the Soviet Union had gone too far in subjecting children and peer-groups to conformity to a single set of values imposed by the 'adult society' (in other words, the communist party), perhaps the United States had allowed excessive autonomy and failed to utilize the constructive potential of the peer-group in developing social responsibility and consideration for others.[20] Peer-group influences were generally secondary to those of the family, but could supersede the latter if parents alienated young adults or failed to give them understanding guidance.

SUGGESTION FOR FURTHER READING

Urie Bronfenbrenner, *Two Worlds of Childhood: US and USSR*, Harmondsworth, Penguin, 1974

9

Women in employment

In this chapter and the next I explore the implications for family life of the growing participation of married women in economic activities and relations other than those of the domestic household economy. From the outset there is a problem about terminology here, and most current and recent usages are inaccurate, objectionable, or both. To refer to 'working women' or 'working wives' as distinct from housewives implies that housework is not work, which is ridiculous and belittles those who do it. The phrase 'economically active', though sanctioned by international official usage, is open to a similar objection; moreover, there is the special irony that the word economy itself is derived from the classical Greek for household management. 'Occupied' is no better, though 'gainfully occupied' is perhaps more acceptable. Most people understand what is meant by 'going out to work', and it will do for many purposes, though it is not precisely accurate since some paid work is done at home. Nor is 'employed' or 'in paid employment' quite right, since some gainfully occupied people are employers or self-employed. With these qualifications in mind, however, and for want of a better short expression, I refer in what follows to 'women's employment'.

Much of the paid work that women do is of a kind that can be done for a while, left, and resumed. Work of a kind that demands continuous application and a lifetime's commitment while holding out hope of advancement, generally known as a career, is the subject of the next chapter.

WOMEN'S EMPLOYMENT IN THE PAST

There is nothing new about women earning an independent livelihood in western societies where, as I suggested in chapter

1, their position has always been relatively favourable compared with other major culture areas. At least, for example, female infanticide was never the practice in the west, as it was in traditional China; nor was clitoridectomy, as in some traditional African and Islamic societies; nor, as in the latter and in ancient Rome, were girls usually married at puberty; nor were most girls married to men not of their own choice, for though child betrothal and arranged marriages did sometimes occur they were not generally characteristic. In pre-industrial western societies, as seen in chapter 2, most women like most men in early adulthood worked for some years as living-in servants in the households of families other than their own, leaving to get married usually in their middle or late twenties. Some never married, and stayed in service to become the trusted family retainers of popular legend, supervising the younger servants.[1] According to Macfarlane, in mediaeval England women whether single, married, or widowed had extensive and well-developed rights and status. Unmarried women were landholders, working the land with hired labour. Some even held land in military tenure, presumably hiring men-at-arms to do service for them. Women agricultural workers were paid the same wages as men, for example at harvest time. Women had full legal rights to sue and be sued in person, not as wards of some male guardian; and they could plead their own cases in court, or those of others including their husbands. And women evidently engaged in business, including money-lending.[2]

It seems possible that before the industrial revolution many married women were not only housewives but also their husbands' business partners, in fact if not in name. Even in recent times, perhaps continuing an older tradition, farmers' wives in the north of England commonly kept the accounts and handled all the bills and money, while the men managed the crops and livestock (the very word husbandry is suggestive) and were content to leave financial matters to the female 'Chancellor of the Exchequer'.[3] While that kind of partnership cannot have prevailed at all social levels, there must have been less and less scope for it with the rise of bigger economic enterprises, the separation of the work-place from the home, and the decline of the household as the primary unit of economic organization.

In the 19th and early 20th centuries substantial numbers of women were employed, albeit in a restricted range of occupa-

tions. By far the biggest number were domestic servants. As
J. A. Banks pointed out, the rise of the middle class in the 19th
century was associated with a corresponding rise in the number
of domestic servants, nearly all of whom were female, and most
of whom lived in.[4] In England and Wales their number grew
from three-quarters of a million in 1851 to over one and three-
quarter millions in 1901, when they were the biggest single
occupational group and comprised over 40 per cent of all
employed females.[5] A second area of predominantly female
employment lay in the textile mills, especially in the north of
England, and in garment making. In a third area, David Lockwood showed how clerical and secretarial work were largely
taken over by women from men during the 19th century as
firms grew bigger, the male counting-house clerk came to have
less and less prospect of promotion to the board-room, and the
transformation of office work into predominantly women's
work was associated with the advent of new machines such as
typewriters and telephones.[6] Other largely female occupations
included the highly skilled near-professions of nursing and
teaching whose status and importance were enhanced by
reforms in the treatment of the sick and in schooling
respectively.

It may possibly have been at that period that employment
came to be regarded as appropriate for 'surplus' women who
'had to' work because they had no husband to support them. In
a society where marriage was monogamous and women outnumbered men there were bound to be many such women,
and, for example, in Britain until well into the 20th century
there were generally about 107 to 109 women for every 100
men aged 15–49. Three factors contributed to this. Mortality
rates in most societies are generally higher for males than for
females, so that when mortality was generally heavy fewer men
than women survived into adulthood. Secondly, more men
than women migrated overseas to settle in the colonies or to
spend their working lives abroad, many of them in tropical
areas of high mortality, as colonial administrators, mission-
aries, soldiers, and the like. With the general improvement of
health following the sanitary reforms of the 19th century, mortality rates fell; but then there were heavy casualties, almost
exclusively among men, in the 1914–18 war, so that by the

1921 census in Britain the number of women for every 100 men aged 15–49 had risen to 113, and the 'surplus female' effect was prolonged into the 1920s and 1930s.[7]

After 1950, however, women's employment ceased to be associated with their singlehood as the numbers of married women workers greatly increased. The circumstances of the Second World War had something to do with this. Although Germany and the Soviet Union suffered appallingly heavy losses, casualties in some western countries including Britain and the United States were comparatively light, and they were not confined to men. In the case of Britain, too, emigration had dwindled to a mere trickle compared with earlier decades. So there was no longer a 'surplus' of 'unmarriageable' females to fill the available jobs at a time of brisk demand for all civilian goods and services, lower unemployment than ever before or since, and acute labour shortages. In these new circumstances, some employers began to take more seriously than before the possibility of employing married women, part-time as well as full-time, and even devising shift arrangements to meet their needs such as meeting children from school. One such firm was Peek Frean's, who made biscuits in south-east London, and whose married women workers were the subject of a pioneer study by Pearl Jephcott, Nancy Seear, and J. H. Smith.[8]

By the 1950s, too, women were marrying younger than in the past, and fewer were remaining single. Thus in England and Wales although the proportion of women aged 45–49 who had never married was still as high as 16.6 per cent in 1950, it fell to 10.2 per cent in 1962 and 7 per cent in 1975.[9] More women workers, therefore, could only mean more married women workers. Thus in Britain between 1951 and 1979, while the number of men officially classed as being 'in the labour force' remained stable, and the number of single women fell, there was a two-and-a-half-fold increase in the number of married women so counted, and the proportion of married women classed as 'economically active' rose from 22 to 50 per cent.[10]

To sum up: there is nothing new about women's employment; the new development since 1950 has been the growing number of *married* women going out to work.

THREE ATTITUDES TOWARDS WOMEN'S EMPLOYMENT

Three attitudes may be distinguished towards the employment of women, especially married women. Each has its outward implications for the wider economy and society, and its inward implications for family life.

First, employment is incompatible with marriage; or, wives should not go out to work.

According to this view, the normal and rightful place for a married woman is at home, supported by her husband, devoting herself to home-making and child-care. It is accepted that some women may 'have to' go out to work if they have no husband or other man, such as a father, to support them. In the wider economy and society, therefore, women's employment is linked to their singlehood. When a working woman marries, she should give up her job to someone who needs it more – either another woman, still unmarried, or a man with a wife and family to keep. Within the family, the husband/father is the breadwinner, responsible for the family's income, supporting wife and children. In recognition of that responsibility he is entitled to look for home comforts to the wife/mother. Men's and women's roles are segregated (in Bott's term: see chapter 5), and there is a clear-cut division of labour between the sexes both in the family and the wider society. Men and women inhabit largely separate worlds, with the further implications mentioned in the last chapter: though boys and girls alike are born into the women's world and live in it as young children, girls stay in it for life while boys at some stage have to cross over, and are initiated into an exclusively male world, as much in recreational milieux ('the club') as at work. Hesitantly, I label this the 'traditional' attitude, though the tradition and the circumstances that gave rise to it may not be of very long standing, going back perhaps no further than the 19th century.

Secondly, the neo-traditional attitude: employment is compatible with marriage, but not with the care of infants and the aged.

This view corresponds largely to the 'three-phase model' of Alva Myrdal and Viola Klein,[11] according to which women do not automatically and at once give up their jobs when they get married, but continue in employment for a while until they start having children. In the second or family phase of their lives, married women withdraw from employment to devote themselves to the care of their young children, as enjoined by Bowlby and his disciples (see chapter 3). Then, in the third or post-family phase when their children are growing up and going to school, they go back to work. Family incomes are increased, especially during the children's school years when the costs of feeding and clothing them are greatest. Non-monetary benefits in addition include the interests and friendships women can find in their working lives outside the home, and the satisfaction of not letting scarce and valuable skills go unused, especially for women trained in occupations with a high ideal of service to others such as nursing and teaching.

However, the break in employment during the family phase of caring for young children seriously handicaps or even virtually precludes women from pursuing careers. In addition, women's working lives outside the home are liable to be curtailed by the need to look after their own and their husbands' aged relatives.

Within the household, according to this view, men are still the principal though no longer the sole breadwinners upon whom falls the prime responsibility for maintaining the family income, while the wife's contribution 'helps'. If there is some blurring of the lines of the division of labour between the sexes, and men do some of the housework, this too is called 'helping' – a key word, indicating that the ultimate responsibility for household tasks lies with women. Likewise, it would be the mother who would absent herself from work to look after a sick child. For this reason, too, women's attendance at work comes to be seen as unreliable, which further handicaps them in the world of employment and especially careers.

Thirdly, the thoroughgoing egalitarian attitude: employment is compatible with marriage and all other family responsibilities.

This follows logically from the principle that women and men should have equal opportunities for continuous full-time employment, and that there is no reason to accept anything short of the equality of the sexes in this as in other fields. To implement this principle, it is important to establish that women are no more likely than men to be absent from work because of family responsibilities, especially if maternity leave is regarded as equivalent to the sick leave to which in many occupations workers of both sexes are entitled without penalty. This attitude involves a radical rejection of the traditional division of labour between the sexes, and entails the sharing of all household tasks and responsibilities on a perfectly equal basis. It is not a matter of him 'helping' her with the housework, but a process of negotiating individual agreements about who does what in the home on the basis of ability and preference, not sex. Likewise, it involves the 'parenting', not the 'mothering', of children (see chapter 3). Men should be just as liable as women to stay at home with a sick child; and the same should apply to the care of the aged. Putting these principles into practice is greatly facilitated if maximum use is made of domestic machinery to lighten household tasks, and also of public or private help with the care of dependants such as nursery schools for infants and welfare services for the aged.

We may reasonably surmise that the first or traditional attitude prevailed in western industrial societies before the Second World War. Though support for it has since declined, it is probably still the view of a substantial minority. The second attitude, or attitudes broadly akin to it, representing a compromise between the competing claims of family life and employment in women's lives, gained currency after 1945, and by the 1960s was the view of the overwhelming majority. The uncompromising egalitarian attitude, which has come to the fore in public discussion since 1960, is still probably the view of a small minority. Though some pay it lip-service, few seem prepared to accept its full implications for their family lives.

WORKING MOTHERS AND THEIR CHILDREN

Public discussion in Britain about married women working, especially those with dependent children, was strongly influenced by John Bowlby's work on maternal deprivation and associated with fears about the children's welfare.

These fears were largely allayed by a study carried out around 1960 by the sociologists Simon Yudkin and Anthea Holme.[12] They found that the pre-school children of working mothers were mostly looked after by relatives, especially their grandmothers, and in some cases their fathers, while for a fair minority day nursery or nursery school was the solution. For children of school age, school dinners solved one important problem for working mothers, many of whom were able to be back at home before the children returned from school. Others returned to a grandmother or father at home, and 'latchkey children' (in the phrase then current), who had to let themselves in to an empty dwelling, were a minority. School holidays and children's sickness presented problems too, which again in Yudkin and Holmes' judgement the majority of parents solved satisfactorily in one way or another, but which a minority did not handle satisfactorily: 'a suspiciously high proportion of children – almost exactly one-third – seemed never to be ill'. According to studies of children's development, especially those of J. W. B. Douglas and his colleagues (to which I refer again in chapter 11 below), the children of working mothers seemed to develop physically just as well as those of mothers who stayed at home, and they were no more liable to accidents, though if injured or ill they were more likely to be admitted to hospital and tended to stay longer once there. There was no difference in the incidence of signs of disturbance, such as thumb-sucking and bed-wetting, between the children of working and non-working mothers; and Douglas and Blomfield concluded that there was 'no reason to believe that the children of employed mothers are in any way at a disadvantage'.[13] Similarly, in his study of young delinquents in Glasgow, Thomas Ferguson found that mothers' employment was not a factor of any importance in relation to their sons' delinquency.[14]

Women in Britain, however, have continued to act according to Myrdal and Klein's three-phase model. Fig. 3 shows that in 1983 close to 70 per cent of women aged 20–24 were classed as 'economically active', as of those aged 40–49, but at ages in between the 'economic activity rates' were lower, as we should expect if many women aged 25–35 had temporarily withdrawn from paid work in order to look after young children. That was not the pattern, however, in other countries of the European community except to a very limited extent.

In her survey of women's employment carried out for the British government in 1968, Audrey Hunt like Yudkin and Holme showed how important was the help given by family members, especially grandmothers, in looking after the children of working mothers. But the grandmothers of the

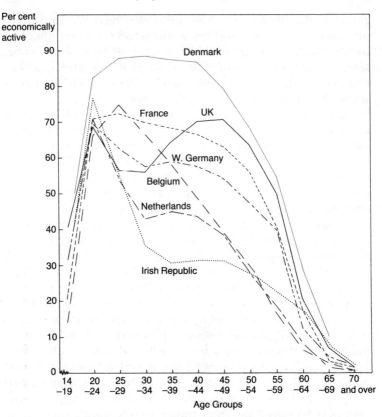

Fig. 3. Female economic activity rates in seven Western European countries, 1983.
Source: EC Labour Force Survey, 1983. Data kindly supplied by the Statistical Office of the European Communities.

1960s included many who had never worked; and it was open to question whether the new generation of working mothers, when they reached their fifties and became grandmothers in their turn, would be so inclined to stay at home and look after their daughters' (or sons') children. Hunt also emphasised how for many women the need to care for the aged was second only to that of young children. The great majority of working mothers thought that their children benefited, mainly financially, from their going out to work. About one in three were the daughters of working women, and most of them had not minded their own mothers' going out to work. There was overwhelming support among Hunt's sample, from working and non-working women alike, for two propositions. On the one hand, a married woman with no children had the right to go out to work if she wanted; but on the other, a woman with children under school age should not go out to work. These considerations seemed to be more important to them than their husbands' attitudes to their going out to work, which were about evenly distributed, one-third approving, one-third disapproving, and one-third with no strong feelings. Though husbands' attitudes evidently had some bearing on wives' choices, Hunt showed that among employed wives one in seven was working despite her husband's disapproval.[15] Her findings seem to confirm what I surmised above, that the traditional attitude still had the support of a sizeable minority, while the neo-traditional view, that a wife has the right to work but not if she has young children, had become that of the prevailing majority in the 1960s.

DISCRIMINATION: SEGREGATION AND UNEQUAL PAY

Despite married women's increasing participation in work outside the household, however, it is far from being the case that women mingle with men on terms of equality in every walk of life. Discrimination in the world of work is manifest in two related ways: women tend to be paid less than men, and women and men do different work.

This has partly been the outward consequence of prevailing views of family life and attitudes towards women's roles in the family. Employers long argued that women's commitment to their work is less than men's, since men are the breadwinners while married women's earnings are a useful but secondary addition to a family's income. In so far as they adopt the three-phase model, too, women have not the same life-time commitment to continuous employment. And when they are working, because of their family responsibilities such as looking after a sick child women's attendance at work is less reliable. Such arguments have often been put forward to justify paying women less than men.

The trade union movement, too, has not always been particularly zealous for equal pay. As Hilary Land pointed out, the unions' prime aim has traditionally been to ensure that every man was paid a 'family wage', enough to keep a wife and children, and they long espoused 'the model of the family based

on the male breadwinner and a wife who puts her domestic responsibilities first.'[16] From the point of view of male trade
unionists, admitting women to men's jobs could be seen as a
form of dilution and regarded with suspicion. Lacking as they
did a lifelong commitment to industry, working (or so it was
sometimes said) for 'pin-money' before and after having their
children, including many in part-time work or working at home
or in small establishments, women were notoriously difficult to
organize into unions, and so were powerless to press for higher
wages and better conditions. No wonder if, from a trade union
point of view, they were so often exploited and under-paid.

Equal pay for equal or similar work has been enjoined by law
in Britain since 1970, and sex discrimination in selection for
jobs and conditions of employment has been generally unlawful, with certain exceptions, since 1975. However, the question
of equal pay and conditions in this strictly limited sense arises
only when men and women compete directly for the same jobs
in the same labour market. This they do only to a very limited
extent, as women's employment is heavily concentrated in
certain predominantly female occupations – almost as much so
as in the 19th century, though there are nothing like as many
domestic servants now. Thus in 1971 in Britain more than 90
per cent of workers in the clothing trade, nurses, secretaries,
domestic servants and canteen assistants were women, and so
were more than 60 per cent of shop assistants, hairdressers,
cleaners, telephone operators, teachers, waiters, and cooks.
On the other hand, 18 per cent of medical practitioners were
women, 17 per cent of accountants, company secretaries, and
senior local government officials, 11 per cent of senior civil
servants, 4 per cent of barristers and solicitors, and just 1 per
cent of engineers.[17]

Such data clearly indicate a high degree of sexual segregation
in occupations, for which in the United States there are precise
numerical estimates in an 'index of dissimilarity'. According to
this measure, if (for example) all male workers were coal
miners and all female workers were shop assistants or hairdressers, the index of dissimilarity would be 100 per cent, representing complete segregation. In fact, United States censuses
from 1900 to 1960 yielded indexes ranging between 65 and 69
per cent, and showing no particular tendency to fall; and the
United States occupational structure has been more segregated

by sex than by race, for which the corresponding index in 1960 was 47 per cent.[18]

Moreover, there is a marked tendency for women to occupy subordinate posts in organizations under the direction of mainly male senior staff: for example, as nurses in hospitals under the authority of doctors, most of whom are men; as teachers in schools with mostly male heads; or as typists in business firms or government offices most of whose managers or senior officials are male. Naturally enough, the difference in responsibility and authority is reflected in pay: and it raises the question: Why so few women in top jobs? to which I turn in the next chapter.

This tendency also has its inward implications for family life. It means that most working wives earn less than their husbands; and for this too we have precise data for the United States where, according to the Bureau of the Census, among couples both of whom worked full-time the husbands typically earned nearly twice as much as their wives (medians $14,826 and $8,696 respectively in 1977), and the wives therefore contributed not much more than one-third of the family income. Moreover, many more women than men work part-time, or do not go out to work at all, so that in American families as a whole the wives' contributions amounted to not much more than a quarter of all family income.[19]

The relationship between men's and women's earnings, therefore, acts as an important factor predisposing men to see themselves as still the main though not now the only breadwinners, and tipping the balance of the division of labour in the household towards the neo-traditional pattern with the wife accepting prime responsibility for the housework and caring for the children and elderly relatives while the husband 'helps'.

SUGGESTIONS FOR FURTHER READING

Simon Yudkin and Anthea Holme, *Working Mothers and their Children*, London, Michael Joseph, 1963

Audrey Hunt, *A Survey of Women's Employment* (Government Social Survey Report no. SS 379), London, Her Majesty's Stationery Office, 1968

10

Careers and couples

In its widest sense a career is a progression or sequence through time, especially in the life of an individual; thus Erving Goffman wrote of 'the moral career of the mental patient'. In particular it means an occupation affording the prospect but not the certainty of advancement. Some careers are to be found in large organizations such as the civil service, the armed forces, and big business corporations, with their opportunities for promotion to higher ranks. Others may be pursued in professional or business partnerships, as in medicine, the law, or architecture; yet others are highly individual, such as those of a novelist or a concert pianist. A career is more than a mere job or livelihood; and commitment to a career is generally regarded as combining ambition, service to others, and self-fulfilment. In various ways it demands uninterrupted, full-time dedication: for some, such as the concert pianist, simply keeping in practice; for others, keeping abreast of current developments such as new scientific discoveries, changes in the law or in business or professional practice; for many, maintaining personal contacts in informal relationships ('old boy networks') with clients, colleagues, business associates, and the like. It generally demands travel, for example to attend conferences, fulfil professional engagements, or promote one's firm's business. In many cases it demands mobility, for as noted in chapter 5 the pursuit of a career generally entails being a spiralist, willing to move at the firm's behest to another branch or establishment, or to seize the opportunity of a higher post elsewhere in a different organization. At other times, however, it may involve the reverse, staying in one place even at the cost of personal or family inconvenience to see a project through to completion, finish a course of study and present a thesis, or fulfil obligations

146

to clients or colleagues. Clearly such exigencies impose constraints upon the family life of the career-oriented.

PARTNERSHIP AND THE SYMMETRICAL FAMILY

In the book that represented the culmination of their twenty years' work at the Institute of Community Studies in east London, Michael Young and Peter Willmott summed up the changes they discerned in family life as a trend towards 'the symmetrical family'. While more women were going out to work, men were spending more time at home. Their working hours were shorter than in the past. Houses were bigger and more comfortable, in contrast to the cramped, unattractive dwellings of the London poor and working classes in the 19th century; so there was less reason for men to seek the warmth and comfort of the 'pub'. Furthermore, the old closely-knit working-class communities had been broken up as the former London County Council had re-housed people in suburban estates. That movement exemplified Young and Willmott's 'Principle of Stratified Diffusion', according to which patterns of life originating among the well-to-do spread down the social scale, with a time-lag; thus 'the slow march' of the middle classes to the suburbs in the 19th century had been succeeded by that of the working classes in the 20th. In those more spaciously-laid-out estates, the local pubs were less accessible, while there was more to do at home, including gardening and home decorating. These and many other household tasks had been facilitated by 'the miniaturization of machines', making for a more home- and family-centred life for the type of working man whom J. H. Goldthorpe had called 'privatized';[1] and there had been a very considerable blurring of the division of labour between the sexes.

Young and Willmott were convinced by what their informants told them that there had been a profound concurrent change in the quality of the relations between the sexes. Along with a de-segregation of roles had gone a greater tendency for husbands and wives to share alike in household work and leisure activities, between which it was increasingly difficult to distinguish. Although it would be premature to use such a term as egalitarian, the trend was in that direction as husbands and wives were more nearly equal than in the past when men were masters, of whom their wives and children went in fear. Neither companionate nor companionship were quite the right words for the tendency and the new relationship, for which they finally hit on the term symmetrical.

MANAGERS AND THEIR WIVES: THE TWO-PERSON, ONE-CAREER COUPLE

At the very top of the socio-economic scale, however, and quite contrary to their Principle of Stratified Diffusion, Young and Willmott found that decidedly 'asymmetrical' relations prevailed in the family life of the 190 managing directors of whom they carried out a special survey. Among their wives, only 2 per cent were working full-time and 8 per cent part-time. As for the majority, their chief role was to look after the home and the children, in nearly every case with the paid help of domestic servants, gardeners, chauffeurs, and *au pair* girls. They were also expected to be available at short notice to entertain, or to accompany their husbands to dinners with business associates; and to provide a relaxing atmosphere at home in a setting in which men subject to intense pressures at work could make the most of their precious, limited leisure time.

The relationship seemed typically to be one of partnership, but of a different kind from that which we have mainly been describing . . . If the wife could accept that she was a junior partner, all could be well . . . These wives were not notable for their superior education and the feminist aspirations that go with it. They belonged to a minority who were prepared to settle for a different sort of compromise in an asymmetrical family, married to a dominant man with whose successes they could to some extent identify, very well-off in material terms, home-centred because their husbands were so much the opposite.[2]

An exactly similar picture emerged from another study of managers and their wives carried out in the London area by J. M. and R. E. Pahl. Among their sample, only 3 out of 86 wives worked full-time and 10 part-time. As married couples, both husbands and wives characterized their relationships as 'close' (the word most often used) and egalitarian, much more so than their parents' had been. Wives saw their most important roles as looking after the house and children, sharing their husband's relaxation, and talking over his problems, and to a less extent being a social asset and entertaining his colleagues. Husbands were on the whole well content with their married lives; wives less so, and some resented the passive, supportive domestic role into which they were thrust, and regretted not making more use of their own skills and the qualifications that some of them possessed. Most wives, particularly younger women, did not mind moving in response to their husbands' career opportunities, but there were sometimes acute conflicts between these and the needs of children settled in school and building up a circle of friends.[3] The great majority of the managers and their wives in this study, then, exemplified the two-person career couple as partners jointly pursuing one career: his.

And in the United States, Martha R. Fowlkes' study of 'wives of medicine and academe' in a New England community yielded precisely comparable findings. Fowlkes distinguished wives' 'adjunct' and 'supportive' contributions to their husbands' careers. As adjuncts, wives helped their husbands directly; thus most academic wives did their husbands' typing. Medicine was viewed unequivocally as a two-person career, and the role of doctor's wife was particularly clearly defined. Two magazines, *MD's Wife* and *Medical Mrs*, in addition to the traditionally female interests of food, family, and fashion emphasized the voluntary roles and social concerns of women. It was taken well-nigh for granted that doctors' wives would participate in voluntary hospital auxiliary activities; nearly all were doing so, and several acknowledged that it benefited their husbands' reputations and careers. Compared with her adjunct work, 'the supportive contribution of the wife is diffuse and pervasive, consisting of a more generalized stance and set of attitudes and responses that simultaneously sustain, nurture, and bolster her husband's career commitment'. All wives sang their husbands' praises at home and abroad, provided them with a supportive environment, and were prepared to move.

Fowlkes went on to state that wives did 'double duty in the rearing of children who belong to both of them, . . . manag [ing] and keep [ing] the homes in which both of them live, . . . organiz [ing] the family and social life in which both of them engage'.[4] This usage of the term 'double duty', however, seems debatable in relation to wives most of whom were not going out to work, and whose husbands too could be said to be doing double duty by earning enough to keep both of them (or all, including the children). Perhaps it would be better to reserve the term for working wives who also shoulder most of the domestic responsibilities, and I return to this point below in discussing the sheer overload problem in the 'dual-career family'.

In sum, then, even though many couples engaged in the joint pursuit of a single career may say that they regard themselves as equal partners, it is questionable whether in this as in other areas of social life the phrase 'equal but different' may not be specious and serve perhaps as a disguise and a rationalization for inequality. Certainly in the studies cited above men seemed to be more content with such a partnership than women. True equality, it may be asserted, means women having as much right to their own independent careers as men; and that brings us to a consideration of the resurgence of feminism since about 1960, and the dual-career family, the topics to which I now turn.

THE REVIVAL OF THE WOMEN'S MOVEMENT

By about 1920, it seemed as though the movement whose beginnings had been signalled in 1792 by Mary Wollstone-craft's *A Vindication of the Rights of Women* had run its course and achieved its main objects. Political franchise, votes for women, had been granted in most western countries except Switzer-land. At various dates in different countries, women had been admitted to universities. Redoubtable pioneers had effected their entry into once exclusively male professions, like Harriet Martineau into journalism, and Elizabeth Blackwell and Elizabeth Garrett Anderson into medicine, respectively in the United States and Britain. Women had gained the right to prac-tise law and to enter all ranks of the civil service.

According to historians of the women's movement, then, 1920 represented its 'moral pinnacle', to be followed in sub-sequent decades by the 'end' or 'decline' of feminism.[5] 'Be-tween 1920 and 1960 public interest in women's rights to all intents and purposes had vanished.'[6] The bastions had fallen, the walls of male exclusiveness had been breached, the first heroic pioneers had entered the citadels. Of course they were few at first, but it could only be a matter of time before they were followed by others in larger numbers. Furthermore, though it was only right that they should have the opportunity, perhaps not all women would want to dedicate themselves to careers and reach the top. Perhaps many, given the choice, would choose to be wives and mothers; and the career women would be the exceptions, thought of as they still were as 'battle-axes' and 'blue-stockings'.

By 1960, however, such arguments were beginning to look thin. Forty years on, the numbers of women in parliament, the professions, business management, and 'top jobs' generally were still to be measured in single figures per cent. It began to be pointed out that 50 per cent or more of the adult population are female; that girls now had well-nigh equal educational opportunities; and that there are no systematic differences in the distribution of intelligence between males and females, old false beliefs about male superiority having been rendered untenable by the work of psychologists in the 1920s. It should follow that the proportion of women in top jobs should be about 50 per cent. Why, after forty years, were there nowhere near as many? And as for the choice between marriage and career, men did not have to make such a choice; why should women?

WHY SO FEW WOMEN IN TOP JOBS?

The entry of women to a ranked professional or occupational structure often seems to go through a series of stages as represented in fig.4. Male exclusiveness, which prevails in stage 1, is breached in stage 2 with the arrival of the women pioneers. Quite quickly, a few of these go right to the top, as in stage 3; but without large numbers of new women entrants, female participation at all levels remains limited. At this stage, there tends to be 'tokenism' and 'the statutory woman'; to demonstrate that women are not being excluded or discriminated against, it is a requirement, often informal or unspoken but sometimes formally laid down, that there should be at least one woman on every official committee or university senate, each business firm should include a woman partner or director, and so on. However, even if there are large numbers of new female entrants, so that women actually outnumber men in the lower and middle ranks, they may still be under-represented at the top, and the whole structure may be skewed, as in stage 4.

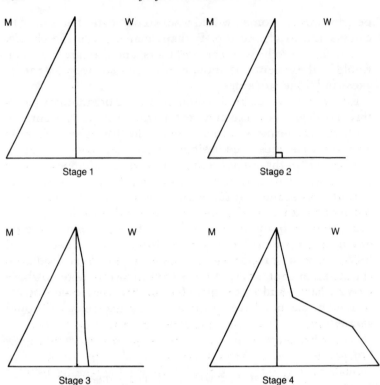

Fig. 4. Four stages in women's entry to a ranked occupation, once exclusively male.

School-teaching in Britain is one example; another is the Soviet medical profession.

If, then, the onward march towards the equality of the sexes seemed to have been checked at stage 3 or stage 4, why was that so? Were women experiencing institutionalized discrimination? Granted that the grosser discriminations had been removed, for example when women were admitted to medical schools and allowed to practise law, were there subtler forms of differential treatment in laws and administrative and business practices that handicapped women, requiring unusual determination to overcome? Were there perhaps systematic differences in opportunity, such as poor mathematics and science teaching in girls' schools? Secondly, were there individual prejudices and preferences that might result in women being denied promotion, or finding it harder to establish the confidence of clients and colleagues? These might work either way, though; for example, some of a law firm's clients might quite possibly prefer to confide in a male partner; but on the other hand many women patients prefer to see a woman doctor, as was clearly demonstrated when it was proposed to close the all-female hospital in London named after Elizabeth Garrett Anderson. Thirdly, was there a tendency for women – some women, at least – to hold themselves back? Were they more conscious than men of family needs and their responsibilities for children and the aged? or aware, perhaps of an incongruity between the image of themselves as wife and mother on the one hand, and as competent professional practitioner or tough, astute business executive on the other? To what extent, indeed, might women be held back by a fear of success?[7] And finally, assuming that careers were not to be restricted to single women 'battle-axes', and that it was unlikely that a new generation of career women might find 'househusbands' willing to stay at home and look after the children, in what circumstances and on what terms was it possible for women to combine an independent career with marriage and motherhood? Few though they might be, what was life like for couples both of whom were pursuing careers? Following the resurgence of feminism in the 1960s, these questions prompted a number of studies of dual-career families (dual-profession families, two-career families, or dual-career couples) from the late 1960s onwards.[8]

DUAL-CAREER FAMILIES

Research into this subject in Britain was initiated under the auspices of Political and Economic Planning (PEP, later renamed the Policy Studies Institute) by Michael Fogarty and Rhona and Robert Rapoport,[9] and continued by the Rapoports.[10]

A noteworthy feature of the PEP studies was the comparison they afforded between western and eastern Europe. On paper, it might seem that career women would be better placed in communist countries in which the equality of the sexes was written into the constitution and where there was official and

Party encouragement of women to go out to work. That indeed was regarded as emancipation from alienated enslavement to household tasks, and was facilitated by the 'socialization' of women's work, especially child care, through the provision of collective nurseries and crèches (as noted in chapter 8). There was ample legal protection for working women's rights, for example to maternity leave with full reinstatement afterwards. And there had been some spectacular successes. More than 70 per cent of medical practitioners in the Soviet Union were women, who were in a majority also in some other professions including economists, and a substantial minority in yet others; for example, engineers, 30 per cent of whom were women (compared with 1 per cent in Britain). On the other hand, even in professions where women outnumbered men, there were more men in higher posts. Thus though 70 per cent of all doctors were women, the proportion dropped to 52 per cent among chief physicians and heads of medical establishments; and while 1 male doctor in 3 or 4 held a senior post, 1 female doctor in 7 or 8 did so. Similarly in schoolteaching, women outnumbered men by 3 to 1 as primary teachers, including heads, but men outnumbered women by the same ratio among the heads of secondary schools. At the top, indeed, there were some indications of 'tokenism' and 'the statutory woman' in the highest posts. As in the west, after 1920 there had been a quick rise in women's participation in fields newly opened to them, followed by a levelling-off especially after about 1950.

Compared with their Soviet and eastern European counterparts, career women in the west enjoyed less formal, legal protection, and there was less public, communal provision for their needs in the form of crèches and nursery schools. On the other hand, their material conditions were more favourable. They lived in better houses with far greater material resources in the way of domestic machinery such as washing machines, whereas not all of their eastern counterparts even had a domestic hot water supply. Above all, western career women could employ *au pairs*, children's nurses, cooks, cleaners, and gardeners to relieve them of many routine domestic tasks. According to the Rapoports, eastern European career women were putting in from four to six hours' housework a day in addition to their professional work; really doing double duty, it seemed, for the formal declaration of the equality of the sexes in the constitutions of eastern countries did not necessarily seem to incline men to do a substantial share of the housework. Thus a group of Romanian women architects, asked why they had let opportunities slip for promotion to higher administrative posts, replied that 'we've enough administrative problems at home'.

In east and west alike, indeed, the central problem of the dual-career couple and the salient feature of their family life was sheer overload. This emerged very clearly from the Rapoports' intensive study of thirteen such couples. Some were business as well as marital partners, others were pursuing careers independently of each other. For all, time and energy were the scarcest resources, and efficient organization the prime imperative. Every minute of every day had to be scheduled to fit in all the requirements of career work, child-care (including taking children to and from school, music lessons, swimming, social events), and housework (shopping, cooking, cleaning, washing clothes). The clear impression to be gained from the Rapoports' studies was that dual-career couples were conscientious parents, determined that their children should not suffer from their career commitments. While routine aspects of children's care might be delegated to paid helpers, their essential needs for parental attention and help with their problems were to be met as a first priority. Sheer overload, however, left little time or energy for casual sociability with neighbours or even with visiting relatives – sometimes to the dismay of the latter. Even 'leisure' had to be meticulously planned and scheduled.

Part of the PEP project was a survey of just over 200 married women graduates and their husbands, whose responses were analyzed by Lotte Bailyn. Most rated their marriages as 'very happy', but among the small group of fifteen couples both of whom were strongly committed to their careers only two did so, and there were special circumstances even about them; both marriages were childless, and both husbands strongly favoured wives pursuing their own careers, and were happy in their own work. In most cases, though, this pattern did not seem conducive to a happy marriage. Bailyn further asked, 'What produces the work-prone woman?' No very clear-cut answer emerged, though it seemed that such women tended to identify themselves with their fathers, and to have experienced family tensions in their childhood. But the question itself is possibly worthy of note.[11]

Fogarty and the Rapoports made it clear that 'the dual-career family is a statistically minor variant'; and although they thought that 'the dual-career families of today are, in a sense, pioneers for families of tomorrow', they were at pains not to exaggerate the extent and importance of this way of life: 'it is not likely to be the pattern of choice for the majority of families in the foreseeable future. Many prefer, and will continue to prefer, a more conventional type of work–family structure. . . . No single pattern of work and family life provides the answer.' Nevertheless, 'high-level careers for women (notably for married women) [could] be practicable and desirable from both the family and the economic point of view', and they certainly need not 'damage the family'. It was important that, at the very least, adventitious obstacles should not be placed in the way of couples who might choose the dual-career pattern. However, 'positive action [was] likely to be required, not merely the removal of barriers'. It was not only a matter of individuals adapting themselves and their family life to the exigencies of their careers, but also of adapting the institutions and practices of the world of work to the needs of women and men and their family life. To take but one example, flexible working hours, progress towards a six-hour day or a four-day week, and the demise of the present distinction between full-time and part-time work, would do much to enable men and women to participate on more equal terms in both work and family life.[12]

Studies in the United States, however, have strongly indicated that genuine egalitarianism in two-career families is rare. Husbands' careers generally take precedence over wives', and few share the responsibility for housework and child-care on anything like equal terms.

In a study of 53 career women and their husbands, Margaret Poloma and Neal Garland began with a hypothesis derived from Parsons and Bales, that since it was the husband-father's occupation that determined the family's socio-economic position, he would be put under some strain when he was no longer the family's main provider. What effect, then, did the wife's professional activities have on role-relations within the family?

Four types of response emerged among the 53 families: traditional (20), neo-traditional (27), egalitarian (1), and mat-riarchal (5; reluctant 3, resigned 2). It will be noted that their usage of the first three terms was slightly different from mine in chapter 9.

In their 'traditional' families, the wife's career was regarded as her 'hobby', equivalent to the unpaid voluntary work con-ventionally undertaken by middle-class women. The husband continued to be the sole breadwinner, and the wife's income was not aggregated with his, nor used for family purposes at all; one wife invested most of hers. With hired help, these wives took full responsibility for child-care, home-making, and other traditionally feminine tasks such as entertaining.

In the 'neo-traditional' type of family, husband and wife were of comparable professional status and shared the breadwinning role, though in every case the husband earned more. Even if the wife's income was not merged with her husband's, it was used for family purposes such as holidays, school fees, or a country home. Much routine housework was done by hired help, and husbands in this type of family did some of the rest, for instance cooking. But both husband and wife regarded child-care as ultimately her responsibility. Only one 'egalitarian' couple regarded it as one to be shared by both parents.

As already indicated, most wives earned less than their hus-bands. A number made it clear that they were determined to keep it that way, and would cut down on their work rather than let their income exceed his. One said, 'The only way that I would ever let that happen would be if we were in dire need. . . Psychologically it would upset the roles. There is enough dif-ficulty in this kind of marriage without disrupting these roles.' According to Poloma and Garland, 'no wife *wanted* to earn more than her husband, but some in fact did in order to meet the family's needs'; and it was those five women who were the 'reluctant' or 'resigned matriarchs'.[13]

Lynda Lytle Holmstrom interviewed 20 couples of whom the wife was pursuing an independent professional career, and a further 7 whom she called 'traditional' of whom the wife had curtailed her career. Mobility had been a problem for the two-career couples; 15 of the 20 wives had at some time been influenced by their husbands' career needs to move, or stay, though in 12 of these 15 cases at another time the wife's need had been decisive. Anti-nepotism rules against husband and wife working in the same organization had often created difficulties; and wives had more often taken risks, for example accepting university posts without tenure. For traditional couples, there was no problem; the wife's willingness to move was taken for granted.

Like the Rapoports, Holmstrom emphasized the overload problem in two-career families. Career women needed physical vitality and powers of organization to control their own time-schedule and co-ordinate it with their husbands'. Most dual-career couples had developed highly rational and flexible ways of sharing child-rearing and household tasks. They hardly ever said 'that's man's work' or 'that's woman's work', but rather 'whichever of us happens to be around'. Many wives spoke warmly of 'sharing evenly', or 'stressed how grateful they were because their husbands were such a tremendous help to them around the home'. Taking her cue from that word 'help', however, Holmstrom nonetheless insisted that 'no matter how much help the woman received, the domestic realm was defined as ultimately her responsibility'.

A second career was not necessarily a source of much additional net income, as two-career couples paid more tax and had to spend freely to enable both to work, especially on hired help for routine child-care. Traditional wives, aware of this, gave it as a reason for not working. However, Holmstrom suspected that there was sometimes 'faulty accounting' and a 'dual standard', attributing to a wife's career needs the expenses for things that were highly desirable anyway, like a second car for a suburban housewife.

Contrary to what Parsons had suggested (as noted in chapter 4), the solidarity of two-career families did not seem to be threatened by competition for status between husbands and wives. It was rather the traditional couples whose solidarity appeared to be at risk from the resentment of wives who had given up their own careers to further those of their husbands.

Virtually all two-career couples habitually discussed each other's work. Between those qualified in different fields, discussion could be only at a relatively superficial 'sounding-board' or educated-lay-person's level. For some it was more, but there were pitfalls. Some topics had to be avoided; there was a danger of professional or intellectual disagreements becoming personal; and sensitivity to implied criticism was hard to handle. For these reasons, joint work was very difficult, and only three couples had achieved it over the years.

Holmstrom's concluding assessment was that compared with traditional wives, and no doubt with other women generally, professional wives fared very well; compared with men, and especially their husbands, less well. Even though both careers were important, typically the husband's was more important. And although two-career couples deviated a great deal from middle-class norms, they were still a long way from equality of the sexes.[14]

Using postal questionnaires, Jeff and Rebecca Bryson surveyed 200 husband-and-wife members of the American Psychological Association, comparing them with 150 male and 150 female members of the APA not married to each other.

Among the couples, a higher proportion both of husbands and wives had been awarded doctorates, and they had earned them a year or two younger than controls. Consistently, too, in terms of career success such as articles published, papers read, and university posts secured, husbands did better than male controls, and wives than female controls. Being married to a professional colleague clearly helped both husbands and wives in their scientific work, therefore. However, while husbands were the best-paid of the four groups, wives were the worst, and they had been in their current posts for a far shorter time than any of the other three groups. So husbands reported themselves well satisfied with their dual-career marriages; wives less so, for although they had achieved more than other women psychologists their scientific productivity had not been duly rewarded either in salary or job stability. It was clear from their detailed responses that wives bore prime responsibility for domestic organization and above all for child-care: 'When the children were small I cared for them; my husband, on the other hand, "babysat".' Indeed, according to the Brysons, 'the only stereotypically female activity for which they did not bear the majority of responsibility was housecleaning, but this was because outside help was employed, not because husbands shared the responsibility'.

The Brysons therefore drew two conclusions. First, 'if you are a male psychologist, you should marry a female psychologist. However, if you are a female psychologist you should not even consider marrying a male psychologist. Unfortunately, the inherent asymmetry in this advice makes it less than helpful.' Secondly, 'we have not progressed to the point of the symmetrical family'.[15]

It is clear from all these studies, then, that dual-career families are rare, and those dual-career couples whose relations can be called truly egalitarian are rarer still. Such studies have been criticised as elitist, but that seems wide of the mark. Given that research such as the PEP project was carried out in response to the question 'Why so few women in top jobs?', attention could hardly have been directed elsewhere than towards the highest socio-economic levels at which some exceptional women had 'made it' to the top without detriment to their family life. That no doubt is why these studies tell of a world of two-car families able to employ paid help with childcare and housework, a world unknown and inaccessible to most of us. It will not be denied that a genuine equality of the sexes requires that there should be no great disparities in the numbers of men and women at all occupational levels. To achieve that clearly necessitates a fundamental reorganization of family life; and the contribution of the dual-career family studies has been to show what that reorganization has involved for those who have achieved it, if not completely, at least to a more or less adequate extent. But at what cost? Despite their material affluence, these couples obviously work extremely hard for very little reward. Financially they seem to be little if any better off than if only one of them worked full-time; and they do not seem to enjoy much marital happiness. Further, the pursuit of the equality of the sexes in careers by women born into the higher social classes may have important implications for social mobility and the class structure generally – a point to which I return in the next chapter.

SUGGESTIONS FOR FURTHER READING

Michael P. Fogarty, Rhona Rapoport and Robert N. Rapoport, *Sex, Career and Family*, London, Allen and Unwin, 1971

Athena Theodore (ed.), *The Professional Woman*, Cambridge, Mass., Schenkman, 1971

Lynda Lytle Holmstrom, *The Two-Career Family*, Cambridge, Mass., Schenkman, 1973

Fran Pepitone-Rockwell (ed.), *Dual-Career Couples*, Beverly Hills, Sage, 1980

Harold Benenson, 'Women's occupational and family achievement in the US class system: a critique of the dual-career family analysis', *British Journal of Sociology*, vol. 35, 1984, pp. 19–41

11

Social class, social mobility,
and family life

It has long been a truism of sociology that the family, not the individual, is the unit of social class. That has been so whether class has been envisaged as a graded system of social stratification, or in terms of classes divided from one another in potential or actual conflict. Fundamentally though the two conceptions of class differ, according to both alike the class position of each nuclear family household is determined by the occupational status of its head, normally the husband/father. As noted in chapter 4, this was unequivocally the view of Talcott Parsons; and it is one with considerable commonsense justification. Members of a nuclear family household inhabit the same dwelling, large or small, sanitary or insanitary. They enjoy similar amenities, or experience the same lack of them. They share common catering and cooking, and sit at the same table to eat meals together. They likewise share a common lifestyle, including leisure activities, in which they often participate as a group especially when the children are young. Thus it makes sense to speak, for example, of 'working-class babies', although strictly the expression is meaningless since infants are not gainfully employed. Differences of class position or socio-economic status, whose most readily ascertainable single indicator is the occupational status of the household head, are related to important demographic differences affecting all family members; as will appear below, these include infant as well as general mortality, fertility, age at marriage, and marital breakdown rates. There are class differences, too, in patterns of interaction among family members. And the processes of family life play their part in engendering and sustaining the social class system itself.

Since about 1970 that conventional wisdom has been questioned. If women really are an oppressed under-class, then we have to think in terms of sexual stratification, and of lines of class division and class conflict cutting right through each nuclear family. While we do not know enough about how resources are distributed among family members, it should not be assumed, for instance, that husband and wife necessarily consume the same diet; she may be slimming and he not, or he may get a preferential share at home and also subsidized meals at work. It is further asserted that the conventional wisdom fails to take account of recent social trends, including the increasing number of lone-parent families without a male head (see chapter 14), and the ever-rising number of married women who go out to work. Compared with single-earner families, working wives' contribution to family income at the very least makes additional resources available to raise the family's material standard of living and consequently their position in any realistic socio-economic scale. And, as a practical problem for sociological analysis, how are we to classify families in which the spouses' occupations are in different categories or grades? – especially if that of the wife is higher, for example an unskilled manual worker's wife working as a secretary?

In what follows I exemplify the relations of family life to social class and social mobility by references to studies carried out in Britain. This is not because class divisions and disparities are particularly well-marked in British society; on the contrary, according to data collected by the World Bank, in 1979 the distribution of income among households was less unequal in Britain than in most other western industrial countries.[1] Sociologists in Britain, however, have long been specially interested in social class, and have made this country a particularly well-documented case of processes that without doubt are paralleled in other industrial societies.

MARRIAGE, BIRTH, AND DEATH: CLASS DIFFERENCES IN LIFE-CYCLES

I	Professional
II	Intermediate
IIIN	Skilled non-manual
IIIM	Skilled manual
IV	Partly skilled
V	Unskilled

Many British studies of social class, academic as well as official, use the Registrar-General's standard classification of occupations (above).

To begin with marriage: homogamy (a statistical tendency for like to marry like) is particularly well marked at the top and bottom of the social scale. A sample study of officially recorded data for England and Wales in 1979 showed that people in class I were 5 times more likely to marry someone of the same class than if mating were independent of social class, and people in class V 6.3 times; in between the ratio was lowest at 1.1 in class IIIM. The association between brides' and grooms' social status was closer when the bride was classified by her own occupation than by her father's, even though, despite increasing women's participation rates, no information on the bride's occupation was given in about 1 marriage entry out of 4. There were wide differences in ages at first marriage. The highest were in class I (median ages 25.8 for men, 26 for women classified by their own occupations, 23.9 for women classified by their husbands'); the lowest in class IV (23.2 for men, 20.4 and 20.8 respectively for women); they were slightly higher in class V than in class IV.[2]

According to a study in Aberdeen in 1970, women whose husbands were in classes III–V were more than twice as likely to become pregnant for the first time before they were 20 as those whose husbands were in classes I and II.[3] In 1975 Ann Cartwright conducted a survey under official auspices of mothers of newly-born babies in 24 registration districts in England and Wales. While she did not find very great class differences in the use of contraceptives, she noted that although earlier surveys had shown classes I and II to be the first to adopt 'the pill', by 1975 they were the first to give it up, possibly in reaction to misgivings about health hazards, and revert to the sheath: an instance, perhaps, of the Principle of Stratified Diffusion. Women in class V were the most likely to describe their recent pregnancy as 'unintended' (no less than 47 per cent) or 'regretted' (18 per cent); mothers in class IIIN gave the fewest responses of 'unintended' (18 per cent) or 'regretted' (5 per cent); mothers in classes I and II slightly more. There were wide class differences in breast feeding; 32 per cent of mothers married to men in class I were doing so at the time of the interview (normally within 5 months of birth), 16 per cent in other non-manual classes, 8 per cent in the manual classes.[4] In a later study, Cartwright found that the proportion of husbands present at the birth of their children varied with social class from 54 per cent in class I down to 16 per cent in class V.[5]

Social class differences in fertility have been noted ever since the 1880s, when it became apparent that the 'middle classes' (actually those near the top of the social scale, inferior only to the landed gentry and nobility) had begun to limit their families, a change associated with and probably stimulated by the trials of Charles Bradlaugh and Annie Besant in 1876–7. By the late 1930s the pattern had shifted from one of a simple class gradient, with manual classes having more children than non-manual, to a U-shaped relationship in which the smallest families are in class IIIN with slightly bigger families in classes I and II and rather bigger again in the manual classes. Now that the small family system has spread down the social scale to all classes, average family sizes range only from just under 2 to just over 3 children, and class differences in fertility are not as obvious as they once were. They are, however, both persistent and consistent, and emerged clearly from an analysis by Jean Thompson and Malcolm Britton of 1971 census data for women married once only aged 35–39 in England and Wales. Working wives as a whole had fewer children (89 per cent of the national average), non-working wives more (110 per cent), and the same was true in each of the Registrar-General's six social classes. Whether working or non-working, however, and whether classed by their husbands' occupation or their own, wives in class IIIN had the fewest children, those in classes I and II rather more, and those in classes IIIM, IV, and V more still. Further, Thompson and Britton showed that the same U-shaped relationship prevailed when family size was related to wives' education, with those who had left school at the legal minimum age having the biggest families, those who had stayed on a year or two the smallest, and those who went on to later ages the next biggest.[6]

The relation between divorce and social class has changed very greatly since judicial divorce was introduced in England and Wales in 1857. Before the 1940s the number of divorces was by present-day standards very small, and the legal costs made divorce the privilege of the well-to-do, while the remedies for marital breakdown among the poor were magistrates' court proceedings for separation and maintenance. By 1950 the relation was less clear-cut, and one study carried out at the time found the social class profile of divorce petitioners to be similar to that of the whole population. By 1961 the pattern had changed again, and in a sample study by Colin Gibson the highest divorce rate was found to be in class V; the gradient was not uniform, however, and the next highest rate was in class IIIN.[7] I take up this subject again in chapter 13.

As in industrial countries generally, infant mortality in Britain has been reduced far below its 19th-century levels. From over 150 at the turn of the century, the infant mortality rate (deaths under one year per thousand live births) was brought down to 11 in 1981. What has not changed much, however, is the *relative* disparity among the social classes; the infant mortality rate in class V has long been about double that in class I, and a difference of that order of magnitude persists. Further, it has long been noted that while there is some disparity among the classes in neonatal mortality (deaths in the first month of life), it is far outweighed by that in mortality during the remaining eleven months of the first year.[8] After that, according to an official report,

Between the ages of 1 and 14 relative class death rates narrow, but are still clearly visible. Among boys the ratio of mortality in occupational class V as compared with I is of the order of 2 to 1, while among girls it varies between 1.5 and 1.9 to 1.... Accidents, which are by far the biggest cause of childhood deaths (30 per cent of the total) continue to show the sharpest class gradient. Boys in class V have a ten times greater chance of dying from fire, falls, or drowning than those in class I. The corresponding ratio of deaths caused to youthful pedestrians by motor vehicles is more than 7 to 1.[9]

These considerations no doubt give depth of meaning to phrases like 'working-class children'.

Finally, mortality among adults shows the same clear class gradient. In England and Wales in 1971, death-rates among men aged 15–64 were two and a half times as high in class V as in class I. To some extent no doubt this difference arose from occupational hazards to which men were directly subject, and to be sure mortality among men of these working ages was nearly double than of women. However, death-rates among women in class V were also just two and a half times those among women in class I, though women's mortality rates were

lower than men's in every class.[10] On this point, a most significant recent finding has been that mortality differentials among
married women are less closely related to their own occupations than to those of their husbands.[11] Taken in conjunction
with the data on class differences in infant and child mortality,
and other demographic measures, such findings appear to
afford considerable justification for the conventional view of
the nuclear family household as the unit of social class, whose
environment largely influences the life circumstances of all its
members, and whose class position is most reliably indicated by
the occupational status of its generally male head.

PATTERNS OF CHILD CARE

As in the demographic studies cited above, social class has been
treated as a positional variable only in some studies comparing
patterns of family interaction at different social class levels.
Thus the psychologists John and Elizabeth Newson found that
many aspects of the care and development of children in
Nottingham, England, were class-related. For this purpose
they adopted the Registrar-General's classification according
to the father's occupation, modifying it on occasions to take
account of a mother's occupation or qualifications.[12]

In infancy, they found breast-feeding and early weaning most
prevalent in classes I, II, and IIIN (the 'middle classes'), bottle-
feeding and late weaning among the working classes. For
obvious reasons, babies in the well-to-do classes were far more
likely to sleep in a room alone. Working-class mothers were
more prone to check their infants' genital play; working-class
babies had more tantrums and were more likely to be smacked.
Fathers' participation in child care was lowest in class V,
highest in class IIIN. The Newsons commented that shop and
office workers have the least excuse for escaping the practical
duties of fatherhood, neither the quantities of evening paper-
work which the young professional man brings home, nor the
sheer physical fatigue of the manual worker.

At four years old, working-class children were more likely to
dislike playing alone. Middle-class children were put to bed
earlier, more of them with bedtime stories and prayers and with
father's participation. In matters of discipline, middle-class
children were considered more likely to confess their misdeeds

voluntarily. Like Goode and other writers (see chapter 5), the Newsons found that physical punishment was somewhat class-related. Working-class parents were more prone to threaten to leave their children or send them away, or hand them over to some authority figure. The extent to which mothers regarded their husbands as stricter than themselves with the children was also strongly class-related.

At seven years old, middle-class children were rather more likely to have their friends come and play with them at home. They did more drawing and painting at home, read or looked at books more, and were more likely to write at home for their own pleasure (particularly girls) or collect things (particularly boys). More working-class mothers believed that all toys should be communally owned. At this age there were no significant class differences in the extent to which children preferred to play alone, though middle-class children were somewhat more likely to engage in solitary fantasy play. Children's proneness to get into fights with other children was to some extent related to sex (girls rather less combative) but not to class. There were, however, class differences in mothers' strategies for dealing with children's quarrels; middle-class mothers tended to counsel justice and to refuse to get personally involved, while working-class mothers were more apt to interfere personally and to urge retaliation. As in their earlier studies, the Newsons found marked class differences, and also sex differences, in physical punishment, working-class boys being smacked oftenest, and for offences such as rudeness and bad language for which fewer middle-class mothers considered it to be an appropriate punishment. The proportion of boys' mothers who had at some time used an implement such as a strap or cane, 26 per cent overall, was much the same at all class levels; but more middle-class mothers of girls (22 per cent in class I) and fewer working-class (10 per cent in class V) had done the same. More working-class parents, however, had threatened this and other punishments without carrying them out, whereas middle-class mothers were more averse to empty threats. And there were well-marked class and sex differences in the proportions of children rated destructive and aggressive, with working-class boys more likely to score high on both counts.

SOCIAL CLASS, CHILD DEVELOPMENT, AND EDUCATIONAL OPPORTUNITY

As has been seen, occupational status has been taken as an independent classificatory variable in studies in which social class differences such as those in mortality, fertility, and child-care have been presented as interesting facts in their own right and little more. Other and perhaps more truly sociological studies, by contrast, have explored the ways in which the processes of family life engender and sustain the social class system on the one hand, while they are related on the other to social mobility, that is the movement of individuals from one class to another up and down the social scale. Much research in Britain has been done on the relations between social class and educational opportunity, in which patterns of child-care at different social levels have been examined for their bearing on children's progress in school and their success in examinations leading to higher education and professional and academic qualifications for highly-rewarded and highly-esteemed occupations.[13] Another obvious way in which family and class are related is through the inheritance of property. Material and educational factors converge to make housing a resource of central importance. Clearly, well-to-do families are more likely to be able to afford a house big enough for each child to have a room of his or her own in which to read and do school homework undistracted. Moreover, since neighbourhoods generally consist of houses of a similar type and standard, neighbouring families tend to be of similar class status. Their children play together and form neighbourhood peer-groups as well as going to the same schools. Later, away from home, people of similar class origins meet as work-mates, or if their schooling continues as class-mates at boarding schools, colleges, and universities. In these largely separate social milieux, many men and women find their marriage partners.

A notable study of some of these processes was the follow-up by J. W. B. Douglas and his colleagues of all children born in Britain during the first week of March 1946, in which the focus of attention, initially medical, shifted as the study progressed to psychology, education, and sociology. Among the voluminous data collected were assessments by health visitors, under the direction of medical officers of health, of standards of infant care and management, and by school nurses of the children's health. Reading, comprehension, vocabulary, and non-verbal picture tests were administered when the children were 8 and 11 years old, and the results were related to the parents' social backgrounds and the children's progress through the school system, including for most of them their fate at the selective 'eleven-plus' examination.[14]

Douglas was critical of the Registrar-General's classification based solely on the father's current occupation. This was liable to vary as men changed jobs, a serious disadvantage in a long-term study; and it could be grossly misleading in individual cases, as in those of fathers who had come down in the world (like one former teacher working as a gardener following a nervous breakdown) and whose children were being maintained at expensive boarding-schools by grandparents or godparents. Moreover, 'in ambitious working-class households it is not unusual to find that the mother comes from a middle-class family and supplies the drive and incentive for her children to do well at school'. In fact, Douglas's data indicated that mothers' education and social background were of equal importance to fathers' in their influence on children's test scores and performance in the secondary selection examinations.

Douglas's own classification emerged from his data; first distinguishing 'middle class' from 'manual working class', he subdivided each into upper and lower sub-classes – not, however, on the basis of occupational prestige, but according to the social origins and education of both parents. Thus his 'upper-middle-class' families were, so to speak, middle-class through and through, both parents having been born into middle-class families and having attended secondary schools (associated at that time with academic education and social prestige). Whatever the father's occupation, whether professional, salaried, black-coated, or self-employed, on the average their children gained high test scores. Other middle-class children, 'whose parents may be said to deviate in their upbringing and education from the middle-class pattern', gained considerably lower average scores. Similarly, the manual working-class families fell naturally into two groups. First, those in which one or both parents came from a middle-class family, or had been to secondary school. 'The great majority of these are skilled workers and we call them the "upper manual working class".' Secondly, those in which both parents came from working-class origins and had attended only elementary schools (those associated at that time with working-class status): the 'lower manual working class'.

The average test scores at 11 years in these four social classes ranged from 57 for upper-middle-class children to 47.5 for the lower manual working class. Quite consistently, too, while middle-class children's scores had improved between the ages of 8 and 11, those of working-class children had deteriorated. Wide class differences emerged in the proportions of families reaching the highest standards of infant care and infant management; in the extent to which they made use of available medical services; in the interest which parents, particularly fathers, took in their children's school progress; and in their ambitions for their children's future schooling. Moreover, these differences were not only class-related, but also cor-related with one another. The parents who made frequent visits to the schools and were seen by teachers as very interested in their children's education were also those who made most use of the available medical services and were regarded by the health visitors as giving their children a high standard of care. Such parents came predominantly from the middle class; within each social class, however, the parents who most encouraged their children in their school work had also given them the best care in infancy. Indeed, the correlation was even closer among working-class parents than middle-class; if they showed a high level of interest in their children's school work then their standards of care and their use of services were also high, and they had middle-class aspirations for their children's future schooling. Children of all classes whose parents showed a high level of interest not only made higher average test scores at 8 and 11, but also improved their performance, whatever their initial ability; and the effect was most marked of all among girls.

Housing was second only in importance to parental interest for children's development. Though obviously class-related, it operated also independently of class. By a combination of criteria – whether or not they were over-crowded, whether the survey children shared beds or slept alone, and whether there was a hot water supply and an unshared kitchen and bathroom—homes were rated 'satisfactory' or 'unsatisfactory'. In all classes, children from 'unsatisfactory' homes achieved lower average test scores, though of course the proportion of manual working-class homes so rated was far higher than middle-class. Moreover, the scores of manual working-class children from unsatisfactory homes tended to deteriorate between 8 and 11, while those of middle-class children similarly disadvantaged tended to recover. Douglas observed that middle-class parents were likely to provide some privacy for their children even if their homes were unsatisfactory; and he gave some weight, too, to neighbourhood influences. Middle-class children, even if their own home circumstances were bad, were likely to mix with other middle-class children from education-minded families; while manual working-class children from similarly unsatisfactory homes tended to live in poor neighbourhoods where there was little interest in learning.

So at the fateful eleven-plus examination, middle-class children were at a marked advantage in selection for the prestigious academic secondary grammar schools; and this was not all explained by their higher average ability as measured by Douglas's tests. At each level of measured ability except the very highest, a higher proportion of middle-class children was selected for grammar schooling. For example, at the middle of the range (test scores 55–57), roughly half the upper-middle-class, children were so selected, 1 in 3 of the lower middle class, and 1 in 4 of the working-class.

These findings give us considerable insight into the processes of family life whereby social class status is maintained over the generations, and in particular to those patterns of child-care and parental encouragement through which middle-class parents transmit their advantages to their children. Well might an American sociologist observe that 'the family is the most powerful single factor counteracting the egalitarian tendency inherent in modern educational systems'.[15] But there is seen to be nothing rigidly deterministic about these processes; and in Douglas's minority of 'ambitious working-class households', with their high standards of child-care, their middle-class educational aspirations, their parental encouragement and their children's improving test performances, we may discern at least one potential source of social mobility.

SOCIAL MOBILITY

The first large-scale inquiry into social mobility in Britain was carried out in 1949 by David Glass and his colleagues at the London School of Economics, using their own occupational classification: [16]

1　Professional and high administrative
2　Managerial and executive
3　Inspectional, supervisory, and other non-manual, higher grade
4　Ditto, lower grade
5　Skilled manual and routine non-manual
6　Semi-skilled manual
7　Unskilled manual

A sample of over 9000 adults in Great Britain were interviewed, and a mass of data was accumulated whose analysis brought to the fore such tendencies as homogamy and class-related differences in age at marriage on which more recent findings have been noted above. The central finding was that at that time – that is, in the decades preceding the inquiry – the numbers who had moved up and down the social scale, and those who had stayed in the class into which they were born, were not very different. Thus among men in England and Wales, roughly 30 per cent were in a higher class than that of their fathers' last occupation, 35 per cent the same, and 35 per cent lower. The tendency for a man to stay in the same class as his father was most strongly marked in class 1 and 2. Class 1 men were 13 times as likely to stay in class 1 as they would have been if recruitment to occupations were independent of men's class of origin; class 2 men were nearly 6 times as likely. The 'index of association' in class 7 was rather over 2, while in class 5 it was not much above unity. This was a large class, making up nearly half the sample, and it may be that at that time it had served as a kind of reservoir for both upward and downward mobility. Another analysis of particular interest for the sociology of family life concerned mobility over three generations. Comparing men in the sample with their fathers and grandfathers, there were nine possible modes: same, same; up, up; down,

down; same, up; etc. The three commonest modes were same, same (18 per cent), up, down (13 per cent), and down, up (15 per cent); the least common were up, up (3 per cent) and down, down (8 per cent). Thus nearly half the sample had finished up at or near the same class level as their grandfathers, if not their fathers, while two successive movements in the same direction were rare. It seemed unlikely, then, that many men would find themselves in a widely different class from their first cousins.

Twenty years after Glass's inquiry, there was an evident need to see what changes, if any, had occurred in the trends and processes he had identified; and a second large-scale survey was accordingly carried out in 1972 under the direction of John H. Goldthorpe (not the present writer: J. E. G.). Goldthorpe devised yet another occupational classification (below: summarized) including a cluster of occupational groups in his classes III, IV, and V of more or less equal status but different character and interests. These he grouped together as an 'intermediate' class between I and II, together the 'service' class, and VI and VII, the 'working' class. His sample consisted of just over 10,000 men in England and Wales, a parallel survey being done separately in Scotland.[17]

I   Professionals, officials, managers and proprietors, higher grade
II Ditto, lower grade

III Routine non-manual
IV Small proprietors, farmers, and self-employed artisans
V Supervisors, and technicians whose work is partly manual

VI Skilled manual
VII Semi- and unskilled manual

The most important conclusion was that the whole situation had indeed changed. Whereas Glass had found upward and downward mobility more or less in balance in a stable class structure, it became clear from Goldthorpe's work that there had been far more upward than downward movement in his sample, and that the whole class structure had changed. Classes I and II had nearly doubled in size in a generation, while the working class had correspondingly shrunk, comprising as it did only 45 per cent of the men in his sample compared with 54 per cent of their fathers. While nearly half (45 per cent) of men born into class I had stayed there, that class had grown by re-cruiting widely from other classes; only 24 per cent of its 1972 members had been born into it, and they were far outnum-bered by the 28 per cent who had come from the working classes VI and VII and the 35 per cent from the intermediate classes III–V. Class II in its origins was even more nearly a microcosm of the population. Such findings clearly gave con-siderable colour to the optimistic view then current that Britain's was an 'open society' with 'room at the top'. However, Goldthorpe was at pains to counter that view, pointing out that the relative chances of being found in classes I and II were several times greater for men originating in those classes than they were for those born into the working classes, and for those starting life in classes III–V around twice as great. The overall picture was not one of increasing opportunity for social ascent, 'but rather of stability or indeed of increasing *in*equality in class mobility chances'. He was clearly concerned, moreover, about what might happen in the future if and when the expansion of the 'service' classes should cease; I return to this point below.

In 1974 a follow-up study was carried out to inquire in more detail into the family life of men who had undergone 'long-range mobility', moving into or out of class I from or to class III and below, and to compare them with other selected groups: men intergenerationally stable in class I and in classes VI and VII, and those in classes III–V who had started their working lives respectively in manual and non-manual occupations. From this study emerged, first, data on class differences in kinship; these proved to be rather slight. More working-class men were in frequent touch, weekly or oftener, with close kin outside their own households, but when contacts over longer periods of a month or a year were counted the class difference largely disappeared. Working-class men were somewhat more likely to turn to kin for help over minor matters, such as borrowing a tool or materials for a job, and to associate with their kin in leisure activities; but over major matters, par-ticularly the birth of a child, the great majority of families at all social levels had been helped by kin.

These findings afforded benchmarks for comparing the kinship relations of mobile men with those intergenerationally stable. Like stable class I men, mobile men did not have frequent contacts with close kin outside their households, and apparently for the same reason: they did not live near them. If anything, however, mobile men saw more of their kin over longer periods than a week; in no way were they isolated from their kin, nor did they tend to drop their distant relations. Similarly, if anything an even higher proportion of the mobile had been helped by kin when a child was born. Despite surmises to the contrary on the part of some other sociologists in Britain and the United States, Goldthorpe found no evidence that mobility disrupted kinship ties. To adopt a saying from another context, the mobile seemed to find that their loyalties had not been divided, but rather multiplied. Far from being isolated, the upwardly mobile man at least was typically involved with two or more sets of primary social relations, one with kin, the other or others with neighbours, colleagues, and friends. If problems arose it was not so much because ties were broken as from the difficulties of 'managing' diverse relationships in two or more social networks. And the mobile person might well have cross-class ties with kin of other class positions.

Goldthorpe was castigated by feminist and other critics for confining his survey to men. Anticipating those criticisms, he gave his reasons. Financial provision on a scale unusual for British social research had been made for the exceptionally large sample of 10,000 in order to permit statistically precise and reliable analyses to be made of both current mobility and trends over time. Including women would effectively have reduced the sample of men to half that number, jeopardizing the investigation of mobility trends in successive birth cohorts, and adversely affecting the study's comparability with other surveys. Moreover, in the period retrospectively covered by the survey, it was difficult to envisage 'any *sizeable* numbers of women occupying *markedly* different class positions' from their husbands whose attributes or activities would 'materially influence the class position of the family unit'. Even in 1971 on the eve of his field-work only a minority of about 40 per cent of married women were in paid employment. In 1951 the proportion had been about 20 per cent and in 1931 only 10 per cent; much of that employment, too, was part-time and intermittent. Goldthorpe acknowledged that information was lacking about those women, unattached or themselves heads of households, whose status was not dependent on or associated with a male; but he doubted whether it would have made much difference if they had been included in his study. The debate has continued, with Goldthorpe firm in his 'defence of the conventional view' of the family as the basic unit of social class, 'most adequately indexed' by the occupational category of its male head.[18]

At the conclusion of his book, Goldthorpe foresaw 'a rather bleak economic future in which competition for higher-level class positions intensifies'; and he added in a final end-note that a development which would sharpen that competition, and probably increase inequality in relative class chances, would be a growth in the number of women seeking permanent careers in high-level occupations. There was little doubt that, for some time at least, 'class influences would bear even more strongly on their selection than on that of men: the "liberation" of the daughters of the service class could well be at the expense of the mobility chances of working-class sons'. 'And their families', he might have added, for it would be consistent with his whole analysis to suggest that upwardly mobile men take their wives and children up with them in a way not exactly paralleled in the case of women.

This prognostication opens up wider questions about the implications for men's mobility of women's increasing participation in paid employment. Is it not possible that, in the decades before Goldthorpe's survey, many men had experienced upward mobility precisely because women, emerging from the statistically invisible category of housewives, had taken their places at lower levels in the labour force? In so far as the cause of the equality of the sexes is successfully promoted, with an increase in the proportion of women in top jobs, will the channels of upward mobility for men (and their families) indeed become blocked? Given the hitherto strong tendency for class homogamy at the top and bottom of the social scale, and the different patterns of child-care and educational advantage, will these developments make the classes more self-recruiting, and Britain a less 'open' society in that respect than it was in the 1950s and 1960s, the decades preceding Goldthorpe's survey? As Goldthorpe said, 'egalitarians do not in fact have any easy options open to them'. It seems clear that this whole extra dimension will have to be included in any serious future research into this subject, together with all the implications for family life that have been explored in earlier chapters of this book.

SUGGESTIONS FOR FURTHER READING

John and Elizabeth Newson, *Infant Care in an Urban Community*, London, Allen and Unwin, 1963; reprinted as *Patterns of Infant Care in an Urban Community*, Harmondsworth, Penguin, 1966

John and Elizabeth Newson, *Four Years Old in an Urban Community*, London, Allen and Unwin, 1968; Harmondsworth, Penguin, 1970

John and Elizabeth Newson, *Seven Years Old in the Home Environment*, London, Allen and Unwin, 1976; Harmondsworth, Penguin, 1976

J. W. B. Douglas, *The Home and the School*, London, MacGibbon and Kee, 1964; Panther, 1967

A. H. Halsey, A. F. Heath, and J. M. Ridge, *Origins and Destinations: Family, Class and Education in Modern Britain*, Oxford, Clarendon Press, 1980

John H. Goldthorpe *et al.*, *Social Mobility and Class Structure in Modern Britain*, Oxford, Clarendon Press, 1980

12

Family life among ethnic minorities

Although this book is primarily about family life in the mainstream, majority culture and society of western countries, it would be seriously incomplete without some reference, however brief, to ethnic minorities in those countries.

These minorities are numerous and diverse. In Canada, for example, thirty-seven 'ethno-racial categories' or ethnic groups were listed in the 1971 census data cited by K. Ishwaran in a volume notable for its recognition of ethnic diversity.[1] Clearly a comprehensive treatment cannot be attempted here.

Some socially and culturally distinct communities in western countries are themselves of western origin, and though their family life may have its distinctive features they tend to fall within the range of variation of western societies generally. French-Canadians are a leading example. Philippe Garigue found that male authority was emphasized, and there was a clear-cut segregation of husband's and wife's roles, she having full-time responsibility for housework and child-rearing while he went out to work. Children were more warmly attached to their mother, who was the centre of affection and played a more important part in parent–child relations, while their father tended to be perceived as rigid, withdrawn, arbitrary, and authoritarian by comparison. Kinship networks were widely extended, covering indeed all Canada and substantial areas of the United States.[2] Ralph Piddington too found a wide range of kinship awareness, far wider than that of English-speaking societies. Migration, urbanization, industrialization, and 'progress' had not resulted in any loss of French-Canadian values and culture, which had, on the contrary, been reasserted in opposition to the materialism associated with Anglo-Saxon models, and in adherence to the French language and to the

Roman Catholic church and its associated institutions. Widely extending and intermarrying kindreds helped to transmit that culture and maintain a French-Canadian ethnic identity. So did large families, *la revanche du berceau*, 'the revenge of the cradle' against their humiliation under the English conquest and subsequent hegemony.[3]

In so far as there are systematic differences between ethnic minorities' family life and that of the majority, 'white', or 'host', society in western countries, these differences may be attributable to two main types of influence: (a) the minority's past and present socio-economic circumstances, (b) their continuing adherence to cultural values and practices at odds with those of the majority society, especially when their distinctive culture is transmitted through a different language and enshrined in a different religion from that of the majority. Both sets of factors may operate together, and they are not mutually exclusive. Though in some cases one seems to preponderate over the other, they can also act in combination. Thus an ethnic minority not fully accorded social and economic acceptance by the majority community, and subject to adverse discrimination, hostility, or harassment, may develop a 'reactive ethnicity' (as it has been termed) in a defiant reassertion of their distinctive cultural identity, where in a more tolerant atmosphere they might have played down their cultural distinctiveness and chosen the path of assimilation or integration.

These factors may be seen at work in two contrasting examples: black Americans in the United States, and south Asian communities in Britain.

BLACK AMERICANS IN THE UNITED STATES

Statistically there are quite well marked differences between black and white Americans, and ethnic questions in United States census schedules enable such comparisons to be made. Demographic studies collated by John Reid,[4] by Thornton and Freedman,[5] and by William F. Pratt *et al.*[6] in the early 1980s showed that, compared with whites, among black people both fertility and mortality, including infant mortality, were higher. Although proportionately more black women became pregnant before marriage, black women on the average married later, and more did not marry at all. Among those who married there was more marital breakdown, followed to a greater extent by separation rather than divorce, so that there was less remarriage. Also, because of black men's higher mortality, there were more widows. For all these reasons, a higher proportion of black children were born out of wedlock, and many more spent all or part of their childhood, not in a two-parent home, but cared for either by their mother alone, or mother supported by female kin. If the term means anything, indeed, there was further evidence of more 'extended family' living among blacks; more black couples lived with their kin during their early married years, and far more black grandparents assumed primary responsibility for their grandchildren.

Such statistics, however, indicate differences of degree rather than of kind. Many white marriages too break down, while many white children are born out of wedlock, and are looked after by mothers alone. It is a very open question whether or not statistical black–white differences arise from distinctive patterns of family life among black people, different from the white American norm. Furthermore, in attempting to account for these differences we are plunged deeply into perennially agonized controversies about the position of black Americans in United States society generally, and about the history of slavery in particular.

Ever since the 1930s there has been a widely-accepted view about black family life to which I refer as the conventional wisdom. The higher rates of illegitimacy and marital breakdown among black people, and the higher proportion of female-headed households, had long been known. They were described in such terms as 'disorganization', 'demoralization', 'instability', 'matriarchy' and 'matrifocality'; and they were attributed mainly to the kind of life black Americans were forced to live under slavery. Slave unions were not accorded the legal status of marriage, since authority over a female slave and her children, and responsibility for their maintenance, lay not with her male partner but with her owner. Although some, perhaps most, slave-owners allowed slaves to choose their own partners, and some even arranged for their unions to be solemnized in a religious ceremony, it was said that others used male slaves as stallions for breeding purposes and forced slaves into unions not of their choosing. Further, power lay with the owners, not with the male heads of slave households. Sexual exploitation of black women by white men involved black men in being powerless to intervene when their partners were seduced or raped, or otherwise ill-used, and black women in begging their menfolk and children not to intervene, enraged, for fear of making matters worse for the whole family. And slave families could be, and sometimes were, broken up by family members being sold separately. In this school of adversity, black women developed their traditional self-reliance, taking sole responsibility for training their children to cope with the hard knocks of a hostile world, and down-playing the importance of marriage. Hence too a traditional tolerance of premarital pregnancy and of illegitimacy.

This conventional wisdom is largely associated with the monumental work of E. Franklin Frazier, himself a black man; more precisely, it represents a somewhat over-simplified version of a view already widely held among social scientists, which Frazier in part adopted and endorsed in his own work, albeit with some qualifications.[7] With Robert Ezra Park as his mentor, Frazier was a foundation member of the influential Chicago school of sociology in the 1920s and 1930s; in the 1940s he was one of the American social scientists associated with Gunnar Myrdal's monumental study of race relations in the United States;[8] and he became a towering figure on the American intellectual scene.

While Frazier identified slavery as the prime formative influence, he went on to show how black family life had responded to later vicissitudes after emancipation, in the migrations from country to city and from south to north. It was about that later period, indeed, that Frazier wrote of demoralization. He emphasized too the diverse patterns of family life among black Americans at all times including his own. Some, such as those he called black Puritans, exhibited much greater stability and conformity to the ideal conventions of American life generally, indicated by a high proportion of home ownership. Likewise among 'the brown middle class' home ownership and conservative attitudes prevailed. In this group there was a reversal of the matriarchate, as the men were well enough off to be sole breadwinners, and conservative enough to prefer their wives to be subordinate and economically dependent. Families in this class inhabited an extraordinarily narrow social world. They shunned lower-class black families, whom they regarded as uncouth, rowdy, and lax in their morals; yet they were also at great pains to shield their children from the rebuffs and humiliations they might experience from white people. Findings of this kind, and the qualifications they implied to the over-simplified conventional wisdom based on Frazier's work, were not always borne in mind in subsequent controversies.

During the 1940s, Frazier's analysis was challenged by Melville J. Herskovits, who attributed many features of black Americans' social life to the heritage of their African origins.[9] His was in part a counterblast against earlier racist and pro-slavery ideas according to which the survival of African culture traits among black Americans only showed how 'primitive' they were, whereas from the culturally relativist standpoint of a social anthropologist there was nothing to be ashamed of about African origins, and indeed an appreciation of the ancestral cultures of the African past could be a source of pride and dignity. Many of the 'Africanisms' that Herskovits traced were in such things as music, dance, supernatural beliefs and magical practices, and speech patterns among isolated rural groups such as the Gullah of the Sea Island region. He did add, however, that 'matriarchal' black family life, with its high illegitimacy rate and the special emphasis on the mother's role, might well have its origins in African polygyny in which the closest bonds were those between a mother and her children, and a 'common-law' relationship was recognized rather than formal marriage. Frazier in reply reiterated the conventional wisdom and the majority view among social scientists. He conceded that many African elements were to be found in the cultures of black people elsewhere in the New World, in the West Indies and especially Brazil; but they were much more difficult to trace in the United States, where for many generations most slaves had lived in small groups on small plantations, isolated from one another, speaking only English, in close contact with their white owners. Retaining only fragmentary memories of their ancestors' African background, they had been stripped of their cultural heritage to an extent suffered by few peoples in human history. In the process, 'the African family system, the chief means of cultural transmission, was destroyed'; and the mother's special role in black family life was attributable to 'the exigencies of life in the new environment'.[10]

Black family life became a matter of political controversy in

1965 when a storm broke out over an official report whose author, Daniel Patrick Moynihan, was both social scientist and public servant; at the time Assistant Secretary of Labor, he later became a United States Senator. The report's political background and the furore that followed it were comprehensively reviewed by Lee Rainwater and William L. Yancey.[11]

Central to the strategy proposed in Moynihan's policy document was the need to focus attention on the black American family in assessing the effectiveness of government programmes to relieve poverty and remedy disadvantage. But that was not all; black family life itself was seen as a problem, a 'tangle of pathology'. Not only was the relative disadvantage of black people in American society widening, but their family life, especially in the inner cities, was 'crumbling'. While a small middle-class group had managed to extricate themselves, the great majority of black families were trapped in a cycle of poverty and disadvantage.

Drawing on the conventional wisdom of social science, and backing it up with official statistics, Moynihan characterized black family life as disorganized and unstable. Throughout their history – alike under slavery, during Reconstruction and the 'Jim Crow' period, and in their more recent experience of discrimination, unemployment, and urban poverty – it was black men who had been most humiliated. That had undermined their position as husbands and fathers, and led to a reversal of the conventional roles of husband and wife in a pattern of female dominance that reproduced itself over the generations; thus black women were better educated than black men, though the gap was closing. Many black fathers were absent, or unemployed, or too poorly paid to support their family. Children deprived of maternal care because of the family's dependence on the mother's income lacked also a strong, competent father-figure. Edward Wight Bakke's study of unemployed men was quoted with approval, to the effect that unemployment put two women in charge of a family: the wife/mother, and the social worker, generally female, with whom she had dealings, while the male was reduced to a mere errand-boy between home and social welfare office.

With all their handicaps and disadvantages, black children under-achieved at school. This led to difficulty in getting and keeping well-paid work, so perpetuating the cycle of disadvantage, and generating disaffection and alienation among young black people. In particular, the failure of 56 per cent of young black men to meet the modest requirements of the armed forces qualification test excluded them from military service, with all its rewards and privileges as well as hazards and sacrifices, and a source of manly pride in much needed contrast to the disorganized matrifocal family life of the urban slum. National action was urgently needed to remedy that family disorganization; and Moynihan concluded with a quotation from Frazier, calling for changes in black family life and in American society generally that would enable the black father to play the role conventionally required of him.

In the long, confused controversy stirred up by the Moynihan report, two leading themes emerged. One was the diversity of family patterns among black people. Thus in his 1965 agenda paper for a White House conference planning session following the report, Hylan Lewis said that it had 'especially overlooked and underrated' the diversity among lower-income black families. [12] It will be recalled that Frazier's work had fully documented that diversity, affording considerable qualifications to the conventional view of black family life that had been based on an over-simplified version of his findings. Jessie Bernard took up the same theme even more strongly in her book which, though not directly addressed to the Moynihan debate, appeared when it was at its height in 1966. [13] She identified two cultures among black Americans, a cleavage, she said, which had nothing to do with economic class, and which had originated even before emancipation. At all income levels, some black Americans had completely internalized the norms of white American society. Religion was an important factor, as the denominations and sects that had gained many black adherents strongly emphasized the Protestant work ethic and stable, conventional family life. Other black Americans, however, conformed outwardly if at all to white norms, and were not unduly worried about unstable unions and premarital pregnancies. Any generalizations were untrustworthy, therefore. Nonetheless, the commonest type of black household centred on a husband and wife living together in their first marriage, and most black children were brought up in such a household. It was quite wrong to regard statistical data on black families as representing deviance from the white norm.

Secondly, and even more fundamentally, it was questioned whether black family life really had any distinctive features at all. Were not the characteristics of black families simply those of poor families? and did not statistical black–white differences arise simply because most black families were poor? Thus Hylan Lewis pointed out that many black–white differences were diminished considerably when controlled for income (that is, when black people were compared with whites at similar income levels), though they did not disappear completely; and income made more difference than colour. Inequities in housing, employment, health, and education likewise accounted for a large part of these differences. The higher proportion of female-headed households among black people was one of the differences largely though not wholly attributable to poverty, along with discrimination in health, housing, and employment. Like Bernard, Lewis pointed out that two out of three black families included two parents, and that this form of household was normal for black and white Americans alike. While the proportion of female-headed households among black people was higher than among whites, it had risen only slightly in the previous fifteen years and not at all in the last five years – scarcely evidence of a rapid 'crumbling' of black family life. Rather than a pathological deviation from normality, it should be recognized as an existing and fairly common form of family life, and the question was how to devise ways of helping 'parents without partners'. In the same way, Hylan Lewis's analysis of data on births out of wedlock tended to shift the explanatory emphasis from 'black' to 'poor'. So did his analysis of child-rearing practices, with a further reminder of the diversity among low-income families which, he said, had been overlooked and underrated, along with the impressive resilience and endurance of the so-called 'culturally disadvantaged' children of the poor.

Like Lewis, Moynihan's feminist critics denied that there was anything intrinsically pathological about 'matrifocal' female-headed households. Why should it be assumed that men should necessarily take responsibility and exercise authority? Moreover, if there was 'matriarchy', it was not necessarily because women wanted it; it could be forced on them by adverse circumstances. Women had saved their families from disasters throughout history, and none more so than black women in American history. Moynihan had underrated them.[14]

One of Moynihan's severest critics was William Ryan, for whom the report was a prime example of blaming the victim; indeed, it largely stimulated him to write his book of that title.[15] By suggesting that part at least of the reason why black people were poor and disadvantaged lay in weaknesses or failures in their family life, the report put the onus of change on black people themselves. They were at fault, though paradoxically it was through no fault of their own. It was a typical victim-blaming argument, too, to explain what was wrong in terms of the past, and so play down the need to remedy current injustices. Black people had suffered terrible wrongs at the hands of cruel slave-owners, but that was long ago; few white people today were even the remote descendants of slave-owners, and none could seriously be held responsible for those past wrongs. Consequently, Ryan was among those who tended to explain the characteristics of black family life as responses to current circumstances of poverty and discrimination, rather than as representing the heritage of slavery. Discounting the notion of a distinctive culture, he drew attention to resemblances rather than differences between black and white families, especially among the poor and otherwise disadvantaged.

Responses to current circumstances, or the heritage of slavery? Racial discrimination against black people, or class differences? After the Moynihan controversy, these seemed to be the key questions for the study of black family life. For Andrew Billingsley, however, they were spurious questions, to each of which the answer was: both. Black people were an ethnic group with their own culture and a distinct history, which it would be quite wrong to ignore; yet the strategies adopted by black families were also well adapted for their survival in contemporary conditons. Female-headed households were an example. In most states, a family with a husband and father at home was inegligible for federally-supported welfare benefits. Faced with the stark choice between having a man about the house, and money in the house, some poor black families chose the latter. So far from exhibiting disorganization, such a strategy seemed quite functional for their survival. Nevertheless, it could not be too strongly emphasized that most poor black people lived in nuclear family households headed by men who worked hard every day trying, often unsuccessfully, to pull their families up out of poverty.[16]

In a similar vein, John Mogey reported from his study of a

slum area of Nashville, Tennessee, that terms like matrifocal, matriarchal, denuded, incomplete, disorganized, and unstable were quite inapplicable to family life there. True, some households had female heads, while many men were 'boy friends' rather than legal husbands: but the families inhabiting the area, though impoverished, were relatively stable, and extended kinship networks helped to solve problems of solidarity and survival. [17]

Extensive, mutually supportive networks of kin (particularly kinswomen) and neighbours pursuing strategies of survival: these too were the salient findings of Carol B. Stack in a social-anthropological study of a slum area she called The Flats in a southern town. [18] Like Mogey, she found preconceived terms like 'matrifocal' unhelpful, and 'unstable' and 'disorganized' downright false, while even 'nuclear family' and 'household' did not quite fit in a society in which a person might eat in one household, sleep in another, and contribute resources to a third. Households had shifting memberships, but that did not indicate instability, and many were in a steady state, composed of three generations – elderly men and women, a middle generation of mothers bringing up their own children or those of near kin, and the children. Some of the perennial features of black family life persisted, evidently. Women whether married or not felt few if any inhibitions about childbearing, and very few were married before they had given birth to one or more children. Relationships between men and women were recognized, but not necessarily expected to endure. There was more than one strategy open to the father of a child, before or after birth. He might deny paternity, and the denial might well be accepted, especially if the mother and her kinswomen reckoned he would probably not do much by way of supporting her and the child. In that case, the mother might find a subsequent partner willing and able to act as father. Or the natural father might acknowledge paternity, in which case he would have to make good his claim by paying the bills, helping in the home, and actively being a father to the child, to the satisfaction of the mother and her kinswomen. So men were on probation because women regarded them as essentially unreliable, if only because many were unemployed or in insecure employment. The people a mother could count on were rather her female kin and neighbours, and it was among them that the strongest ties were formed through child-minding arrangements, swapping material goods, helping out in times of crisis, and pooling resources generally. Female kin, indeed, would often discourage women from forming long-lasting relationships with men. Even the meagre resources provided by AFDC (Aid to Families with Dependent Children) were at least controlled by women. So people in The Flats were involved in networks with many kin and friends upon whom they could rely, and census statistics indicating a high proportion of single-parent, female-headed households did not adequately reflect the complexities of family and neighbourhood organization. These features of urban black family life were highly adaptive, and constituted their resilient response to the problems posed by poverty, unemployment, and the vagaries of the welfare relief system.

While American sociologists were concentrating attention on black family life in response to contemporary conditions, American historians were engaged in a reappraisal of slavery. That reassessment was associated above all with the work of Robert William Fogel and Stanley L. Engerman, though they were not alone in adopting a new approach to the subject, relying on the quantitative analysis of primary sources such as plantation registers and records of slave sales rather than on the subjective accounts of the experience of those involved as slaves, ex-slaves, owners, or northern abolitionists. Most of their work on the economics of slavery lies outside the scope of this book. However, one of their ten 'principal corrections' to the traditional view of the slave economy was:

The belief that slave-breeding, sexual exploitation, and promiscuity destroyed the black family is a myth. The family was the basic unit of social organization under slavery. It was to the economic interest of planters to encourage the stability of slave families and most of them did so. Most slave sales were either of whole families or of individuals who were at an age when it would have been normal for them to have left the family.[19]

Slavery in the United States differed from that elsewhere in the New World in some important respects. Whereas in a wider perspective by far the greatest slave crop was sugar, grown on big estates in Brazil and the West Indies, in the United States slavery was associated with first tobacco, then cotton, grown mainly on small estates. Thus in the late 18th century the average number of slaves on plantations in Jamaica was 180; in Virginia and Maryland, 13. Furthermore, elsewhere in the New World slave mortality exceeded fertility, mainly because of tropical diseases which afflicted also the white population, so that the slave labour force had continually to be replenished by fresh imports from Africa. In the United States by contrast, and again largely because of the climate, fertility exceeded mortality, so that few imports were needed relative to the total black population, and few also compared with Brazil, Spanish America, and the Caribbean colonies. When the foreign slave trade was made illegal in 1808 only some 20 per cent of black Americans were foreign-born, and the proportion had dropped almost to zero by 1860 on the eve of general emancipation; the great majority were the children, grandchildren, and great-grandchildren of those originally enslaved in Africa. Such data afforded the economic and demographic background to much that had already been known, and had emerged, for instance, in the debate between Frazier and Herskovits about African origins.

For slave-owners in the United States, therefore, it was both possible and profitable to breed their own slaves, while for slave-owners elsewhere in the New World it was not. Slave fertility represented an excellent long-term investment, provided slaves could be expected to live long enough to repay the heavy cost of rearing them; for they could not be expected to make much contribution to the work of the plantation till they were in their teens, and did not reach maximum productivity till they were in their twenties. The break-even point occurred about the age of twenty-seven, according to Fogel and Enger-man's calculations, which incidentally also vindicated the gradual emancipation schemes enacted in some northern states ahead of general emancipation in the United States as a whole. In the United States the life expectation among slaves well exceeded twenty-seven; elsewhere, in colonies such as Jamaica, it fell considerably short, making it more economic for slave-owners to use slave women as labourers, discourage fertility and family formation, and import fresh slaves from Africa.

So it was one of an American slave-owner's prime concerns to encourage pregnancy among his female slaves.[20] However, this was in general achieved by promoting stable family formation rather than by less savoury methods. According to Fogel and

Engerman, systematic breeding of slaves for the market was a myth, and there was 'not a single authenticated case of the "stud" plantations alleged in abolitionist literature'. Nor was it done by the owner or his agents themselves, or not to any great extent. Although the sexual exploitation of slave women did occur, especially perhaps by owners' sons, and there was no legal redress against it, it was contrary alike to economic sense and moral sensibility. Evidence that it was the exception rather than the rule was afforded by the remarkably low proportion of mulattos (people of mixed descent) in 1860, after 230 years of close contact on small plantations; and by latter-day statistical and genetic studies suggesting that no more than 1 or 2 per cent of slave children were fathered by whites.

Slaves' material conditions of food, housing, and clothing, though meagre by latter-day standards, on the whole compared favourably with those of free white wage-workers in Europe, Britain, and the northern United States. Their medical care was poor, but so it was for whites too: and sick slaves were looked after to the best of their owners' ability. It was through their control of these basic resources that owners acted to encourage stable family life, believing that to be the surest way to promote slave fertility and provide for the care of slave children, their most precious long-term assets. They recognised male slaves as husbands in fact if not in law, listing them as household heads, and through them distributing houses, garden patches, clothes, and other resources to their families. Promiscuity was encouraged neither by slaves nor their owners, and very young pregnancies were rare. It was clear enough that African family forms were discarded as quite inappropriate to the new conditions and the nuclear family household became the norm; it was an open question how far that pattern was imposed by slave-owners and how far it was a response by slaves to their own perceived needs. The strength of slaves' attachment to their families was amply evidenced in their anguish when families were sold apart, and their struggles to be reunited, even though it was only rarely that slave-owners broke up families in this way.

Fogel and Engerman believed that misapprehensions about slavery had arisen from the profound and long-enduring cleavage in the whole American intellectual tradition between abolitionists and defenders of that 'peculiar institution'. When the movement to abolish it began, notably among Philadelphia Quakers in the mid-18th century, it was based on one simple moral postulate: no-one ought to have so much power over another. That remained irrefutable, and should have sufficed, but as the movement grew in the early 19th century two other and more disputable arguments were added. First, that those who had such power over others were almost bound to misuse it, and the allegation that slaves were denied a proper family life formed part of the general abolitionist charge that they were systematically ill-used and cruelly treated. Secondly, that slavery as an economic system was inefficient and wasteful.

These two arguments had confused the debate and weakened the abolitionists' case. The belief that the slave economy was inefficient was not borne out by the evidence. Further, it was associated with the view that black labour was inefficient, and so contributed to a racist 'myth of black incompetence' that was, paradoxically, largely an abolitionist invention. On the contrary, slave labour was in general both efficient and well managed, not least by those black men who came to assume managerial responsibility as 'drivers' or overseers.

In the same way, the abolitionists' emphasis on abuses raised the question whether these were common events rarely reported, or exceptional instances frequently and luridly reported. It enabled defenders of slavery to point out, with some truth, that on the whole slaves were better fed, housed, and clothed, and no less humanely treated, than free white wage workers at the time – as if that justified slaves' total subjection and the restraints upon their liberty. Moreover, if it were also true that the system was inefficient and unprofitable, slave-owners could almost be portrayed as benevolent philanthropists who at some cost to themselves kept the plantations going out of kindness to their slaves. As for family life, their emphasis on abuses involved abolitionists in a serious inconsistency. On the one hand they alleged that slavery had destroyed black people's family life, reduced parenthood to mere breeding, and through sexual exploitation and selling apart engendered a casual attitude towards marriage in which husbands and wives failed to develop deep and enduring affection. On the other hand, by accurately representing the anguish caused when slave families were sold apart, they showed, on the contrary, how deep and enduring was the affection between slave spouses.

Fogel and Engerman concluded that black people endured worse material hardships after the civil war than before. Their life expectation fell by 10 per cent, their diet deteriorated, and their sickness rates in the 1890s were 20 per cent higher than on the slave plantations. Black families who as slaves had been maintained by their owners now had to find money to live on; and employment was available to black men only at the lowest of low wages. Even those who as slaves had acquired skills, such as blacksmiths and carpenters, were squeezed out of employment in competition with white workers in a market in which black men were more and more narrowly confined to the least skilled and most menial jobs. Well might Frazier write of demoralized family life after emancipation.

Eugene D. Genovese confirmed and amplified many of Fogel and Engerman's findings, while qualifying some of them. Many slave-owners had seen themselves as authoritarian fathers of a large family, white and black, though this involved them in an inconsistency as they also recognized and actively encouraged family life among their slaves. With such close contact, especially between the white family and their house servants, it was not surprising that sexual exploitation sometimes occurred, as it did, enough to constitute a scandal and to make life hell for some black women and their menfolk, yet not enough to be other than exceptional. The restraint generally shown by white men in the southern United States contrasted sharply with the behaviour of their counterparts in, for example, Brazil. Selling apart was rare, and many slave-owners accepted financial loss for the sake of keeping slave families together; however, even if it actually happened to few, many feared it might happen to them. Slave children, whatever miseries might await them as adults, mostly had 'a real childhood' in an age when some English children worked up chimneys and down mines. They did not generally lack the image of a strong, competent black father, as sensible masters recognized and strengthened male authority and responsibility in slave households; while in less-well-conducted plantations some slave fathers stood up bravely to defend their families against ill-treatment, and sometimes paid a terrible price for their courage. From their own experience, slaves came to value family life in a male-headed two-parent household, no matter what difficulty they might have in achieving that ideal.[21]

Genovese's general conclusion was that the strength of

family life in 'the world the slaves made' had been greatly underestimated by many authorities, including even Frazier. Historians and sociologists had been led astray by reading history backwards, and assuming that if things were bad in the 20th-century urban ghettos they must have been even worse under slavery. If black family life had been disoriented, it was in the 20th-century migrations to the north; rural black family life in the south, remaining closer to the patterns developed under slavery, seemed always to have been much stronger.

One of Fogel and Engerman's severest critics was Herbert G. Gutman, who in an exceptionally lengthy and adverse review poured scorn on, for example, the calculations that had led them to conclude that few slave families were broken by being sold apart.[22] Yet Gutman's substantive findings seemed not so very different from Fogel and Engerman's, and on some points seemed to amplify and reinforce them. Slave communities neither approved nor to any great extent practised promiscuity; trial marriages were tolerated, but marriage generally followed prenuptial pregnancy. As for the slave-owners, the simple biological reproduction of the slave labour force required only that slave mothers should have children, yet many owners encouraged the formation of completed slave families for reasons both moral and economic, finding them indeed conducive to labour discipline and a source of incentive. However, this did not apply equally at all stages in the development of a plantation. When a young owner was buying in slaves to assemble a labour force for a newly-acquired plantation, many family and kin networks might be broken. Similarly when an owner grew old or died the labour force might be dispersed by sale or divided by inheritance among several heirs. Only in the middle phase of the plantation cycle would there be much prospect of stability for the slaves' family life. So '*all* slave marriages were insecure', and there were good reasons for the abolitionists' charge that slavery weakened the slave household.[23] Nevertheless, Gutman's evidence showed how slaves kept up extensive kin networks, together with naming practices and an avoidance of cousin marriage possibly of African origin. Once again there were unequivocal indications of the tenacity of black family life despite adversities under slavery.

Coming to more recent times, Gutman took issue with the Moynihan report and the conventional wisdom it embodied, not exonerating even Frazier's contribution. In 1880 most black people in the southern states lived in husband- or father-present households, and most black women were not household heads. The so-called matrifocal family was hardly to be found at that time; nor was it the predominant pattern at later dates, despite the upheaval of the early 20th-century migration from the rural south to the urban north. Sample data for 1900 indicated more male-absent households than in 1880, but studies in two New York City districts showed that in 1905 and 1925 the great majority of black households included a husband or father. Throughout the period 1880–1925, Gutman concluded, 'the typical Afro-American family was lower-class in status and headed by two parents.'[24] Neither weak nor disorganized, black family life had not been destroyed under slavery, nor had it been shattered by the 20th-century migrations.

To sum up: among sociologists and historians alike, there has been a strong trend in recent thought in the United States to question the old conventional wisdom, to down-play the heritage of slavery, and to attribute black–white demographic differences and the characteristics of black family life to conditions of unemployment, poverty, and discrimination in the more recent past.

SOUTH ASIAN COMMUNITIES IN BRITAIN

People of south Asian origin, along with other non-white people especially from the West Indies, first migrated into Britain in substantial numbers during the late 1940s and throughout the 1950s, a time of full employment and an unsatisfied demand for labour; that migration was checked by new immigration laws in 1962. The first south Asian migrants were mostly men, many of whom intended to stay for only a few years while saving or remitting as much money as possible to augment or restore a family's fortunes at home. During the 1950s, therefore, many lived frugally in all-male households, sharing cramped accommodation in inner-city areas with kinsmen, co-religionists, or men from the same village. As time went on, expectations of an early return receded, though for many it remained an ultimate goal; and gradually during the 1960s and 1970s men sent for their wives and children to join them, so that this became a period of consolidation when Asian communities and family households were reconstituted in Britain and linked even more closely with those in the homelands. Also during the late 1960s and early 1970s more Asian families arrived in Britain fleeing from persecution in and expulsion from first Kenya and then Uganda. Subsequently, in the course of nature, all these families and communities have been augmented by younger members born in Britain and having no other home.

Generalization about these communities and their family life is possible to only a limited extent. Within the population of south Asian origin the larger categories of Hindus, Muslims, and Sikhs are sub-divided by language, region of origin, and in some cases caste; thus the Mirpuri community, for example, are Muslims originating from a group of villages in the Mirpur district of Pakistan. The traditional kinship systems of these different groups are far from uniform. Thus among Hindus and Sikhs marriage is generally permissible only to one of a different *gotra* or kin group but of the same or a similar caste; in other words, kin groups are exogamous while castes are endogamous, or largely so. Among Muslims in Pakistan, by contrast, the all-important kin group, the *biraderi* or brotherhood, is an endogamous patrilineage within which cousin marriages are preferred. Traditional ideas about divorce differed widely, too; impossible for Hindus, it was easy for Muslim men. However, there are similarities as well as differences. All are authoritarian patriarchal systems in which men exercise authority over women, parents over children, and the old over the young. Marriages are arranged between kin groups, girls are strictly chaperoned, and the sexes are segregated. The idea of family honour is strong. Although the concept of the joint family is elusive and somewhat controversial,[25] it is manifested in a preference for living in large multi-generational households, often including brothers and their wives and children, as far as circumstances permit; and in mutual aid networks and business partnerships linking related men, whether co-resident or, as in many cases, widely dispersed about the world.

Besides religious differences and those of kinship organization, the diversity of south Asian communities, together with the wide cultural gap between all of them and the British host society, have been further accentuated by the widespread use of languages such as Gujerati, Punjabi, and Urdu within communities and families. Newspapers circulating in Britain in these languages with their distinctive scripts have reinforced each community's sense of ethnic identity and its links with the homeland on the Indian sub-continent. Language differences have played their part in family life, too. Many Asian women, not at all fluent in English, have had to rely on their children born and schooled in Britain as interpreters and advisers in their dealings with the host community, so reversing the customary patterns of authority in the family. Yet other differences have arisen between those south Asians who migrated directly from the sub-continent and those who came from East Africa and who, after a two or three generation separation from the homelands and participation in the modern sector of a colonial economy, tended to be less traditionalist in their attitudes.

Studies carried out during the 1970s included those by Roger and Catherine Ballard of Sikhs in Leeds;[26] by Verity Saifullah Khan of Mirpuris in Bradford;[27] by Muhammad Anwar of Pakistanis in Rochdale;[28] and by Arthur Wesley Helweg of Sikhs in Gravesend (or 'Gravesindia').[29] These studies are remarkable for their unanimity about the leading features of south Asian family life in Britain, and also for the wide agreement they recorded among the great majority of south Asians themselves about their family life in an alien western society and culture.

For all reported a widely-held conviction that western ways are bad. Thus according to Khan, prospective migrants in Mirpur were admonished to seize the economic opportunities of life in Britain but not to succumb to the bad ways of the west. Anwar put it even more strongly: Pakistanis had been taught from childhood to despise western ways as morally bankrupt. They resisted change, adopted an attitude of non-participation in British institutions, and depended rather on kin, friends, and ethnic institutions in encapsulated communities closely linked with the homeland. Just how closely was exemplified when a dispute in Pakistan over land bought with money remitted from England led to a fight in Rochdale between kinsmen of the disputants in the home village. Similarly, Helweg related how even in the early days of all-male migration tight social controls were exerted through gossip and letters upon Sikh men in Britain, and mothers in the Punjab threatened to go on hunger strike if errant sons did not mend their ways. These controls were reinforced and the gossip network – a persistent feature of south Asian societies generally – was drawn even tighter when men in Britain were joined by their womenfolk, zealous to uphold the family honour upon which depended, among other things, their daughters' marriage prospects.

Prominent among the features of western society that south Asians found most repellent were family life and related issues of schooling, relations between the sexes, marriage, and the care of the aged. Evident, indeed, from all accounts is a quite explicit rejection of just about all the distinctive features of western family life that I set out in chapter 1. Thus according to both Catherine Ballard and Verity Khan, south Asians perceived English family life as cold and insecure, lacking in affection and in respect for the older generation. Families were small, young adults left home to make their own way, old people lived alone or were put into homes without good reason; marital breakdown and sexual licence were rife. By Asian standards it all seemed outrageously immoral and inhumane.

English schooling likewise was seen as puzzling and threatening. According to Khan, Mirpuri parents misunderstood British education, expecting as they did a regime of set books, homework, discipline, and no parental involvement. Similarly, according to Catherine Ballard, Asian parents were mystified by the very idea of pre-school education, by the informality of British schools, by the free mixing of boys and girls, and by the practice of letting children learn at their own pace and not by rote, encouraging them to be questioning and assertive, and to develop their potential aptitudes in their own way. The paramountcy of individual development that inspired such educational practices was quite incompatible with Asian ideas, according to which relations between children and their elders should be affectionate but hierarchical, group interests should prevail over those of the individual, and no great emphasis was to be placed on the development of a personal identity.

It seems clear, indeed, that schooling has posed most difficult problems for south Asian family life in Britain. Sending children to school has been much more than a matter of complying with the law; residence in Britain has been sought and valued for its educational as well as its economic opportunities, and indeed the two can hardly be separated. But schooling, perhaps more than anything else, has made it impossible for south Asian communities to inhabit their own worlds in matters of religion, language, and family life while limiting their dealings with the host society to purely instrumental transactions. As Helweg pointed out, schools taught children both formally and informally about western ideas of courtship and love-marriage; thus children could hardly be taught English without exposing them to a whole literature in which those are perennially prominent themes. Informally, too, schools exposed Asian children to English peer-group pressure, which challenged unquestioning obedience to parental authority.

Thus Anwar described how Pakistani parents in Rochdale, who had brought their children to Britain for a good education, nonetheless feared that the children would be spoiled by forces beyond their control, especially television and the school environment. Parents, and also relatives in Pakistan, were worried about co-education and the permissive atmosphere in British schools. Along with western influences generally, these were seen as threats to parents' authority and control and the respect due to them, and to the children's attachment to Islam and to Pakistani culture. In addition to their English schooling therefore, and to counteract its influence, parents considered it important for their children to receive religious instruction both formally in Islamic centres and informally, mainly from their mothers, at home. In a typical instance, Anwar related how a father warned his son to come home early and not waste time with English friends, whom he regarded as a bad influence. In a similar vein, Helweg stated that Sikh parents openly taught their children not to associate with or emulate their English class-mates, and formed an intelligence network, watching and telephoning if, for instance, a girl were seen talking to boys on her way home, even Punjabi boys she had grown up with; while Khan described how Asian children in Bradford congregated at bus stops and stuck together at school, fearful of English children.

These tensions between south Asian communities and the host society have been reflected within south Asian families in tensions between the younger generation, born or at least schooled in Britain, and their elders. According to Anwar, three leading issues arose between young Pakistanis and their parents: western dress, especially for girls; arranged marriages; and freedom, by which was meant mainly young people's desire to be free to do as they like in their own spare or leisure time. However, they were far from unanimous about how strong these disagreements were. Fewer than half of the young Pakistanis questioned in his nation-wide survey, and only one in three parents, reported any family disagreements at all. Fewer than half of the young people saw nothing wrong with girls wearing western clothes. Three out of four thought young English people had more freedom than they had, but only one in three wanted more freedom than their own parents gave them. However, 60 per cent thought that more and more young people would rebel against the arranged marriage system.

Other writers too reported no lack of teenage rebellion in Asian families, but also that it was limited and controlled. According to both Catherine and Roger Ballard, many young Asians disagreed with their parents about specific issues and envied British teen-agers' freedom and independence, yet they also valued the supportiveness, the economic co-operation, and the clear morality of their families. For their part, some Asian parents maintained a flexible and open-minded approach, making every effort to explain their attitudes, and trying to discuss problems in an atmosphere of mutual trust and affection in which a shared religious faith helped. Others, however, were inconsistent, taking up positions without thinking through the consequences, for example encouraging academic achievement at school and then not allowing a girl to go on to college but keeping her at home pending an arranged marriage; or, according to Helweg, overlooking minor manifestations at first but changing their attitude when they came under community pressure through the gossip network. Severe difficulties arose when some excessively authoritarian fathers, seeing themselves as embattled upholders of righteous morality, interpreted the slightest move towards greater freedom as a headlong rush into western ways, and became heavily repressive.

Distressed by family rows, and in some cases fearing being locked up, beaten, or even killed by their father and his kinsmen, many young Asian women have turned for help to sympathetic members of the British host community, including professionals – doctors, teachers, social workers – as well as personal friends. Such outside helpers, imbued with the values of western individualism, often advised them to leave home, set up on their own, and lead an independent life. But few did so, and most confounded their western helpers by going back. English friends tended to suspect that they did so under duress or emotional blackmail. In the Ballards' opinion, however, outside helpers tended to underestimate young Asians' attachment to their families, and Catherine Ballard quoted one such girl as saying 'I missed my family terribly in spite of all the rows . . . Who's going to marry a girl who has run away? When I tried to explain to my doctor why I'd gone back he thought that I was barmy or that my parents had threatened me . . . He just didn't get it.'[30]

At the heart of the matter lies Asian rejection of western individualism. This has little or nothing in common with socialism, and indeed many Asians have shown themselves fully equal to their British counterparts in industry, thrift, and initiative in a private-enterprise economy. According to Asian principles, the larger group to which individuals are required to subordinate their interests is not society as a whole, as in the European socialist tradition, but the family or kin group. Thus Helweg reported that British social workers' proposals to set up refuges for runaway Asian girls were vigorously opposed by Sikhs who felt very strongly that social workers had no right to undermine parental authority in that way. There was tension over how the British social services should deal with such situations, and how far, in a country such as Britain, cultural relativism could prevail.

Arranged marriage is in many respects the crucial issue, both within south Asian communities and between them and the host society. For the latter, it runs directly counter to the whole western conception of marriage as a union based on the freely consenting individual choice of responsible adult partners. It has been officially deprecated: thus Catherine Ballard quoted a British government minister as saying that 'We would want to discourage the arranged marriage system . . . [We hope] that more and more parents will respect the rights of their children.'[31] And it has had important, and often highly contentious, implications for British immigration policies and prac-

tices, especially when one of the prospective spouses is still
resident in the sub-continent and the couple have not even
met.

For Asian parents, no doubt, the whole point of preserving a
daughter's chastity and reputation throughout her girlhood
was to uphold the family's honour and enable them to make a
good marriage for her when the time comes. More than any
other single factor, this justified all the chaperonage, the surveillance, and the restrictions upon Asian girls in contrast to
the free-and-easy lives of their English counterparts. As for
young Asians, Catherine Ballard stated unequivocally that all
knew throughout their childhood and adolescence of their
parents' intention to arrange their marriages. Some managed
to meet boy or girl-friends clandestinely; some were able to
defer an arranged marriage, pleading that they did not feel
ready; many in recent years had played at least some part in the
arrangements themselves, through long informal meetings or
telephone conversations with the designated partner. Many,
perhaps most, accepted the prospect without demur from the
first; practically all eventually acquiesced.

Many articulate Asians defend the practice. Citing data of the
kind I set out in chapter 11, they contend that arranged
marriages merely ensure explicitly and overtly that like marries
like, that marriage partners are suitably matched according to
their family backgrounds and personalities, the same effect as
that achieved tacitly and unavowed in most cases in the so
called love-marriages of the west. Moreover, arranged marriages
are said to be no less affectionate, and certainly no less
stable.

These are, however, more deeply underlying factors in
young Asians' eventual acquiescence. According to Roger
Ballard, for young Sikh men in Leeds arranged marriage was a
test, even a personal identity crisis. In their teens, many had
shaved their beards, left off their turbans, polished up their
English, and made English friends, including girl-friends. That
'Anglicizing' period in their lives came to an end, however, only
partly in response to family pressure to marry correctly. That
indeed had much weight, as they respected their parents and
were most reluctant to sever family ties. Some hoped for a kind
of cultural bilingualism, in which they might switch between
Punjabi and English in more than language, reforming and

modifying their parents' ways rather than abandoning them. Above all, however, was the dawning realization that however completely they adopted western ways they would never be fully accepted as British because of the colour of their skin. Some racial discrimination they had encountered, indeed, from their school-days onwards; but even if they were fortunate enough to have avoided the grosser manifestations of racial prejudice on the part of some of the native British population, knowledge of that eventual non-acceptance was enough to prompt a reactive ethnicity in which they decided after all to be Sikhs, grow their beards again, put their turbans back on, accept an arranged marriage, and cultivate family and community relationships.

SUGGESTIONS FOR FURTHER READING

E. Franklin Frazier, *The Negro Family in the United States*, revised edition, Chicago, Chicago University Press, 1966

Jessie Bernard, *Marriage and Family among Negroes*, Englewood Cliffs, NJ, Prentice-Hall, 1966

Lee Rainwater and William L. Yancey, *The Moynihan Report and the Politics of Controversy*, Cambridge, Mass., MIT Press, 1967

Robert William Fogel and Stanley L. Engerman, *Time on the Cross: The Economics of American Negro Slavery*, 2 vols., Boston, Mass., Little Brown, 1974

James L. Watson (ed.), *Between Two Cultures: Migrants and Minorities in Britain*, Oxford, Blackwell, 1977

Verity Saifullah Khan (ed.), *Minority Families in Britain: Support and Stress*, London, Macmillan, 1979

Muhammad Anwar, *The Myth of Return: Pakistanis in Britain*, London, Heinemann, 1979

Arthur Wesley Helweg, *Sikhs in England: The Development of a Migrant Community*, Delhi, Oxford University Press, 1979

13

Marital adjustment, marital breakdown, and divorce

Why do some marriages break down and not others? Why are there so many more divorces nowadays? – and presumably therefore more broken marriages? Research into this subject has generally been addressed to one or other of these two questions. They are to some extent related: an increase in some factor associated with marital breakdown, such as marriage at a young age, will at least partly account for the rise in the number of divorces. However, they are largely separate questions, and studies addressed to one do not necessarily shed much light on the other.

STUDIES IN THE UNITED STATES

Marital adjustment and marital happiness

Early work in the United States was mainly directed to the first question, and sociologists looked into the factors making for marital adjustment and marital happiness. According to Ernest W. Burgess and Harvey J. Locke, between 1925 and 1945 more than a dozen such studies were carried out. The first, apparently, was that of Hornell Hart and Wilmer Shields, who focussed on the age at marriage and concluded that a high proportion of marriages contracted at young ages (men under twenty-four, women under twenty-one) turned out to be unhappy – a finding consistently replicated in later research. Factors associated in other early studies with satisfactory marriage were homogamy (partners of same ethnic group and religious affiliation and approximately equal education), parents' marriages happy, sociability, and conventionality as evidenced by church attendance and a wedding by a minister of religion.[1]

Several of those early studies were directed or supervised by Burgess, a colleague of Robert Ezra Park at Chicago, then the world's leading sociology school. Prominent among them, and highly influential, was his work with Leonard S. Cottrell in 1931–3 on the prediction of marital adjustment.[2] By today's more rigorous standards, the provenance of their data was somewhat questionable; some 7000 copies of an 8-page questionnaire were distributed, and about 1300 couples responded, 526 of whom were residents of Illinois married at least 1 and not more than 6 years. With 14 late additions, the responses of these 540 couples provided the data base for the analysis. Compared with the United States population as a whole, they were predominantly white, Protestant, urban, young, educated, and of high occupational status.

Burgess and Cottrell analysed four main variables: a happiness rating, an adjustment score, a prediction score, and the current formal state of the marriage.

For the happiness rating, in a procedure that has since become a standard commonplace, each subject was asked to assess the marriage on a five-point scale as very happy, happy, average, unhappy or very unhappy. Husbands and wives were asked to make these judgements independently of each other, and in some cases an outsider's assessment was also available. There was close agreement among these independent ratings, with correlation coefficients of over 0.8 (perfect correlation = 1).

For the adjustment rating, a battery of questions covered five main areas of family life: common activities; agreement or disagreement over matters such as money, caring for the children, recreation, friends, religion, relations with in-laws, manners; the extent to which affection was demonstrated; the extent to which the partners confided in each other; and any complaints each partner had about the other, or about the married relationship. An adjustment score compounded out of the responses to these questions proved to correlate very closely indeed (0.92) with the happiness rating.

The prediction score was compounded from information about such things as age, health, occupation, earnings, amount saved at time of marriage, religious affiliation and activity, sociability, length of courtship and engagement, relations with parents, and the happiness of parents' marriages. This score correlated fairly closely (0.51) with the adjustment score.

Finally, the prediction score was related to the current formal status of the marriage, which was assessed in four categories according to whether the couple were divorced, separated, had contemplated divorce or separation, or had never contemplated divorce or separation. More than 90 per cent of those with a high prediction score had never contemplated parting, while the majority of low scorers were already divorced or separated.

These two studies showed that the probable outcome of different marriages could be predicted with a fair degree of reliability from information about the relevant background factors. Further, although their authors themselves did not make the point, it was evident that much of the requisite information was quite objective and factual in nature. In so far as it consisted of externally verifiable facts such as age, length of engagement, education, occupation, and church attendance, much of it could even conceivably have been supplied by a well-informed outsider without enquiring into the couple's subjective personal feelings and judgements.

Early in the 1930s, the psychologist Lewis M. Terman carried out two studies in California using a marital happiness index largely derived from Burgess and Cottrell's adjustment scale.[3] In the first he divided a sample of 341 married couples into those more and those less happily married, and compared both with a third group of 109 divorced couples. His original aim was to investigate the 'opposites attract' hypothesis, according to which it makes for marital happiness when unlike personalities marry. He concluded that it does not. In both his married groups, husbands and wives were more likely to be similar than different in traits such as dominance/submission and verbal fluency, while among the divorced the personality scores of husbands and wives tended to be unrelated. However, there were wide differences between the happily married group and the less happily married and divorced groups on some individual items in the psychological tests he used, such as the extent to which spouses agreed to try and avoid arguments. To explore these further he carried out a second and larger study of 792 married couples, preponderantly of the upper and upper-middle occupational and educational levels of urban Californian society, and including no divorced or separated and few unhappily married couples. Terman analysed the correlates of marital happiness under three heads: personality factors, background factors, and sexual adjustment. He went into great detail about sex relations, finding for example that passionate wives who liked intercourse 12 times a month or more enjoyed far greater marital happiness than those at the other extreme who preferred only 2, 1, or 0, and that the marital happiness of both husband and wife was liable to be seriously adversely affected if she seldom or never attained orgasm. Among background factors, he came to some conclusions that have been confirmed in later studies, for instance that the presence or absence of children made no difference to marital happiness; others that now seem strange, for instance that age at marriage made no difference, even though those of his sample who had married youngest (women under twenty, men under twenty-two) did show rather lower average marital happiness scores than the rest. And he found strong indications that people who were unhappily married were temperamentally unhappy in other ways too.

Following the Burgess–Cottrell and Terman studies, between 1939 and 1944 Harvey J. Locke compared a divorced group (drawn from courthouse records) with a happily married group (recommended by a married relative or friend as 'one of the most happily married couples I know') in Monroe county, Indiana.[4] Unlike the highly unrepresentative samples of the earlier surveys, Locke's samples were similar in education, income, and religious affiliation to each other and to the populations both of the United States as a whole and Indiana in particular. His findings, however, were in close agreement with those of the earlier studies. Compared with the divorced, his happily married group had married later after a longer engagement. Only 3 of the 200 happy marriages had been precipitated by pregnancy, compared with 41 of the 324 that had ended in divorce. Contrary to popular belief, the number of children born to a marriage made little or no difference to marital adjustment. Parental approval of the marriage was a positive factor, and so were sociability and conventionality, both of which in rural and small-town Indiana in the 1940s meant active church membership and Sunday school attendance, and a wedding in a place of worship by a minister of religion. Happy couples' personal relationships approximated to the model of 'the companionship family'; freely showing affection for each other, they 'talked things over' together, participated jointly in socially approved activities inside and outside the home, rated each other as of equal status and equal intelligence, and made joint 'democratic' decisions over such matters as disciplining the children (firmly but not harshly), money, religion, and recreation.

Re-analysing Locke's data and adding that from her own survey in 1948, Muriel Mackeprang found no difference between the average marital adjustment of working and home-making wives, nor of their husbands[5] (though, as noted in chapter 10 and again below, later studies have suggested otherwise).

In another study directed by Burgess with Paul Wallin, 1000 engaged couples were interviewed in 1937–9, and 666 of them were followed up in 1940–3 after they had been married for three to five years. Most of the men were or had been university or college students in Chicago, so the sample was not representative of the United States population as a whole. The findings were very similar to those of the Burgess–Cottrell and other early studies. However, widening somewhat the concept of marital adjustment, Burgess and Wallin pointed out that 'adjustment to marriage needs to be distinguished from adjustment of husband and wife to each other'. Most marriages meant a somewhat different adjustment to husband and to wife, he to the breadwinner role, she to that of home-maker. 'In one sense women fit into marriage more easily than men since home, husband, and children tend still to be more central in their interests, except those to whom a career is more important.'[6]

Homogamy, heterogamy, and adjustment

A question much discussed in the older American studies was whether 'like marries like' or 'opposites attract', and which was more conducive to marital adjustment and happiness. Robert F. Winch essayed to resolve the paradox by combining sociological and psychoanalytical approaches.[7] Marriages in the United States were strongly characterized by homogamy in respect of a number of sociological variables including age, previous marital status, ethnic origin, religious affiliation, and socio-economic status; and also of some psychological variables, including intelligence, interests (religious, aesthetic, political), attitudes, and temperament. Such variables largely determined the 'field of eligibles', the potential partners whom a person might meet. Falling in love was different. Contrary to Terman's earlier findings, noted above, Winch maintained that it involved heterogamy and complementary needs, and occurred when one of a pair engaged in behaviour aroused by his or her own needs which was found to gratify the relevant needs of the other. For example, in a dominance-submission relationship, one partner would delight in assuming the dominant decisive role and being a tower of strength to whom the other found reassurance and a sense of security in submitting. Within the field of eligibles it was in this sense that opposites attract.

Class: a neglected factor

Social class differences were largely overlooked in the early studies of divorce and marital adjustment, as indeed they were quite generally in American sociology of that period. In part they were missed because of the unrepresentative nature of some of the samples; class differences can hardly appear in a sample drawn essentially from one class, as were those in the Burgess–Cottrell, Terman, and Burgess–Wallin studies. Locke, on the other hand, was at such pains to match his divorced and happily married samples with each other and with the population as a whole that the class composition of his two samples was similar, and any class differences in the risk or prevalence of divorce were rendered undetectable by his research design. Furthermore, the ecological analogy that dominated the thought of the influential Chicago school tended to obscure social class variables by bringing them into the analysis only implicitly. The Chicago practice, widely followed elsewhere, of plotting everything on a map led to some areas of the city being identified with 'social disorganization' characterized by mobility (frequent changes of address), low home ownership, divorce, juvenile delinquency, suicide, and many forms of illicit activity and 'vice'. It was quite commonly assumed that the 'instability' of divorced persons was shown by their tendency to 'drift' into such areas – which, incidentally, were also areas of low average incomes.

Marital breakdown and divorce

When in 1948 William J. Goode began his study of the subject, therefore, he was quite unprepared to find a negative correlation between class ranking and the divorce rate (that is, higher divorce rates at lower socio-economic levels); he had expected it to be the other way about, and even discarded a pilot sample as aberrant for that reason.[8] Confirmation was found, however, partly in his own analysis of United States official statistics, and partly from other independent studies previously unknown to him, including one carried out under Burgess's supervision that had shown higher marital happiness ratings at higher occupational levels. Quite consistently, whether class was indicated by occupational status, education, or income, divorce rates were higher at lower socio-economic levels except the very lowest.

That apart, Goode's findings were in general accord with those of the earlier studies. His own sample was of 425 divorced mothers aged 20–38 at the time of the divorce, drawn from courthouse records of Wayne county, Michigan, and followed up mostly within 2 years of the divorce. Though there was no control sample, comparisons where appropriate could be made with samples such as those of Burgess and Terman, mostly happily married, and with the United States population as a whole from official statistics. Thus the median age at first marriage (19.4 years) of Goode's divorced women was lower than that in a United States registration area of 18 states (20.4 in 1953), and 93 per cent of Goode's sample compared with 78 per cent of all once-married women had married under 25. Their courtships and engagements had been markedly shorter than those in the Burgess–Cottrell and Terman samples, and as many as 19 per cent had had no engagement at all. So far as he could tell from within his own sample, Goode suggested that engagement was somewhat class-related, with longer engagements at higher occupational levels. Without much to go on by way of comparison, Goode was struck by the evidence from divorced women of the number whose families and friends had disapproved of the marriage or been indifferent to it; the high proportion who had had no friends in common with their husbands; and the association between disapproval or indifference on the part of relatives and friends on the one hand and short or non-existent engagement on the other. Presumably in many cases those 'significant others' did not know about the marriage until it had happened, and there had been no opportunity for their reactions, seen or sensed, to have any influence upon the couple's decision.

Besides a class gradient in the incidence of divorce, there was some evidence from Goode's study, compared with others, to suggest that a higher proportion of marriages ending in divorce were heterogamous (of unlikes) in respect of class, and also of religion. For instance, his sample seemed to include a more than proportionate number of mixed marriages of a Catholic to a non-Catholic.

Asked what in their view caused the breakdown of the marriage, the divorced wives gave lengthy, various, and overlapping answers. Goode made it clear that his analysis was based only on their accounts; had the ex-husbands given theirs, a different picture would no doubt have emerged. The commonest single complaint was that of non-support; the husband had not provided adequately for her and the children. Staying away, drinking, gambling, and 'out with the boys' – together 'the complex' – also figured prominently, along with lack of affection and excessive assertion of authority. 'Another woman' was less often mentioned. Few wives complained of desertion, mentioned sex problems, or admitted to having another man. Goode remarked that the causes of divorce so defined by the women themselves bore little or no relation to the formal legal grounds on which divorces were granted, in which adultery and desertion figured prominently along with cruelty and to a less extent drunkenness.

Marital breakdown had been a traumatic experience for most of them, resulting in loss of sleep, poorer health, and loneliness, though some came through unscathed. The worst part was the final actual separation, not the legal proceedings, nor the post-divorce period. Most answers to the question 'How would your life have been today if you had not got a divorce?' were: Worse; in health, in happiness, financially, or for the child. In other words, marital breakdown had been the problem for which divorce was a solution, at least in part.

MEASURING MARITAL BREAKDOWN

The measurement of marital breakdown bristles with statistical difficulties. Borrowing terms from medical statistics, we may distinguish the annual incidence, the prevalence at any one time, and the lifetime risk. To begin with divorce: the simplest measure of its annual incidence is the crude divorce rate, the number of divorces per 1000 population per year. This is open to the objection that the whole population are not at risk of divorce, only the married population. The divorce rate per 1000 married couples (or existing marriages, as in fig. 1) per year is a sounder measure, but it is not as readily available for as many countries as is the crude divorce rate; moreover, the two measures are closely correlated, and range out different countries in much the same 'league table' order,[9] so I adopt the crude rate in table 1. Estimates are sometimes made of the proportion of marriages ending, or likely to end, in divorce, which may be termed the lifetime risk; but this proves to be a highly elusive figure. One completely fallacious procedure is to relate current divorces to current marriages, since the latter are pre-

Table 1. *Divorce rates in selected countries*

	Divorces per 1000 population	
	1960	1980
N. America		
United States[a]	2.18	5.19
Canada	0.39	2.59
W. Europe		
UK: England and Wales	0.51	2.99
Scotland	0.35	2.04
N. Ireland	0.07	0.58
Irish Republic		
France	0.66	1.59[b]
W.Germany	0.88	2.68
Italy		0.21
Belgium	0.50	1.47
Netherlands	0.49	1.82
Denmark	1.46	2.65
Norway	0.66	1.62
Sweden	1.20	2.39
E. Europe		
Hungary	1.66	2.59
Poland	0.50	1.12
Romania	2.01	1.54
USSR	1.27[c]	3.50
Japan	0.74	1.21

Sources: UN Demographic Yearbooks, 1976, table 34, and 1982, table 33.
Notes: a. Estimates, based on returns of sample divorce records, for a varying number of states in the United States Divorce Registration Area; data include annulments. *b.* 1979. *c.* 1961.

sumably just those currently least at risk. Another way is to relate current divorces to the number of marriages some years back, say ten; however, there is often a wide spread of durations of marriages to divorce, and the choice of an interval is an arbitrary one. Yet another is to compare in each year the number of marriages dissolved respectively by death and divorce. Even this is not wholly satisfactory; marriages terminated by the death of one partner mostly last longer than those ending in divorce, so one is comparing the outcome of two overlapping groups of marriages, one contracted on average longer ago in the past than the other. Changes may have taken place in the attitudes and expectations of those marrying at different times, so one is neither strictly comparing like with like, nor gaining a reliable indication of the probable outcome of current marriages. However, the comparison can be highly illuminating, as was seen in chapter 2, Fig 1.

There are even greater difficulties about measuring the total extent of marital breakdown, of which divorce is not the only possible outcome. In some countries and at some periods divorce has not been available, or hardly so to most people. We may need to distinguish between the annulment of a marriage and its dissolution. Some legal and ecclesiastical systems provide for the former while finding no place for the latter; and though there are no doubt profound theological and legal issues involved, of great moment in countries such as Italy and the Irish Republic, from some other points of view that is a distinction without a difference. Thus in British official statistics the small number of legal annulments are included with dissolutions in the total of divorces. [10] Further, not all petitions for divorce are granted, yet all presumably indicate some degree of marital unhappiness or dissatisfaction. In some studies therefore the petitioning rate rather than the divorce rate is taken as the indicator of marital breakdown.

Short of divorce, there are various forms of separation without the right to remarry. In English law, for example, there are judicial separations by a court order that usually includes provision for maintenance payments, and separations by private legal deed or agreement, as well as *de facto* separations when a couple simply live apart without recourse to the law. Statistics are available about judicial separations but not about the others. Furthermore, some separated spouses later proceed to divorce, others stay separated, while yet others are later reunited. So there is a statistical tangle of double counting on the one hand and unknown quantities on the other impeding attempts to estimate the total extent of marital breakdown. Even more elusive are other manifestations: the 'job desertions' of men who, in order to escape from unhappy marriages, take work that keeps them away from home for long periods; and the 'empty shell' marriages of couples who continue to live under the same roof and occasionally appear in public together, yet have little or nothing to do with each other at home and nothing that could be called a married life. We have no idea how many such marriages there are.

DIVORCE IN ENGLAND AND WALES

Before 1957, very little sociological research was done in Britain on this or indeed on any subject. With only one professorial post in the entire country, the Martin White chair at the London School of Economics, and a mere handful of scholars able to devote themselves full-time to it, sociology in Britain before the Second World War was supported on the most exiguous of shoe-strings, so that in his pioneering study of divorce in 1934 David Glass was able to do little more than a laborious pencil-and-paper analysis of official statistics. The ten-fold rise in divorces in the ten years from 1937 to the post war peak in 1947 aroused much concern among informed public opinion, and alarm was expressed about the decline in family stability that was inferred from that rise; but pompous pontifications from bench and pulpit were not always well grounded on facts, nor were they matched by any great interest in scientific inquiry to ascertain and interpret the facts. And when sociological studies began to appear in the late 1950s, they were not all of the highest quality. Some were marked by a parochialism in which it sometimes seemed almost as if divorce was regarded as an English disease, a problem of one national society to be explained only in terms of the circumstances of that society. Comparisons were lacking with other industrial countries, in relation to which the divorce rate in England and Wales was by no means exceptional, and in most of which virtually identical trends were occurring. And little or no reference was made to the wealth of studies in the United

States, to which I have referred above. In the better studies the debt to American sociology was apparent, though not always acknowledged, in their concepts and hypotheses; naturally enough their findings were sometimes different from those in the United States.

1957: a centenary study

To mark the centenary of judicial divorce in England and Wales in 1957, Griselda Rowntree and Norman Carrier of the London School of Economics analysed and interpreted a century's official statistics.[11] Among the factors that had affected the incidence of divorce, some were peculiar to this country; thus Rowntree and Carrier estimated that the introduction of a special poor persons' procedure in 1914 had increased the divorce rate by 40 per cent, and its extension in 1926 had added a further 15 per cent, while the widening of the grounds for divorce under the 1923 Act had contributed another 25 per cent. The effect of the 1937 Act promoted by A. P. Herbert, however, had been swallowed up in that of the war; and the extension of legal aid to divorce petitioners after 1949 (a subject of later controversy, as will appear below) had had no measurable effect. Secondly, and not confined to Britain, the profound disturbances of family life in two world wars had had both immediate and more lasting consequences, as noted in chapter 2. Thirdly, there had been a steady underlying rise. It was widely agreed that the public had become increasingly 'divorce-minded', even though some who noted the tendency bitterly deplored it while others accepted or welcomed it. The social as well as the economic barriers to divorce were lower than ever before; and although by 1957 the divorce rate had fallen from its post war peak and appeared to be stabilizing, Rowntree and Carrier saw no reason to predict a further substantial fall.

Interpreting these trends, Rowntree and Carrier emphasized the growing public acceptance of divorce. Since the 1937 Act there had been no need to prove adultery; and the whole concept of the matrimonial offence had come to be widely regarded as a legal fiction, with the rise of 'hotel' divorces and evidence manufactured to afford the requisite proof. The growing use of civil marriage procedure indicated diminishing acceptance of the religious view of marriage as sacred and indissoluble, and afforded a by-pass for many to the Church of England's 'increasingly intransigent attitude' towards the remarriage of divorced persons in church.

In a longer historical perspective, the rise in divorce went with the decline of land and the rise of industrial capital as the main source of wealth, power, and prestige. The property involved in landowning families' dynastic marriages had been hard to disentangle, and marital breakdown among the upper classes may often have taken the form of the empty-shell marriage. The division of assets at divorce presented fewer difficulties to the rising class whose wealth consisted of stocks and shares; and it was largely in response to the needs of that class that the 1857 Act – 'not a great legal innovation', according to Rowntree and Carrier – had simplified the procedure and made it less costly and more accessible. However, among the less well-to-do, maintenance payments to their ex-wives made it difficult for men to enter second marriages, and so made divorce pointless, unless those ex-wives could largely maintain themselves. Very few Victorian middle-class women could do that, because the strength of the convention that they should devote themselves entirely to home and family made them totally financially dependent on their husbands. That, perhaps even more than the still high cost of the legal proceedings themselves, was what made divorce largely the privilege of the well-to-do in the late 19th and early 20th centuries.

That position gradually changed with the rise of women's employment, as noted in chapter 9, in 'white-blouse' occupations in shops and offices and, for middle-class women, nursing and teaching. Two world wars with their exceptional demands on female labour gave vast numbers of young women of all social classes experience they could turn to account if the need for self-support should arise. So, where a Victorian middle-class wife could see only destitution as the alternative to an unhappy marriage, her 20th-century counterpart could contemplate separation and divorce with comparative equanimity except in times of heavy unemployment. Even though women's pay was still relatively low, divorce no longer need spell destitution from the ex-wife's point of view, and might well be regarded as less reprehensible on that account from the point of view of others.

1959–60: the PIC survey

In 1959–60, the Population Investigation Committee of the London School of Economics commissioned a systematic survey of marriage and marital breakdown, the first of its kind in Britain, in which 3055 adults were interviewed, 2338 of whom were or had been married. The results were analysed by Rachel Pierce[12] and by Griselda Rowntree.[13]

Concentrating her analysis on marriage, Pierce remarked that it had never been more popular; in all advanced industrial countries, more people were marrying, and at younger ages, while those divorced or widowed were remarrying increasingly. Among the sample interviewed, comparing those married during the successive decades of the 1930s, 1940s, and 1950s the proportion of wives marrying before their twentieth birthdays ('teenage brides') had doubled from 10 to 20 per cent. There was a tendency for the manual-worker classes to marry younger, the occupation of the husband and of the bride herself being apparently more closely related to marriage age than their social origins. Courtships were shorter than in the 1930s though they had been shorter still during the war decade of the 1940s. Among couples married in the 1950s marriages precipitated by pregnancy were commonest among the working class and among teenage brides, and marriage at young ages was a working-class pattern that prevailed for the 'prudent' as well as the pregnant.

Analysing marital breakdown in the same sample, Rowntree classified the survey marriages in five categories, four derived from Burgess, one added by herself:

1   Couple divorced
2   Couple separated at time of interview
3   Couple had separated earlier but re-united
4   Informant had contemplated separation
5   Couple had remained together

Those in categories 1, 2, and 3 together were said to have 'parted', and with the addition of the borderline category 4 comprised all who had experienced serious marital difficulties. Rowntree confined her analysis to the 1340 informants married between 1930 and 1949. Only 79 of their marriages had ended in divorce, the number who had divorced or ever separated was 114, and a further 51 had contemplated separation. In percentage terms, then, 8.5 per cent had parted and a further 3.8 per cent had contemplated doing so, giving a total of 12.3 per cent or about 1 in 8 who had experienced all degrees of difficulty in marriages that had taken place between 10 and 30 years before the survey. These percentages presumably represent somewhere between the prevalence and the lifetime risk of marital breakdown.

Comparing sample couples by the husband's own occupation at marriage, Rowntree found little difference in the percentages parting or contemplating parting among non-manual, skilled manual, and other manual workers. Comparing them by their social origins, however, the highest rates of marital difficulty were among couples both of whose fathers' occupations were non-manual, and both of whom had attended selective schools (associated with middle-class status). Homogamy in respect of social class, education, and religion, associated with marital stability in the American studies, appeared not to be so in this sample; the lowest, not the highest, rates of parting were among couples of dissimilar schooling, and in the analysis by religious affiliation the highest rate of parting was that of couples both of whom were Roman Catholics (but the numbers were small; see below). Wives' continuing employment after marriage was associated with higher rates of marital difficulty than those experienced by couples of whom the wife stopped work at marriage. There was a strong association between the number of children born to a marriage and its stability; the percentage parting dropped from 13.6 per cent of the childless to 0.6 per cent of couples with 4 or more children. It made no difference, though, whether contraception had been practised or not during the marriage. Most clear and striking was the evidence linking marital difficulty with early marriage and with pre-marital pregnancy: 21.1 per cent of teenage brides had parted, compared with 3.8 per cent of those married at 25 or over; 12.2 per cent of the pregnant had parted, compared with 6.4 per cent of the prudent whose first child had been conceived after the wedding.

Analysing in more detail the combined effects of the bride's age and whether she became pregnant before or after the wedding, or never, Rowntree found as expected that the proportion of pregnant teenage brides who had later parted was high,

26 per cent, while that of childless teenage brides was even higher. However, the numbers in these categories were very small. The 26 per cent of pregnant teenage brides who had parted represented 13 women out of 50, while the 56 per cent of childless teenage brides represented 13 out of no more than 23. Similarly, the above-average rate of parting of 11.7 per cent among couples both of whom were Roman Catholics, referred to above, represented just 7 couples out of 60. With such small numbers, sampling errors are obviously liable to be appreciable, well illustrating the problems of research design in inquiries of this kind. Although the initial 'sample in the PIC inquiry had been as large and as representative as is usual in such surveys, only a minority of 1 in 8 had experienced any serious marital difficulties; and when that minority were further divided into smaller categories for more detailed analysis, the numbers in some of the sub-samples proved to be too small for statistically reliable conclusions to be drawn. I take up this point again at the end of the chapter.

Class: a changing factor

The relationship between divorce and social class in England and Wales has undergone a complete reversal since the days when divorce was largely the privilege of the well-to-do. Analysing the social class composition of 1871 petitioners, Rowntree and Carrier found that only 17 per cent of them were manual workers. (By contrast, in Scotland with its centuries-old system of legal aid, in 1901 59 per cent of petitioners were of the working class.)[14] The special poor persons' procedure introduced in 1914 made a difference, and according to Glass's estimates poor persons' decrees constituted 23 to 37 per cent of all decrees in 1917–21 and some 31 per cent in 1922–30.[15] In a sample of 1951 petitioners, Rowntree and Carrier found that of those whose occupation was known 70 per cent were manual workers, and the class composition of the sample corresponded very closely indeed to that of the married population as a whole. Ten years later the balance had swung the other way; and in a sample study of 1961 petitioners (published in 1974), Colin Gibson found a higher incidence of divorce among the lower paid.[16] For the first time, then, the relationship between divorce and social class in this country seemed to resemble that in the United States, though as seen in table 2 the gradient was not uniform; the highest incidence was in class V, but the second highest was in IIINM. This last finding was later disputed, however.[17]

Table 2. *Divorces per 10,000 married women aged under 55, England and Wales, 1961*

	Social class of husband						
	I	II	IIINM	IIIM	IV	V	All
Divorce rate	22	25	43	29	25	51	30

Gibson's explanations were, first, the now familiar association of high risk factors, particularly early marriage and pre-marital pregnancy, with working-class occupational status; secondly, the severe material difficulties encountered by many young working-class couples over money and housing. These were enough to explain a higher incidence of marital breakdown at lower social class levels. Since the Second World War, higher wages, the introduction of legal aid, and a greater acceptance of divorce had led to an increased readiness on the part of working-class people to petition for divorce as a means of ending dead marriages.

The 1970s: the rising trend

In the early 1970s, Robert Chester was concerned to dispel the rosy glow of optimism about family stability that had suffused the work of some sociologists including Ronald Fletcher and O. R. McGregor against a background of falling divorce rates in the 1950s.[18] Between 1959 and 1969 the number of petitions in England and Wales had more than doubled, over-topping the postwar peak; and a cohort analysis showed that marriages contracted in each successive year from 1960 onwards had been more liable to end in divorce at all durations, and more than the previously most unstable marriages, those contracted in the war years of 1942–3. Explanations in term of changes in the law and administrative practice applicable to England and

Wales alone seemed quite inadequate to explain so massive a trend, and he was particularly scathing in his criticism of the view that it was the result of extending legal aid to divorce petitioners (which, as noted above, Rowntree and Carrier too had found to have had no measurable effect). Chester asked three questions:

1 Are more contemporary marriages ending in divorce, or are they merely ending in divorce earlier?
2 If more marriages are ending in divorce, is that because more modern couples are experiencing marital breakdown, or merely that those who experience marital breakdown are resorting more readily to divorce?
3 Whether it is more breakdown or merely more divorce in the event of breakdown, in this a temporary effect due to pass like the post war peak, or is it a new pattern related to contemporary conditions?

The evidence available to Chester did not enable him to give a clear answer to his first question. However, official statistics published since leave no doubt that the great increase in divorce between 1960 and 1980 was very largely an increase in early divorce.[19]

His second question involved Chester in the statistical tangle I mentioned above surrounding the problem of estimating the total incidence of marital breakdown. Divorces, annulments, and judicial separations (including in England and Wales magistrates' court orders) together constitute the total of publicly known breakdown, allowing for a proportion of people who get a magistrates' court order first and petition for divorce later. With that allowance, Chester estimated that while between 1959 and 1969 the annual number of divorce petitions had increased by 133 per cent, the divorce rate per 1000 married couples had increased by 100 per cent, the number of recorded breakdowns by 75 per cent, and the breakdown rate by 65 per cent. The answer therefore was: both more breakdown and a greater readiness to resort to divorce.

Thirdly, and rather more speculatively, Chester thought that this represented a new pattern likely to persist, not a generational effect destined to pass. There was an analogy with the wartime delinquent generation; children born between 1935 and 1942 were more prone to delinquency than those born before or immediately after, but cohort delinquency rates among succeeding age-groups rose again to levels that over-topped those of the war generation. Likewise, the same genera-tion born in 1935–42 began to marry in the mid-1950s and began divorcing about 1960 at just about the time when the number of divorce petitions reached its lowest and began to rise again. Subsequent generations, however, showed no rever-sal of this trend, but rather a steady increase in cohort divorce rates indicating a rising lifetime risk. In other words, the war generation had proved to be 'precursory rather than peculiar' in these as in many other ways. Clearly, Chester's judgement has been amply vindicated by subsequent trends.

The 1970s: who divorced?

In 1970–2 Barbara Thornes and Jean Collard of the Marriage Research Centre at the Central Middlesex Hospital compared a newly-divorced with a 'continuing married' group.[20] They were unable to carry out a nation-wide survey as no national list of divorcees was available, nor could they compile one because of official restrictions on the use of court records. Instead, their sample of 520 divorced persons was drawn from lists published in a local newspaper of petitioners granted decrees at a court in the West Midlands. For comparison, interviews were also con-ducted with 570 'continuing married' persons drawn from elec-toral registers in the same area.

To summarize their findings: contrary to those of American studies, there was no evidence to suggest that the offspring of marriages broken by divorce, separation, or death, were any more likely than others to experience marital breakdown. Although those who had been children under five when their parents' marriages broke down seemed more likely to divorce, the remarriage of one parent seemed to have been more stress-ful than the loss of the other.

On social class, their findings confirmed Gibson's in attribu-ting the high divorce rate in class V largely to severe and wide-spread 'environing disadvantage'. The high rate in class IIINM, however, called for a different explanation; it might be 'due to their greater risk of stress arising from their aspirations, "marginality", and ambiguity of social position'. 'Social mobility did not emerge in this study as a correlate of divorce.'

Nor, contrary to United States findings, was dissimilarity either of social class background or of education linked with divorce. The marriages of highly educated husbands were relatively stable. On the other hand, 'marriages in which the wives were in a higher grade occupation at marriage than were their husbands, appeared to be more prone to divorce.'

As in the United States, 'marriages in which both partners were affiliated to a particular religion, and especially those in which the partners were churchgoers, appeared . . . to be most set for marital stability'. Marriages preceded by short courtships, with no engagement or honeymoon, and towards which there was strong opposition (usually parental), were all at an increased risk of divorce.

As in other studies, 'teenage marriages tended to include a pre-marital pregnancy, and to be working-class'; and when the two first-named high risk factors occurred together, the marriage seemed particularly likely to founder. However, those teenage marriages that had lasted were characterized by strong parental support both before and during the marriage, in sharp contrast to the teenage marriages that had ended in divorce. Much the same could be said about pre-maritally pregnant marriages; those that had ended in divorce were marked by courtship disruption, lack of kinship support, and personal and environmental stresses, in contrast to those that had lasted, which seemed to have begun in an atmosphere more conducive to marital adjustment.

Disadvantaged housing, friction in shared accommodation, and frequent unplanned moves, especially in the early years of the marriage, were more characteristic of the divorced than of the continuing married.

Children 'probably do not enhance the marital relationship'; they reduce marital happiness levels, and bring financial burdens and interpersonal stress. If, as was clear from this study as well as from official statistics, divorced couples have fewer children than the continuing married, and more of them are childless, this may well be due to their relatively short periods of cohabitation. Thornes and Collard gave no support to the conventional views, either that big families are happy families, or that children hold a marriage together in the sense that though the parents may not be very happy they stay together for the children's sake. They found, on the contrary, that 'there was little evidence from this study to suggest that the majority of couples whose marriage is breaking up delay separating until their children are independent'.

The great majority in both samples said that their married lives had been sexually satisfactory, at least at the start of the marriage. As might be expected, rather more of the divorced than of the continuing married said it had not been satisfactory; more, too, spoke of a deterioration after a satisfactory start, for which they blamed the other partner. More of the divorced had had pre-marital sexual experience, especially with a partner other than the spouse-to-be; and more of them admitted to extra-marital sexual experience. It did not emerge, however, whether the extra-marital affair generally contributed to the breakdown of the marriage, or whether, conversely, it was a needed source of consolation during an unhappy marriage or after it had broken down.

Finally, Thornes and Collard's study greatly extended our knowledge of the time factor in marital breakdown and divorce. Chester had already shown that the *de facto* duration of marriage to its actual breakdown when one partner moved out was much shorter than the *de jure* duration to final legal dissolution, and official divorce statistics therefore gave a misleading impression of the durability of marriage. In his study of court files for 1966–8, he found that 'separations reach their peak in the third year of marriage, two years before the peak of divorces is reached, and . . . the most hazardous years are those lying between the first and fourth anniversaries of the wedding'.[21] Thornes and Collard's findings tallied exactly with Chester's on that point; in their interviews, however, they were able to go further and ask their divorced sample when their marital problems started; 37 per cent said it was in the first year, and a further 15 per cent that it was during the second; a majority, therefore, had experienced serious marital problems within two years of the marriage. Divorced women were aware of difficulties even earlier than men, possibly 'because marriage *per se* appears to make more demands upon women and to be more stressful for them'. But that early perception of marital problems was followed in many cases by a long period when they were tolerated, perhaps in the hope that they would be resolved. And even when those hopes had proved groundless, and cohabitation ceased, there was another interval between final separation and divorce. So, although it may be inferred from Thornes and Collard's data that the median duration of presumably happy marriage from the wedding to the start of serious marital difficulties was just under 2 years, the median *de facto* duration was 8 years, and the median interval between final separation and divorce was a further 3 years. Typically, therefore, a marriage perceived as unsatisfactory within a year or two dragged on for 9 more miserable years before its final dissolution. At the same time, though, Thornes and Collard noted a tendency towards both more divorce and earlier divorce among more recent cohorts, a trend that has become even more strikingly evident since. And early breakdown, early divorce, or both, were associated with marriages involving a teenage bride or groom, a pre-marital pregnancy, early fertility, infertility, or a couple in social class V.

CONCLUSIONS

The study of marital breakdown poses a dilemma for research design. Some studies (e.g. Burgess–Cottrell and Terman in the United States, PIC in Britain) have started with a sample, whether representative or not, of a population spanning the whole spectrum from the happily married through every degree of marital difficulty to the final breakdown represented by divorce. As Rowntree found, the disadvantage of this procedure has been that, unless a very large and therefore expensive sample is taken, at the end of the analysis there prove to be too few cases in each sub-group to permit statistically reliable conclusions to be drawn, for instance about risk factors such as working-class status, early marriage, and bride's pregnancy. To overcome this difficulty, some other studies (Locke in the United States, Thornes and Collard in Britain) have started with two adequately-sized samples, one of divorced persons and the other of the happily, or at least continuing, married. While this design permits statistically reliable comparisons to be drawn, it has other disadvantages. Intermediate ranges of marital difficulty are not considered; no estimate can be given of the prevalence or lifetime risk of divorce, or any other manifestation of marital breakdown; and there is a danger of overlooking important related variables such as social class, as

Locke did in his concern to match his two samples as closely as possible.

As for the findings of these studies, enough has no doubt emerged to answer the first question posed at the beginning of this chapter, and it would be tedious to reiterate the factors that have been repeatedly shown to be associated with a high risk of divorce. More perhaps remains to be said about the second. In England and Wales at least, the great rise in divorce rates has been associated with an increasing readiness to resort to divorce on the part of working-class people, whose marriages are at above average risk of breakdown for all the reasons reviewed above. That contribution to rising divorce rates must come to an end when working-class people are no less likely to petition for divorce than anyone else in similar circumstances, a time that has perhaps already arrived. Secondly, the divorce revolution in industrial countries after 1960 followed a long period of falling marriage ages, and a corresponding increase in the numbers of teenage brides and grooms. Since about 1970, however, marriage ages have risen again; and this may be partly why divorce rates seem to have steadied around 1980, though it would be premature to say at the time of writing that they have passed their peak.

Another factor, which has not gone entirely unnoticed in the literature but which may not have had the attention it deserves, is lengthening life. According to Peter Laslett, the average duration of marriage to the death of one partner in pre-industrial England was about twenty years.[22] Now it is more than twice that. So whereas in the past many an unhappy marriage was ended by death – and there was practically no other way in which marriages were dissolved – or endured in the expectation that it would soon be so terminated, now people with a far longer expectation of life are correspondingly less willing to accept the prospect of long-continued marital unhappiness and more inclined to take action to end it. And divorce is available and accessible. The social and moral stigma once keenly felt by many divorced persons[23] has, it would seem, been largely dispelled since 1970 in countries like England and Wales and most of the United States by the enactment of 'no-fault' divorce laws, giving further reason for the tendency Rowntree and Carrier noted towards a growing public acceptance of divorce.

Moreover, most divorced persons remarry (a subject I take up in the next chapter), and the ages of both divorce and remarriage have fallen. Many an unhappy spouse must have reasoned that if the fateful decision is to be made, the sooner the better, while the partners are in a better position to maintain themselves without relying on spousal maintenance payments, often not honoured, and while they are still young and active enough to have good prospects of a second and happier marriage. Why prolong the misery?

SUGGESTIONS FOR FURTHER READING

William J. Goode, *Women in Divorce*, New York, Free Press, 1969

Barbara Thornes and Jean Collard, *Who Divorces?* London, Routledge and Kegan Paul, 1979

Arland Thornton and Deborah Freedman, 'The changing American family', *Population Bulletin*, vol. 38 no. 4, Washington DC, Population Reference Bureau, 1983

Griselda Rowntree and Norman H. Carrier, 'The resort to divorce in England and Wales, 1858–1957', *Population Studies*, vol. 11, 1958, pp. 188–233

14

Departures and rejections

In this chapter I attempt to deal, however summarily, with departures from and rejections of that pattern of conventional family life, the autonomous nuclear family household based on lifelong monogamy, that has been the norm in western societies since the Christian revolution. Departures from the norm represent the inadvertent and even unintended consequences of other trends, most of all the divorce revolution since 1960. They can to some extent be distinguished from deliberate rejections of the norm. While the two categories overlap, and hard-and-fast distinctions certainly cannot be drawn, the extent to which different trends and movements involve coherent, consciously worked-out principles is not the same in every case, as will appear; it is a matter of degree.

AFTER DIVORCE

Divorce is followed by lone parenthood for some, by bitterness for many, by remarriage for most.

Lone parenthood

From time immemorial widows and unmarried mothers have been left to care for their young children. One of the consequences of the divorce revolution, however, and a considerable departure from the conventional nuclear-family norm, has been a big increase in the numbers of children living in the care of one parent alone for at least part of their childhood. Thus in Britain in 1981 lone-parent families accounted for over 900,000 households, 1 in 8 of those with at least 1 dependent child. Since custody of children at divorce or separation has generally been given to the mother in recent times (perhaps reflecting the continuing influence of Bowlby's ideas), lone mothers out-numbered lone fathers by about 7 to 1.[1] Similarly in the United States, where until the mid 19th century custody almost automatically went to the father, nowadays mothers obtain custody in about 9 cases out of 10. It was estimated that with the dissolution rates of the late 1970s the parents of over a million children under 18 divorced each year, and that 40 to 50 per cent of all children would live in a fatherless family some time before they were 18, most of them for at least five years.[2]

The severe difficulties facing many lone mothers were amply documented in a major official report in Britain in 1974. For the divorced and separated much of the trouble was due to a widespread non-compliance with maintenance orders, as fewer than half their husbands or ex-husbands kept up their payments anything like regularly.[3] In the United States, too, Goode found that fewer than half of his divorced mothers 'always' or 'usually' received their child payments.[4] But lone mothers who endeavour to gain a securer income under their own control face daunting problems of sheer overload as they try to combine child-care and housework with paid employment. Moreover, like women generally they are low-paid; and many lone mothers were full-time housewives lacking marketable skills before they had to seek whatever work they could find. It is not surprising therefore to find that many single-parent families live in poverty, and that on both sides of the Atlantic they loom large among those needing state welfare benefits. Well might Goode observe that 'our kinship system permits divorce, but does not provide for its consequences'.

Bitterness

Yet maintenance payments present great problems for ex-husbands too, and perhaps even more for their second wives. In most cases the problem is simple: there is not enough to go round. What may appear to an ex-wife no more than minimal provision for her needs and those of the children may seem ruinous to the ex-husband and cut deeply into the resources he might bring to a second marriage. Disputes about maintenance, the matrimonial property and its division, custody and access to the children, all compound and perpetuate the bitterness engendered by the original process of marital breakdown.

Goode found that about 1 in 4 of his respondents 'frequently wanted to punish' their ex-husbands at the time of the divorce. In an intensive study of 92 divorced men in the south of England, 51 of them were found to be 'fairly' or 'very unaccepting and angry'; and the greater the financial impact of the divorce had been the greater their anger.[5] The majority of the most angry group were in manual jobs, nearly all had children in their ex-wife's custody, and most rejected the idea of remarriage, burdened as they were with maintenance payments that seemed to rule out the possibility. By contrast the least angry group were mostly in non-manual jobs and mostly childless, and all were either keen or at least neutral about remarriage. And the anger stemming from a marriage failure did not abate with time, but concentrated into 'a hard knot of feeling that remains lodged in the mind'. Divorced men had mixed feelings about new friendships with women, on the one hand more sexually interested than before, on the other less confident and extremely mistrustful. Longing no doubt for a new partner with whom to enjoy the sex and companionship they had lost, they were nevertheless wary, more aware than a first-timer of the pitfalls and dangers, anxious not to make the same mistakes again, and perhaps even more anxious to avoid other unsuspected traps.

Divorced women experience similarly mixed feelings. As Goode put it, three things are obvious about a divorced woman: she is adult, sexually experienced, and unattached. No wonder men are interested! If she has property too, she has even more reason to suspect base motives for men's advances. Yet there are pressures to remarry. Many divorced women are lonely; many need someone to help support them and look after the children; some feel socially isolated in a world of couples in which they are the odd ones out;[6] sympathetic friends may express concern and attempt helpful match-making.

Remarriage

Like lone parenthood, remarriage is not new, but the divorce revolution has brought it sharply to the fore. The remarriage-able population at any one time consists of widowed and divorced women and men, and the circumstances of the four categories are different. As Jessie Bernard pointed out, a marriage dissolved by death leaves one person remarriageable; by divorce, two.[7] Especially in the United States, where as noted in chapter 2 more marriages end annually in divorce than in death, the numbers of people becoming remarriageable each year through divorce far exceeds those widowed. Moreover, divorces make exactly equal numbers of men and women remarriageable, whereas far more women than men outlive their spouses. The widowed therefore consist largely of elderly widows, whose chances of remarriage are poor. Those of widowed men are better; women generally outnumber men in the older age-groups, and since many are monogamously married the numbers of widows far exceed the numbers of men or comparable age available to marry them. (I return to this point below). By contrast, the divorced are generally much younger, and they predominate among remarriageable people in their thirties and forties. Their remarriage chances are very high, far higher than those of single people of comparable age. Overwhelmingly, therefore, remarriage in recent times has been the remarriage of the divorced.

Thus in the United States it was estimated in 1976 that most young divorced women remarried within three years and 60–70 per cent within five, while in 1977 43 per cent of all marriages were second marriages for one or both partners, and in 1980 one married couple in five included at least one previously divorced spouse.[8] Such trends had not gone quite so far in Britain, but in 1981 one marriage in three was a remarriage for one or both parties, and among those remarrying the divorced outnumbered the widowed by over 5 to 1. Of women under 35 who had separated in the early 1970s, just over half had remarried within 6 years. Most divorced people who remarried did so in their thirties, the median ages in 1981 being 35.8 for men and 33.4 for women. As noted below, most cohabited before remarrying. However, second marriages are more likely than first marriages to end in divorce; according to British statistics, about one and a half times as likely for men, twice as likely for women.[9]

Noting this tendency in the United States also, Bernard pointed to an apparent paradox: though more ended in divorce, second marriages had been shown in a number of studies to be at least as happy as first marriages if not more so. Part of the explanation no doubt lay in the greater promptitude with which a second marriage was likely to be dissolved if it proved unsatisfactory, so that unhappy second marriages were quickly weeded out leaving the happy ones to figure in the sociologists' surveys. Further, while some divorced persons never remarried, those who did included no doubt some who were 'divorce-prone', unable for whatever reason to sustain a lasting relationship. Most people who remarried, however, were men and women capable of at least average marital success who had simply made a wrong first choice.

Viewed in one way, the increasing practice of divorce and remarriage can be seen as setting a socially accepted lifetime pattern of being married successively to more than one spouse that has been named 'serial monogamy' or 'sequential polygamy'. Already by the 1950s Bernard thought that plural marriage in this sense, within the framework of legal monogamy, was more widespread in the United States than polygamy was in populations among whom it was the cultural norm. For large numbers of people in western countries, perhaps as many as one in three, it constitutes a significant departure from the norm of lifelong monogamy.

'Divorce chains'

Another aspect of 'serial monogamy' is the ramifying complexity it introduces to our once rather simple bilateral kinship system. Divorce is not generally followed by a complete severance of relations even between ex-spouses, let alone their respective kin. In some cases the affinal relationships are strengthened; for example, a divorced woman may find that her ex-husband's parents blame him for the breakdown, and redouble their affectionate attention to her and, more especially perhaps, the children. If she remarries, she gains a second set of in-laws. More pertinently perhaps, the children have perforce to form a new relationship with their step-father (of which more below). However, though most children of divorced parents remain in their mother's custody many fathers also maintain contact with their children, even if it may be under access orders that in many cases are matters of anguished and acrimonious dispute between the parents. If the now-absent father remarries, the children acquire a non-co-resident step-mother, whom they at least meet on occasional visits to their father's home. If she brings with her children of a previous marriage, they acquire step-siblings; if she and their father have children of their own, half-siblings. Sometimes a man's current wife and ex-wife are acquainted, find they have something in common, and even co-operate for purposes such as joint family outings and holidays with the children of both marriages. In ways such as these, as the American anthropologist Paul Bohannan has pointed out, a number of households may be linked in 'divorce chains'.[10]

Households of remarriage

The household formed by a remarriage, especially when it includes children of a previous marriage or marriages, has been variously termed a family of remarriage, a step-family, or a reconstituted family. Relationships become quite complex when both spouses bring children from their previous marriages and proceed to have a third set of children of their own. In such a household some of the children are full siblings, some half-siblings, and some step-siblings; and though individually each child has two parents and four grandparents, collectively they have four parents (present or absent) and eight grandparents.

However, many parents and step-parents in that situation are at pains to minimize rather than accentuate the different formal relationships in which they and the children are involved. Thus the American sociologist Lucile Duberman, who probably coined the term 'reconstituted family', wrote of her own experience: 'My second husband and I retained custody of my three children and his two sons. We . . . proceeded to become a "family".'[11] Making every effort themselves to avoid partiality, they asked grandparents and friends to treat all the children alike, tried in public to give the impression of being one family, and whenever possible sidestepped inquiries as to which child belonged to which parent.

Step-relationships

Step-relationships are difficult both to study and to practise. It has even been argued that we need a new terminology; the 'step-' terms have survived in the English language from an earlier age when remarriages were preceded by death, not divorce, and are not generally appropriate today.[12] A divorced mother's second husband does not exactly step into the role of father to her children; their father is someone else, still living, and in most cases keeping up some kind of a relationship with them. Moreover, the roles of natural parents and siblings are diffuse and ill-defined in our society. Although, following Bowlby, there has been a good deal of debate about the maternal role, there has been much less about that of fathers, while sibling relationships are largely uncharted. There are no reliable bases, therefore, for comparison with the roles of step-parent and step-sibling.

Thus the central problem for many a step-father is: should he try to be 'just like a father' and treat his step-children as if they were his own? and if so, what would that entail? Natural fathers vary enormously in the ways they act towards their children; and besides, these children already have a father, though now absent. One difficult area is that of discipline. Given that all children need sometimes to be checked and corrected, a step-father who is too zealous in this respect risks arousing his wife's protective feelings towards her chidren, and endangers his marital relationship. Aware of this, it seems, many step-fathers refrain from correcting their step-children, and so treat them much as a visiting friend or detached outsider might do, leaving that aspect of their upbringing entirely to the mother, and making the child an outsider rather than one of the family.

Then there is the question of names. Should his step-children call him Father? or some variant such as Pa or Daddy-John? or simply by his first name? Should they change their surname to his, as their mother has done? It seems that many children want to do so, to avoid tiresome and possibly embarrassing explanations. Behind these questions with all their symbolic significance lie important legal and financial issues. In countries where a man is legally obliged to maintain his wife and his own children, but not hers by another union, the more a step-father accepts the children and treats them as his own, the more he is impelled to assume financial responsibility for them, and the more he erodes that of their natural father. Yet many families can ill afford to forgo the latter's maintenance payments; so this issue is fraught with possible conflicts between fathers and step-fathers, giving rise to tensions that affect the wives and marital relationships of both. A related question is whether step-parents should go all the way and irrevocably assume complete responsibility for their step-children by legal adoption – a move that in most states generally requires the consent of the natural parents. And finally, little discussed in the literature, there is the question of inheritance.

In the foregoing I have focussed on step-fathers because there are more of them. But though there are fewer step-mothers, it is generally acknowledged that theirs is an even more difficult role. 'Wicked step-mother' myths – Cinderella, Snow White – abound not only in our own culture but also in many others. From one point of view they are misleading and harmful. Of course most step-mothers are not wicked but on the contrary well disposed and affectionate towards their step-children; yet childish apprehensions are reinforced by the stories and in some cases may be hardened into well-nigh implacable hostility. From another point of view, however, it may be important to search for the kernel of truth in the myth, the universal preoccupation to which, like myths in general, it gives expression. Jessie Bernard attempted an explanation in her detailed analysis of different forms of conflict in families, and the different possible alliances that can be involved. Although it is well-nigh inconceivable that a mother might be won away from her natural children into an alliance against them with her second husband, it is altogether more possible that a step-mother might form an alliance with her husband against his natural children. So children may well feel less secure and more anxious about a step-mother than about a step-father. But even apart from the myths, step-mothers' difficulties are at least as great as those of step-fathers over discipline, for example, if only because they are around more; while they also face more often the problem of scarce resources. Thus in Bernard's example, it is difficult enough if Mary and Helen are sisters to convince Mary that Helen needed a new tennis racket when Mary had just been denied a new bathing suit; if they are step-sisters, how much more difficult can readily be imagined.

As had been noted, many step-parents try to treat their step-children as if they were their own, and to create a family life as much as possible like that of an unbroken family. This may make them rather resistant to sociological inquiry; though not all are averse to talking about step-parenthood themselves, many prove reluctant to let an inquiring sociologist interview the children and remind them of a relationship whose distinctiveness the parents had been at pains to minimize. Thus in some studies only the remarried couples have been interviewed, while in others young adults (mostly students) have recalled their experiences as children when their parents divorced and remarried, but much difficulty has been experienced in collecting data from all three of the parties involved in the same step-family relationship: the natural parent, the step-parent, and the child or children. Yet we need such research, if only because of the increasing numbers of children and adults who live through this experience.

COMMUNES[13]

The communal ideal is not new. For thousands of years men and women in Christian and Buddhist societies have renounced family life to enter religious communities. For hundreds of years some people in western countries have rejected their society's prevailing values and norms and founded new communities based on radically different principles. Many such dissident groups have fled from oppression in Europe and taken refuge elsewhere, in North America or in Israel. In the 1960s a fresh wave of enthusiasm for the communal ideal followed a mood of radical disaffection among many young adults, engendered most of all by the Vietnam war, and extending widely to other aspects of western society including conventional family life. Hostile criticisms such as those reviewed in chapter 5 stimulated many to ask, 'if family life is so awful, what's the alternative?'

The kibbutz

In Israel some 100,000 people live in kibbutzim, rural communes founded very largely on the initiative of European socialist Zionists. They were not only anti-capitalist but also anti-family, rejecting above all the closed, formal Jewish family life of the ghettos from which they came; and feminist, rebelling against the inferior status of women in traditional Jewish life, and rejecting the traditional role of the Jewish mother protectively doting on her children and managing their lives. In the kibbutzim, according to the accounts of Bruno Bettelheim[14] and of Lionel Tiger and Joseph Shepher,[15] men and women were to do the same work and have the same rights and duties.

'They would equally be politicians and cooks, equally have the freedom to make love with whomsoever they wished, unbound by the old association of sex, marriage, and procreation. Indeed, they would be free not to marry at all'; though after 1947 marriage came to be rather reluctantly accepted as a necessary concession to the laws of a Jewish state.

Both symbolically and practically, the central institution of the kibbutz was the communal dining-room; where, however, food was eaten unceremoniously and even hastily, in another rejection of the formal family meal of the Jewish tradition. Cooking, serving, and clearing away were done by men and women alike on a rota basis, and there was no individual shopping for food. Couples living together, married or not, did not work together, and they were quite independent of each other. Rewards and sustenance were collective and shared among all kibbutz members, not individual and effort- or enterprise-related. So no woman depended on any man; her sustenance was hers by right as a commune member. Women rejected all their traditionally female roles, including in the heroic pioneer days that of making themselves attractive to men. Child-birth they could not escape, but even then they handed over their children as soon as possible, after no more than two to six weeks, to be communally brought up. To fuss over one's own child would be uncomfortably like being a possessive Jewish mother and taking a step back to the ghetto. All that was conceded was the two hours' play period after work in the evening; and even over that, too, there was keen debate in some kibbutzim over whether parents should put their children to bed afterwards in the communal nursery, or hand them straight over to the metapelet. As for taking a family meal together in the parents' quarters, that would have seemed well-nigh indecent, and a betrayal or everything the whole kibbutz movement stood for. Later, it seems, there was some relaxation; Tiger and Shepher stated that in 10 per cent of kibbutzim, children actually slept in their parents' quarters, but they returned to the metapelet's care during the day, and spent most of their waking hours in a communal, not a family environment.

Utopian communities in North America

In North America many Utopian communities have been founded in the past by dissident groups endeavouring to start a new life in the vast open spaces of the New World. Some have been short-lived, others have endured like the Hutterites and the Dukhobors both in Canada and the United States. Tracing their history back to 1680, Rosabeth Moss Kanter stated that something like a hundred such communities were founded in the United States in the nineteenth century, mostly before 1850.[16] Many were inspired by the religious convictions of widely different Christian sects; some were secularist; a few, like Robert Owen's New Harmony, were socialist. Nathaniel Hawthorne was one of a number of leading intellectuals who were involved in a utopian experiment in communal living named Brook Farm at West Roxbury, Mass., in the 1840s, and he drew on that experience in his *Blithedale Romance*, 1852. Some, notably the Hutterites, practised a strict monogamy and a highly patriarchal family life.[17] Others dissented from orthodox sexual morality and conducted their relationships on other principles. A leading instance was the Oneida community, founded in 1846–8 by John Humphrey Noyes (b. 1811), who believed that the perfect love all should have for Christ and for one another demanded not only the sharing of all material possessions but also 'the abolishment of exclusiveness' in sexual relations and child-care. Under strict community supervision, and by mutual consent, Oneida men and women were able to express that love in sexual caresses. Conception was avoided by 'male continence' (*coitus reservatus*, or withdrawal without ejaculation), a method demanding extraordinary self-control, yet so effectively was it practised that no children were born between 1849 and 1869. Then it was decided that each male could father one child, and preferred males could have more than one, most of all Noyes himself. Children ('stirps') were brought up communally for the most part; parenthood, especially motherhood, was recognized, but just as relations between men and women were not to become so close and 'special' as to detract from the general love that pervaded the whole community, so parents and children were warned against 'stickiness' or excessive and exclusive love for each other. During the 1870s there was much trouble with the outside world. Oneida children venturing into neighbouring communities were taunted as 'bastards', and Methodists and Presbyterians denounced the community's alleged immorality. Anticipating arrest, Noyes fled to Canada in 1879, and in 1881 the community abandoned its controversial practices and resolved itself into a joint stock company; according to Kanter, 'a small fraction of the old community spirit' survived in the firm which later became famous for its silverware.

Analysing the varied outcomes of these attempts to create new forms of communal life, Kanter's central concept was that of commitment or, briefly, the identity of internal motivation and external demands to support the social order. 'When a person is committed, what he wants to do (through internal feeling) is the same as what he has to do (according to external demands).' Utopian communities had many problems, including how to get the work done, but without coercion; how to make decisions to everyone's satisfaction; how to build close, fulfilling relationships, but without exclusiveness; how to choose and socialize new members; how to allow for autonomy, uniqueness, and even deviance; and how to ensure agreement and shared perception about community activities and values. To solve all these, the community had to find ways to engender and sustain its members' commitment if it were to endure and continue to satisfy their needs. Commitment was increased by sacrifice and investment; the more a member had given up, and put into the community, the greater the commitment. Committed membership entailed renunciation of the world. Siting the community in a geographically remote place, or literally building a wall around it, were ways in which communities sought to sever their members' outside ties; but problems continually arose from relationships within the community potentially disruptive of its group life, especially intimate friendships between two members that weakened their commitment to the group as a whole. There were two extreme solutions: celibacy, as in the age-old monastic tradition; or free love and group marriage, as in some 19th-century communities like Oneida and others more recently. Commitment was further enhanced by communion, sharing possessions and working together as well as partaking in ritual celebrations. Many of the older communities practised mortification, symbolized by the adoption of a uniformly drab unattractive dress. They took a close interest in each member's behaviour and promised love and support if misbehaviour were corrected; hence confessions, mutual criticism, shaming offenders, and ranking systems based literally on the 'holier than thou' principle. All these contributed to a transcendental experience of great power and meaning residing in the community, whether that took the form of the personal charisma of its leader, a common attachment to its ideology, or faith in the guidance of a divine power.

By these tests, Kanter considered that many of the communes that sprang up in the 1960s had failed to arouse deep commitment in their members. Their boundaries were weak and their membership ill-defined, as people joined and left at frequent intervals, sacrificing and investing little, and taking their possessions with them when they left. They were ineffectively organized, an absence of rules regulating individuals' work and conduct being indeed part of their *raison d'être*. So they were mostly evanescent – 'small, dissolvable, structureless' – and though they might provide some individuals with welcome interludes from social pressures, they were 'nevertheless a problematic way of creating community in contemporary America'.

However, there were some 'communes with a mission' to which these strictures did not apply, for example the one named Synanon devoted to the care and rehabilitation of those affected by drug abuse. With its strictly organized regime, Synanon 'illustrates the ways in which the commitment mechanisms found in nineteenth-century communes such as Oneida occur in modern dress'.

Communes in Britain

Communes in Britain newly founded in the 1960s were studied by Andrew Rigby[18] and by Philip Abrams, Andrew McCulloch, and their colleagues[19]. Rigby distinguished six types: self-actualizing, mutual support, activist, practical, therapeutic, and religious. It was clear from both studies, however, that communes took so wide a variety of forms as to defy classification. Some represented little more than practical arrangements on the part of couples, mostly with children, to share a large house in a rural setting and combine economies of scale in the bulk buying of household supplies with a vague commitment to the imagined advantages of 'extended family' living, especially shared child-minding and the availability of substitute parents. Such communes were clearly quite different from those which people joined as individuals, or – not uncommonly – as lone-parent families. A related question was whether sex relations were to be paired, or communal and in principle freely available. In communes with sexual sharing, many women were disconcerted to find men just as predatory as those in the world outside.

Some communes, like Abrams' 'Red Dawn', were avowedly political, regarding themselves as cells of revolutionary activity. Most, however, represented a rejection of the world of politics and a withdrawal from the wider society rather than an attempt to change it, unless it were by a gradual dissemination of 'alternative' ideas demonstrated as 'viable'. All communes faced the problem of the division of labour among members, and how to decide arrangements to everybody's satisfaction. All likewise faced the problem of possessions, and the extent to which they should be surrendered by the recruit and shared by the group, or whether they should be recoverable when a member left. Differences in commitment were equally clearly related to those of stability of membership and turnover; most communes proved to have a 'core' of members who owned most of the property, and a 'fringe' with a fairly rapid rate of turnover. And these questions were further related to those of the ultimate dissolution of the commune, and whether it was long or short-lived. However, duration was not to be confused with success; a commune might have a relatively transitory existence for only a few months or years, yet serve a valuable purpose and meet some of its members' needs at critical junctures in their lives.

According to Abrams and McCulloch, the commune movement of the late 1960s had arisen in response to a number of deeply-felt concerns of the time. First, 'the problem of the generations'; there was much talk of a 'generation gap', and recruits to communes were 'primarily and assertively young'. Secondly, 'the problem of the family. Although most people living in families at that time would have thought of their existence in that respect as entirely natural and not at all problematic, a remarkable array of moralists ... had ruled otherwise', including (as noted in chapter 5) R. D. Laing and Edmund Leach. The family was seen unequivocally as a 'setting in which people were bound to transgress one another's freedom'; and the commune movement offered 'a reconstruction of intimacy of a kind which would not entail the constraints and perversions these moral authorities had stigmatised'. Thirdly, 'the problem of women . . . separating the social process of mothering from the exploitation of biological mothers'. Fourthly, redressing the balance of work and play against a society unduly dominated by work. Fifthly, identity; 'the collective making of a more authentic type of self'. Sixthly, 'intentional community', that is, creating a society deliberately to meet its members' needs, as distinct from accepting one ready-made by outside agencies. Finally, and obliquely, the politics of revolution. 'Communes would change their own members.' Whereas the French communist party, the London School of Economics, and the Mayor of Chicago had proved resistant to change in the student rebellions of 1968, 'communes were to be demonstration projects for a gentle revolution of the individual'.

Intrinsic to the ideology of the commune movement was a rejection, not only of the particular social structures of western societies, but also of the very notion of a social structure itself, along with its associated concepts of role, status, social control, and the like. This entailed an explicit rejection of sociology, and Abrams' team's task was not made easier by a baffling combination of seemingly genuine welcome and hospitality for themselves as persons with a total antipathy to their work as social scientists, and indeed to science generally. Life in general, and communal life in particular, was not to be typified or analysed; it could only be experienced.

This is the paradox: the social stifles the self; but the self can only realise itself in a society. The only known society is a monstrous offence; a new society must be created, but the only account of it that can be given is that it should be not society – that is, not the society that is known.[20]

However, though specific social relationships were denied, in the more successful communes social structure was 'smuggled back in – often in the form of a religion'.

The commune movement impressed Abrams as 'a serious, open-ended attempt to achieve a radical alternative to the nuclear family'. Talents conventionally ascribed to males and females respectively could be 'dispersed' between the sexes; but 'the crucial difficulty in this respect, and not just for communes, appears to be that of dispersing mothering. . . . Women in communes broadly go along with everything that femininity, motherhood, etc., ordinarily connote'. Some alleviation of women's lot was achieved by essentially passive female co-operation, such as a rota of mothers to feed the children. And men did some of the women's work, but always with the guarantee that in the last resort the women would see that it was done.

Of the three links that compose the basic family unit, wife–husband, father–child, mother–child, the first two are often seriously opened up in communes, but the third is hardly touched; motherhood remains an all demanding and totally female role. The notion that communal relationships are intentional ... breaks down in the face of child-rearing.[21]

For women, then, when monogamy and the distinction be-tween wage-work and housework were relaxed, deeper ob-stacles emerged to the equality of the sexes. 'The commonest worry of women in communes, so far as we could tell, was still "What shall I do if he leaves me?"' Although communal living afforded some protection, it did not in itself provide a setting in which women could be sure of not being left in the lurch. There were exceptions, however; at Findhorn, a commune later to become famous, monogamous marriages were celebrated and the family was seen as the essential building-block of the New Age.

Children from most communes went to school, attempts to give them tuition in the commune to the satisfaction of the local education authority having failed. This had two import-ant consequences. It led them to ask why they did not live in a 'normal' family group with two identifiable parents, like their classmates; and it made inescapably clear their true status as dependants, less than fully 'intentional' members alike of the commune and the wider society.

Almost all adult commune members, along with many out-siders, believed that communal living was better for the children. 'Our attention was often drawn in an obviously deliberate way to the merits of communal child-rearing: "You can see what a good place this is for kids." But what we tended to see actually was a remarkable gap between the promise and the practice.' Spreading children's dependence and emotional attachments suited the adults – "nearly always someone to cover you" – enabling them to get away from time to time and lead lives of their own. Quite often, however, the child's life was 'haphazard at best, manifestly insecure at worst'. That impelled women back into mothering, to ensure that at least their own children came to no harm; worse, in some cases the most maternal and conscientious woman ended up as 'the effective mother of the whole commune'.

The attempt of communes to do the basic work of the family better. . . is not commonly very successful. Typically, pair relations between adults both threaten and are threatened by the commune as a whole; the more stable they become, the more this is the case. Typically, children find themselves at sea in the flux of adult relationships: whether the sea is calm or tempestuous is beyond their control, and often beyond that of the adults, too.[22]

DIVERSE LIFE-STYLES

If the ideal family life in western societies since the Christian revolution has been that of the autonomous nuclear family based on lifelong monogamy with chastity before marriage and 'faithfulness' (= sexual exclusivity) after, it seems clear beyond doubt that it has come to be 'more honoured in the breach than the observance'. Whether or not it was ever the moral norm, it is certainly not now the statistical norm. I have dealt above with some of the more important departures from and rejections of the norm; it remains to put these into perspective with others in surveying the diverse patterns according to which people in western societies may shape their lives. These diverse lifestyles may be adopted sequentially by individuals at different times in their lives, and are therefore not mutually exclusive.

Moreover, lifestyles radically at variance with the conventional norm may be practised behind the 'monogamous front' of a 'cereal-packet family'. A case in point is afforded by Nigel Nicolson's study of the lives of his parents Harold Nicolson and Vita Sackville-West, prompting the question how many more such cases there are among people less affluent and less articulate who do not leave private diaries to be discovered by their literary progeny.[23]

Cohabitation without marriage

'Don't marry until you are at least 25 and have lived with your intended for at least two years', said one mother to her teenage daughters.[24] In so far as the aim is to avoid marital breakdown and divorce, clearly in the light of the facts set out in chapter 13 that was excellent advice.

Trial marriage, companionate marriage, or marriage in two steps have long been advocated by eminent western intellectuals. In the 1920s Judge Ben B. Lindsey raised a storm of controversy in the United States by advocating that instead of clandestine sexual liaisons young people should be able to enter openly and honourably into a form of 'companionate marriage' if they had no intention of having children. To that end, the best birth-control advice should be made available to them. So long as the wife did not become pregnant, divorce would be by mutual consent, and involve no alimony (maintenance payments). The English philosopher Bertrand Russell, who was in the United States at the time, thought that was a step in the right direction but one that did not go far enough. Explicitly advocating 'trial marriage', he considered that 'all sex relations which do not involve children should be regarded as a purely private affair'. Pre-marital sexual experience was highly desirable. It was absurd to expect people to enter into a lifelong relationship without knowing if they were sexually compatible, as absurd as buying a house without seeing it. No marriage should be legally binding until the first pregnancy. Contraceptives had altered the whole aspect of sex and marriage. Men and women might now come together for sex alone; for sex and companionship, as in Judge Lindsey's companionate marriage; or for the purpose of rearing a family. No morality could be adequate to modern conditions that failed to distinguish these three different relationships.[25]

Such ideas seemed outrageous at that time, though they passed with less comment when they were revived by the American anthropologist Margaret Mead in a magazine article in 1966 advocating 'marriage in two steps': individual and parental.[26] Individual marriage with no children, easily revocable, would appeal mostly though not exclusively to young people. It should be convertible at a second step into parental marriage in contemplation of children; this would be harder to break off, and would entail continuing responsibi. y for the children.

Although arrangements of this kind have not been formally instituted, it seems clear beyond doubt that growing numbers of young people in western countries have quietly taken matters into their own hands and acted according to the spirit of those proposals. Thus in the United States it has been estimated that the number of unmarried couples sharing a household more than tripled between 1970 and 1977 and nearly doubled again between 1977 and 1982, when nearly 1.9 million couples were so living, or 4 per cent of all couples. As usual, too, the prevalence is less than the lifetime risk; 18 per cent of a sample of men in their twenties in 1974–5 had lived with a woman without marriage, even though only 5 per cent were doing so currently, and the proportions must be much higher today.[27] Similarly in Britain in 1981–2, according to the official general household survey, the prevalence of cohabitation without marriage among widowed, divorced, or separated women aged 18–49 was 18 per cent, and among single women 10 per cent. Furthermore, 21 per cent of recently-married women had cohabited with their husbands beforehand where the marriage was the first for both, and no less than 67 per cent where one or both partners had been married before, a big increase over figures for the early 1970s.[28] And in Sweden in 1974 more couples aged 18–24 were living together unmarried than married.[29]

It remains briefly to mention some other possible lifestyles which were extensively discussed in the more ebullient literature of the 1970s.

'Creative singlehood'

Singlehood is not new in western societies which, as noted from the outset, were characterized for centuries by fairly high proportions of men and even more of women who never married. One reason why some women remained single was to look after their aged parents, in some cases in the expectation of inheriting the greater part of their property, like the maiden aunts of Jack Goody's Scottish childhood.[30] In recent decades fewer women have stayed single; thus for example in England and Wales the proportion of women who reached the age of 45 without ever marrying fell from 16.6 per cent in 1950 to 7 per cent in 1975.[31] Even more recently, however, marriage ages have risen again, possibly presaging a rise in the proportion who will remain single, and a reversion to older patterns. Meanwhile, what has been called 'creative singlehood' has been

identified as a possible lifestyle other than conventional monogamy, raising a small question-mark against the taken-for-
granted assumption that since most people marry all should,
and the practical implication that we live in a social world of
couples in which the single are the odd persons out.[32]

Polygyny after sixty?

As noted above (p. 231), women far outnumber men in the
older age-groups, and the imbalance is even greater among
elderly remarriageable people, mostly widowed. Towards
remedying it, and solving at least some of the problems of the
elderly, 'geriatric polygyny' has been seriously proposed; that
is, men over (say) sixty should be allowed to take two or more
wives also over sixty.[33] But as far as I know this proposal has not
been put into effect, either legally or to any appreciable
extent informally.

Extra-marital and co-marital sex

As already mentioned, pre-marital sex relations (PMS), trial
marriage, and living together without (or in many cases before)
marriage have come to constitute one important departure
from the monogamous norm. After marriage, there is nothing
new about extra-marital sex (EMS); since time immemorial
some married people have had clandestine affairs with other
partners. Conventionally they were the subject of the notorious
dual morality, condemned in wives, less severely so in
husbands.

Co-marital sex (CMS) is different, involving an agreement
between monogamously married couples to accept or even
encourage each other's sex relations with other partners.[34]
Essentially they renounce and proscribe jealousy. Possibly the
title of Nena and George O'Neill's book *Open Marriage* may
have given a name to this kind of relationship, though the
O'Neills did not advocate sexually open marriage (SOM) but
rather urged couples to be open and frank with each other in all
things, and let each other grow and change without conform-
ing rigidly to stereotyped role models.[35] One study of sexually
open marriages found most to be happy and stable, and some
marked by 'a sparkle and extraordinary vitality'. Wives gained

equality with their husbands, as sexually open marriage eliminated the conventional double standard and with it fears about their husbands' clandestine affairs.[36] Associated with sexually open marriage has been the catch-phrase 'Compartment Four', that is, the time left when a person has paid proper attention to spouse, children, work, and community activities; it has been urged that to use this time for sex relations with another partner is as legitimate as any other recreation.[37]

Swinging

Another variety of co-marital sex is 'swinging', in which a number of couples meet and make love with other partners in a convivial party setting, usually in each other's houses. For some reason this activity has attracted a good deal of research attention and there are several published accounts by American sociologists.[38] 'Single dating' outside swinging sessions was frowned on in most groups as possibly conducive to jealousy; the key phrase was 'sex for recreation, not procreation', and not, it seemed, for personal and emotional involvement either. Swingers were characterized as people who started early and always found sex most rewarding and satisfying; some even expressed a kind of missionary zeal for a practice which they believed did nothing but good and much increased the sum total of human happiness. Couples joining swinging groups generally did so on the husband's initiative, but after a while wives enjoyed it even more. Though sociable, with many friends, swingers tended to be estranged from parents and kin, and not to engage much in neighbourhood or community activities. They practised their hobby discreetly for fear of adverse consequences on career, credit ratings, and relations with friends and neighbours, and did not allow it to be associated with illegal activities such as drug abuse. They did not let their children know about it, either, and those with young children made sure they were locked in their bedrooms or sent away to stay with relatives before the party started.

Group marriage

Genuine group marriages (so regarded by the partners, not of course in law) appear to be rare, and perhaps hardly distinguishable from communes with sexual sharing. According to one sympathetic account, they typically involved four adults and about three children, usually from previous unions, in rather more stable relationships than the extra-marital experiences or swinging which the adults had tried, hoping for more than sex, and found disappointing.[39]

CONCLUSIONS

Obviously 'sex for recreation not procreation', and with it many of the activities and lifestyles described above, have depended upon and taken for granted safe, reliable, and above all unobtrusive contraceptives of the kinds that came into general use during the 1960s.[40] Not that that was the only significance of the contraceptive revolution, as it has been called, and it seems reasonable to surmise that a heightened sexuality within some marriages too may have been among its consequences.

Indeed, the reader can hardly fail to have been struck by the many profound changes that were affecting western family life at that time. Much has been said in earlier chapters about the divorce revolution of the 1960s. It was during the 1950s and 1960s that adolescent peer-groups came into prominence in western societies (chapter 8), and married women entered employment in large numbers (chapter 9). The rebirth of feminism took place in the 1960s, with many profoundly important consequences including the rise of the dual-career family (chapter 10). At the same time, family life itself was assailed by hostile criticisms (chapter 5), prompting serious experiments in other forms of intimate domestic life in the new communes as mentioned earlier in this chapter. If, as I suggested in chapter 4, the 1950s were a golden age of stable family life and functionalist sociology, the end of that era may have been not entirely unwelcome to some for whom it came as a relief, even a liberation, from the staid conventionality of the one and the bland complacency of the other. By contrast, as seen in chapter 5, the 1960s were a time of turmoil when no guidelines seemed to remain; not even reason, as the prevailing mood was also anti-rational and anti-scientific.

But the scope for experiment with different ways of living has proved not to be infinitely wide, most of all in providing for the care and upbringing of children. True, in the most success-ful communes such as the kibbutz and Oneida children have led happy lives and grown up normally in a largely communal setting; but even there an irreducible part has been played by parenthood, especially motherhood. In the less successful, as Abrams *et al.* observed, children were manifestly insecure. While it may not be the only way, the autonomous nuclear family household supported by the three-generation kindred network seems to have proved to be one reasonably satisfac-tory way of meeting this vital human need while affording an acceptable compromise with the individualism that is integral to western values.

Furthermore, open-minded experiments with different ways of sharing affection and domestic intimacy, inspired by some-thing like Bertrand Russell's uncompromising iconoclasm and clarity of thought, depend upon a tolerance of diversity requir-ing much forbearance and self-restraint on the part of some interested bodies. It seems clear that greater tolerance has in fact been extended towards living together unmarried, par-ticularly among young adults, and even more among the for-merly married. At the same time it has to be remembered that ethnic minorities constitute another and quite different source of diversity in family patterns. Changing legal and other institutional forms in relation to that diversity presents dif-ficult problems, only some of which have been touched on above. Even if there is acceptance in principle of the need to deal even-handedly with people adhering to diverse lifestyles and family patterns, there are difficult dilemmas in practice between exercising the tyranny of the majority on the one hand, and failing to protect basic human rights in the other. The problem posed by runaway south Asian girls in Britain, as described in chapter 12, is one example. Another, referred to in chapter 7, is the difficulty of reconciling greater tolerance for relationships hitherto prohibited, such as inadvertent brother–sister incest or the marriage of a step-father to his adult step-daughter, with calls for greater protection of girls from sexual molestation within the family.

Debates on these and other issues continue at the time of writing; and it may be, as I suggested at the end of chapter 2, that the full implications have not yet been grasped of all the changes that have occurred since 1960. Yet it has been apparent throughout that there has been continuity as well as diversity and change, alike in the recent and the remoter past, in the whole history of family life in western societies as it has evolved over the centuries and as people have changed their ways of meeting basic human needs in response to new ideas and changing circumstances.

SUGGESTIONS FOR FURTHER READING

Bertrand Russell, *Marriage and Morals*, London, Allen and Unwin, 1929

Jessie Bernard, *Remarriage*, New York, Russell and Russell, 1971

Paul Bohannan (ed.), *Divorce and After*, New York, Doubleday, 1970

Peter Ambrose, John Harper, and Richard Pemberton, *Surviving Divorce: Men Beyond Marriage*, Brighton, Wheatsheaf, 1983

Lucile Duberman, *The Reconstituted Family: A Study of Remarried Couples and their Children*, Chicago, Nelson-Hall 1975

Bruno Bettelheim, *The Children of the Dream*, New York, Macmillan, 1969

Lionel Tiger and Joseph Shepher, *Women in the Kibbutz*, Harmondsworth, Penguin, 1975

Rosabeth Moss Kanter, *Commitment and Community*, Cambridge, Mass., Harvard University Press, 1972

Philip Abrams, Andrew McCulloch, *et al., Communes, Sociology, and Society*, Cambridge, Cambridge University Press, 1976

Herbert A. Otto (ed.), *The Family in Search of a Future*, New York, Appleton-Century-Crofts, 1970

James R. Smith and Lynn G. Smith (eds), *Beyond Monogamy*, Baltimore, Md., John Hopkins Press, 1974

Nona Glazer-Malbin (ed.), *Old Family/New Family: Interpersonal Relationships*, New York, Van Nostrand, 1975

Roger W. Libby and Robert N. Whitehurst (eds.), *Marriage and Alternatives: Exploring Intimate Relationships*, Glenview, Ill., Scott Foresman, 1977

Notes

1 FIRST PRINCIPLES

1 Leov Nikolayevich Tolstoy, *Anna Karenina* (orig. Russian, 1873–6); English trans., anon., London, Vizetelly, 1887, and by Rosemary Edmonds, Harmondsworth, Penguin, 1954.
2 Norbert Elias, *The Civilizing Process: The History of Manners* (orig. German, 1939); English trans. by Edmund Jephcott, Oxford, Blackwell, 1978.
3 Jack Goody, *The Developmental Cycle in Domestic Groups*, Cambridge, Cambridge University Press, 1958.
4 Meyer Fortes, Introduction to *ibid.*
5 Raymond Firth (ed.), *Two Studies of Kinship in London*, London, Athlone Press, 1956, p. 42.
6 W. M. Williams, *The Sociology of an English Village: Gosforth*, London, Routledge and Kegan Paul, 1956, p. 67.
7 Eugene Litwak and Ivan Szelenyi, 'Primary group structures and their functions: kin, neighbours, and friends', *American Sociological Review*, vol. 34, 1969, pp. 465–81.
8 William J. Goode, *World Revolution and Family Patterns*, New York, Free Press, 1963; revised edition, 1970, pp. 7–21; Peter Laslett, 'Characteristics of the Western European family', *London Review of Books*, 16 October – 5 November 1980, pp. 7–8.
9 J. E. Goldthorpe, *An Introduction to Sociology*, 3rd edition, Cambridge, Cambridge University Press, 1985, ch. 4.
10 J. Hajnal, 'European marriage patterns in perspective', in D. V. Glass and D. E. C. Eversley (eds.), *Population in History*, London, Arnold, 1965, pp. 101–43.
11 Michael Mitterauer and Reinhard Sieder, *The European Family: From Patriarchy to Partnership from the Middle Ages to the Present*, (orig. German, 1977); English trans. by Karla Oosterveen and Manfred Hörzinger, Oxford, Blackwell, 1982, ch. 2.

2 FAMILY LIFE IN THE PAST

1 Alan Macfarlane, *The Origins of English Individualism: The Family, Property and Social Transition*, Oxford, Blackwell, 1978.

2 Hajnal, 'European marriage patterns.'
3 Peter Laslett and Richard Wall (eds), *Household and Family in Past Time*, Cambridge, Cambridge University Press, 1972; Peter Laslett, *Family Life and Illicit Love in Earlier Generations*, Cambridge, Cambridge University Press, 1977.
4 Jack Goody, *The Development of the Family and Marriage in Europe*, Cambridge, Cambridge University Press, 1983.
5 Michael Drake, *Population and Society in Norway, 1735–1865*, Cambridge, Cambridge University Press, 1969.
6 Edward Shorter, *The Making of the Modern Family*, Glasgow, Fontana/Collins, 1976.
7 Philippe Ariès, *Centuries of Childhood* (orig. French, 1960), trans. Robert Baldick, London, Cape, 1962.
8 Lawrence Stone, *The Family, Sex and Marriage in England, 1500–1800*, London, Weidenfeld and Nicolson, 1977.
9 Linda A. Pollock, *Forgotten Children: Parent–Child Relations from 1500 to 1900*, Cambridge, Cambridge University Press, 1983.
10 This view was most explicitly expressed in William Fielding Ogburn and Clark Tibbits, 'The family and its functions', originally published in *Recent Social Trends* by the President's Research Committee on Social Trends, New York, McGraw Hill, 1934, reprinted in R. Freedman *et al.*, *Principles of Sociology*, New York, Holt Rinehart and Winston, 1963, pp. 421–32; see also W. F. Ogburn and M. F. Nimkoff, *Sociology*, Boston, Mass., Houghton Mifflin, 1950, pp. 469ff., and *A Handbook of Sociology*, London, Routledge and Kegan Paul, 1960, ch. 21. But Ogburn was not alone in his view, which permeated much of the older sociological literature.
11 Goode, *World Revolution and Family Patterns*, p. 6.
12 Lorraine Lancaster, 'Kinship in Anglo-Saxon society', *British Journal of Sociology*, vol. 9, 1958, pp. 230–50, 359–77.
13 Goody, *The Development of the Family and Marriage in Europe*, pp. 37–9.
14 *Ibid.*, p. 204.
15 *Ibid.*, pp. 40–6, 82, 152.
16 *Ibid.*, pp. 45, 62, 91, 99–102, 123, 133, 142–6, 164–5, 181.
17 Macfarlane, *English Individualism*, pp. 82–3.
18 Goody, pp. 95–6, 129–31, 164–6.
19 *Ibid.*, pp. 168–73.
20 Max Rheinstein, 'Divorce law in Sweden', in Paul Bohannan (ed.) *Divorce and After*, New York, Doubleday, 1970, pp. 143–70.
21 *Report of the Committee on One-Parent Families* (the Finer report), Cmnd 5629, London, HMSO, 1974, pp. 224–5.
22 Margrit Eichler, *Families in Canada Today*, Toronto, Gage, 1983, pp. 48–9.

23 Clifford Kirkpatrick, *The Family as Process and Institution*, New York, Ronald, 1955, chs. 5 and 21.
24 Bohannan, *Divorce and After*, p. 43.
25 Phyllis Deane and W. A. Cole, *British Economic Growth, 1688–1959*, 2nd edition, Cambridge, Cambridge University Press, 1967, pp. 142, 161; J. H. Clapham *An Economic History of Modern Britain, 1: The Early Railway Age*, 2nd edition, Cambridge, Cambridge University Press, 1939, pp. 66–7, 536.
26 Carlo M. Cipolla, *The Economic History of World Population*, 7th edition, Harmondsworth, Penguin, 1978, p. 28; W. W. Rostow, *The Stages of Economic Growth*, 2nd edition, Cambridge, Cambridge University Press, 1971, p. xx.
27 E. A. Wrigley and R. S. Schofield, *The Population History of England 1541–1871*, London, Arnold, 1981, pp. 335–55, 389–91, 664–70.
28 Michael Anderson, *Approaches to the History of the Western Family, 1500–1914*, London, Macmillan, 1980, p. 46.
29 Laslett and Wall (eds.), *Household and Family in Past Time*, pp. 126, 135, 136, 142.
30 Laslett, *Family Life and Illicit Love*, p. 34.
31 E. A. Wrigley and R. S. Schofield, 'English population history from family reconstitution: summary results, 1600–1799', *Population Studies*, vol. 37, 1983, pp. 157–84.
32 Laslett and Wall (eds), *Household and Family*, pp. 240, 265, 309–10.
33 Drake, *Population and Society in Norway*, pp. 131–2.
34 In Laslett and Wall (eds), *Household and Family*, pp. 552, 562.
35 *Ibid.*, pp. 267–81.
36 *Ibid.*, pp. 335–73.
37 Alan Macfarlane, *The Family Life of Ralph Josselin, a Seventeenth-Century Clergyman*, Cambridge, Cambridge University Press, 1970.
38 Laslett, *Family Life and Illicit Love*, pp. 65–75.
39 Macfarlane, *English Individualism*, pp. 67–8, 76–7.
40 Pollock, *Forgotten Children*.
41 C. P. Blacker, *Eugenics, Galton and After*, London, Duckworth, 1952, ch. 8; Geoffrey Hawthorn, *The Sociology of Fertility*, London, Macmillan, 1970, pp. 24–5; Cipolla, *The Economic History of World Population*, 7th edition, 1978, pp. 102–3.
42 T. R. Malthus, *An Essay on the Principle of Population*, London, J. Johnson, 1798, facsimile reprint for the Royal Economic Society, London, Macmillan, 1926.
43 Drake, *Population and Society in Norway*, p. xvii.
44 G. M. Trevelyan, *English Social History*, London, Longmans Green, 1944, pp. 341–6; T. S. Ashton, *The Industrial Revolution 1760–1830*, London, Oxford University Press (Home University Library),

1948, pp. 3–6; H. J. Habakkuk, 'The economic history of modern Britain', *Journal of Economic History*, vol. 18, 1958, pp. 486–501.

45 Pollock, *Forgotten Children*, p. 231.

46 V. Fildes, 'Neonatal feeding practices and infant mortality during the 18th century', *Journal of Biosocial Science*, vol. 12, 1980, pp. 313–24.

47 Wrigley and Schofield, 'English population history'.

48 Alva Myrdal, *Nation and Family*, London, Kegan Paul Trench Trubner, 1945, pp. 17, 21.

49 Wrigley and Schofield, *The Population History of England*, pp. 228–48, and ch. 10 esp. p. 422; E. A. Wrigley, 'The growth of population in eighteenth-century England: a conundrum resolved', *Past and Present*, no. 98, 1983, pp. 121–50.

50 David Levine, *Family Formation in an Age of Nascent Capitalism*, New York, Academic Press, 1977; 'Industrialization and the proletarian family in England', *Past and Present*, no. 107, 1985, pp. 168–203.

51 Malthus, *Essay*, 1798 repr. 1926, pp. 68–9.

52 Ann Kussmaul, *Servants in Husbandry in Early Modern England*, Cambridge, Cambridge University Press, 1981.

53 In Laslett and Wall (eds), *Household and Family*, p. 233.

54 Michael Anderson, *Family Structure in Nineteenth-Century Lancashire*, Cambridge, Cambridge University Press, 1971, p. 142.

55 Laslett and Wall (eds), *Household and Family*, p. 143.

56 *Ibid.*, p. 141; Wrigley and Schofield, *The Population History of England*, p. 450 and appendix 3.

57 R. A. Lewis, *Edwin Chadwick and the Public Health Movement 1832–1854*, London, Longmans Green, 1952, esp. pp. 41ff.

58 Goode, *World Revolution and Family Patterns*, pp. xvi, 22.

59 Anderson, *Approaches to the History of the Western Family*, pp. 47–8.

60 Robert Roberts, *The Classic Slum*, Manchester, University of Manchester Press, 1971; Harmondsworth, Penguin, 1973.

61 E. A. Wrigley, 'Family limitation in pre-industrial England', *Economic History Review*, vol. 19, 1966, pp. 82–109.

62 Richard B. Morrow, 'Family limitation in pre-industrial England: a reappraisal', *Economic History Review*, vol. 31, 1978, pp. 419–28; E. A. Wrigley, 'Marital fertility in seventeenth-century Colyton: a note', *ibid.*, 429–36.

63 Ronald Lee, in Wrigley and Schofield, *The Population History of England*, pp. 367–8, 400.

64 Joel Mokyr, *Why Ireland Starved: A Quantitative and Analytical History of the Irish Economy, 1800–1850*, London, Allen and Unwin, 1983.

65 K. H. Connell, *The Population of Ireland, 1750–1845*, Oxford, Clarendon Press, 1950, esp. chs. 3, 5 and 6.

66 D. V. Glass, *Introduction to Malthus*, London, Watts, 1953, pp. 30–8; see also C. Arensberg and S. T. Kimball, *Family and Community in Ireland*, Cambridge, Mass., Harvard University Press, 1940, esp. ch. 6.

67 A. M. Carr-Saunders, *World Population*, Oxford, Clarendon Press, 1936, p. 90.

68 Etienne van de Walle and John Knodel, 'Europe's fertility transition', *Population Bulletin*, vol. 34, no. 6 (Population Reference Bureau, Inc.: Washington, DC, February 1980).

69 J. A. Banks, *Prosperity and Parenthood: A Study of Family Planning among the Victorian Middle Class*, London, Routledge and Kegan Paul, 1954.

70 Paul C. Glick, *American Families*, New York, Wiley, 1957, pp. 54–5.

71 *Encyclopaedia Britannica*, 11th edition, Cambridge, 1910, art. 'Divorce: United States'.

72 Cited in David V. Glass, 'Divorce in England and Wales', *Sociological Review* (old series), vol. 26, 1934, p. 302.

73 Griselda Rowntree and Norman H. Carrier, 'The resort to divorce in England and Wales, 1858–1957', *Population Studies*, vol. 11, 1958, pp. 188–233.

74 *United Nations Demographic Yearbooks*, 1968, table 34, and 1982, table 33.

75 *Putting Asunder: A Divorce Law for Contemporary Society*, the report of a group appointed by the Archbishop of Canterbury in January 1964, London, SPCK, 1966.

76 Arland Thornton and Deborah Freedman, 'The changing American family', *Population Bulletin*, vol. 38, no. 4 (Population Reference Bureau Inc.: Washington, DC, 1983).

77 UK Registrar-General's *Statistical Reviews* to 1963: Office of Population Censuses and Surveys, *Marriage and Divorce Statistics*, 1981, table 2.1; UK Central Statistical Office, *Social Trends 14*, 1984, pp. 35–6.

3 MATERNAL CARE AND MATERNAL DEPRIVATION

1 John Bowlby, *Maternal Care and Mental Health*, Geneva, World Health Organization, 1951; *Child Care and the Growth of Love*, Harmondsworth, Penguin, 1953; 2nd edition, with two new chapters by Mary Ainsworth, 1965.

2 John Bowlby, *Attachment and Loss*, 3 vols., London, Hogarth, 1969–80.

3 S. A. Barnett, *'Instinct' and 'Intelligence': The Behaviour of Animals and Man*, Harmondsworth, Penguin, 1970, pp. 236–43.

4 Ann M. Clarke and A. D. B. Clarke, *Early Experience: Myth and Evidence*, London, Open Books, 1976, pp. 4–8.
5 Bowlby, *Maternal Care and Mental Health*, p. 11.
6 Barbara Wootton, *Social Science and Social Pathology*, London, Allen and Unwin, 1959, ch. 4.
7 John Bowlby and Mary Ainsworth, 1954, quoted in Wooton, *ibid.*, p. 147.
8 Wootton, *ibid.*, pp. 138–9.
9 *Ibid.*, pp. 155–6.
10 Bowlby, *Maternal Care and Mental Health*, pp. 68–9.
11 Michael Rutter, *Maternal Deprivation Reassessed*, Harmondsworth, Penguin, 1972, p. 26.
12 *Ibid.*, p. 125.
13 In Clarke and Clarke, *Early Experience*, chs. 4–5.
14 *Ibid.*, p. 272.
15 Mia Kellmer Pringle, *The Needs of Children: A Personal Perspective*, 2nd edition, London, Hutchinson, 1980, pp. 59–70, 156, 161.
16 Pollock, *Forgotten Children*.
17 Hannah Gavron, *The Captive Wife: Conflicts of Housebound Mothers*, London, Routledge and Kegan Paul, 1966; Harmondsworth, Penguin, 1970.

4 SOCIOLOGICAL MODELS OF WESTERN FAMILY LIFE IN THE 1950s

1 Talcott Parsons, *The Structure of Social Action*, New York, McGraw Hill, 1937; repr. Glencoe, Ill., Free Press, 1949.
2 In a lecture at the London School of Economics, 29 January 1949.
3 Bronislaw Malinowski, *A Scientific Theory of Culture*, Chapel Hill, University of North Carolina Press, 1944.
4 Talcott Parsons and Robert F. Bales, *Family Socialization and Inter-action Process*, Glencoe, Ill., Free Press, 1955; London, Routledge and Kegan Paul, 1956.
5 George Peter Murdock, *Social Structure*, New York, Macmillan, 1949, p. 2.
6 Morris Zelditch, Jr, 'Role differentiation in the nuclear family: a comparative study', in Parsons and Bales, *Family*, ch. 6.
7 While British anthropologists focussed their debate on the definition of marriage and whether it is universal, in the United States there was also discussion of the related issue of the definition of the family and its universality. See Melford E. Spiro, 'Is the family universal?' *American Anthropologist*, vol. 56, 1954, pp. 839–46; E. Kathleen Gough, 'The Nayars and the definition of marriage', *Journal of the Royal Anthropological Institute*, vol. 89, 1959, pp. 23–34 (both reprinted in Norman W. Bell and Ezra F. Vogel (eds.), *A Modern Introduction to the Family*, revised edition, New York, Free Press,

1968, pp. 68–96); William N. Stephens, *The Family in Cross-Cultural Perspective*, New York, Holt Rinehart and Winston, 1963, pp. 1–32; Jack Goody, 'The evolution of the family', in Laslett and Wall (eds.), *Household and Family*, pp. 103–24; *The Development of the Family and Marriage in Europe*, p. 31.

8 Robert F. Bales, *Interaction Process Analysis*, Cambridge, Mass., Addison-Wesley, 1950.

9 Talcott Parsons, 'The incest taboo in relation to social structure and the socialization of the child', *British Journal of Sociology*, vol. 5, 1954, pp. 101–17.

10 *Ibid.*, p. 113.

11 *Ibid.*, p. 114.

12 Parsons and Bales, *Family*, pp. 18–20.

13 *Ibid.*, pp. 11–15.

14 Talcott Parsons, *Essays in Sociological Theory*, revised edition, New York, Free Press, 1954, pp. 79–90, 94–5, 190–3; 'The social structure of the family', in Ruth Nanda Anshen (ed.), *The Family: Its Function and Destiny*, revised edition, New York, Harper, 1959, pp. 264–7.

15 Talcott Parsons and Edward Shils (eds.), *Toward a General Theory of Action*, Cambridge, Mass., Harvard University Press, 1951, pp. 49, 77.

16 Christopher Lasch, *Haven in a Heartless World: The Family Besieged*, New York, Basic Books, 1977.

17 Goode, *World Revolution and Family Patterns*.

18 J. E. Goldthorpe, *The Sociology of the Third World: Disparity and Development*, 2nd edition, Cambridge, Cambridge University Press, 1984, pp. 172–4.

5 CRITICISMS AND CRITICS OF THE 1950s MODELS

1 Michael Young and Peter Willmott, *Family and Kinship in East London*, London, Routledge and Kegan Paul, 1957, Harmondsworth, Penguin, 1962.

2 Peter Willmott and Michael Young, *Family and Class in a London Suburb*, London, Routledge and Kegan Paul, 1960.

3 Peter Townsend, *The Family Life of Old People*, London, Routledge and Kegan Paul, 1957.

4 Michael Young and Hildred Geertz, 'Old age in London and San Francisco: some families compared', *British Journal of Sociology*, vol. 12, 1961, pp. 124–41.

5 Raymond Firth, 'Family and kin ties in Britain and their social implications', *British Journal of Sociology*, vol. 12, 1961, p. 306.

6 Colin Rosser and Christopher Harris, *The Family and Social Change: A Study of Family and Kinship in a South Wales Town*, London,

Routledge and Kegan Paul, 1965, pp. 199–204. See also C. C. Harris, *The Family: An Introduction*, London, Allen and Unwin, 1969, p. 71.

7 Colin Bell, *Middle Class Families: Social and Geographical Mobility*, London, Routledge and Kegan Paul, 1968.

8 Elizabeth Bott, *Family and Social Network*, London, Tavistock, 1957; second edition 1971.

9 Eugene Litwak, 'Occupational mobility and extended family cohesion' and 'Geographic mobility and extended family cohesion', *American Sociological Review*, vol. 25, 1960, pp. 9–21 and 385–94; 'Extended kin relations in an industrial democratic society', in Ethel Shanas and Gordon F. Streib (eds.), *Social Structure and the Family: Generational Relations*, Englewood Cliffs, NJ, Prentice Hall, 1965, pp. 290–323.

10 Elias, *The Civilizing Process*.

11 Sigmund Freud, *Civilization and Its Discontents* (orig. German, 1930); English trans., London, Hogarth, 1955, and in standard edition vol. 21, London, Hogarth, 1961.

12 *The Listener*, 30 November 1967, p. 695.

13 D. H. J. Morgan, *Social Theory and the Family*, London, Routledge and Kegan Paul, 1975, p. 204.

14 Michael Z. Brooke, *Le Play: Engineer and Social Scientist*, London, Longman, 1970, pp. 80–1, 106–7.

15 F. Le Play, *L'Organisation de la famille*, Paris, Téqui, 1874, p. xvi (my translation, J.E.G.).

16 C. C. Zimmerman and M. E. Frampton, *Family and Society: A Study of the Sociology of Reconstruction*, London, Williams and Norgate, 1936, pp. 449–50.

17 Quoted in Morgan, *Social Theory and the Family*, p. 205.

18 In Anshen (ed.), *The Family: Its Function and Destiny*, pp. xvi–xvii.

19 Ronald Fletcher, *Britain in the Sixties: The Family and Marriage, An Analysis and Moral Assessment*, Harmondsworth, Penguin, 1962, reprinted as *The Family and Marriage in Britain*, 1967, pp. 12–17.

20 Barrington Moore, Jr, *Political Power and Social Theory: Six Studies*, Cambridge, Mass., Harvard University Press, 1958, ch. 5, 'Thoughts on the future of the family'.

21 Morgan, *Social Theory and the Family*, p. 205.

22 *Ibid.*, 190–2.

23 Herbert Marcuse, 'A study on authority' (orig. German, 1936), in his *Studies in Critical Philosophy*, London, NLB, 1972, p. 78; *Eros and Civilization*, Boston, Mass., Beacon, 1955, pp. 96ff, 201.

24 William J. Goode, 'Force and violence in the family', *Journal of Marriage and the Family*, November 1971, pp. 624–35, reprinted in Arlene Skolnick and Jerome H. Skolnick, *Intimacy, Family and Society*, Boston, Mass., Little Brown, 1974, pp. 72–92.

25 *Ibid.*, pp. 77–9, 89–90.
26 *Ibid.*, pp. 80–1.
27 *Murder, 1957 to 1968*, UK Home Office Research Study no. 3, London, HMSO, 1969.
28 Ray E. Helfer and C. Henry Kempe (eds.), *The Battered Child*, Chicago, University of Chicago Press, 1968; 3rd edition, revised and extended, 1980; *Child Abuse and Neglect: The Family and the Community*, Cambridge, Mass., Ballinger, 1976; Jean Renvoize *Children in Danger*, London, Routledge and Kegan Paul, 1974; Marie Borland (ed.), *Violence in the Family*, Manchester, Manchester University Press, 1976; National Society for the Prevention of Cruelty to Children, *At Risk*, London, Routledge and Kegan Paul, 1976; Alfred White Franklin (ed.), *The Challenge of Child Abuse*, London, Academic Press, 1977; *Child Abuse, Prediction, Prevention, and Follow Up*, Edinburgh, Churchill Livingstone, 1977; John M. Eekelaar and Sanford N. Katz (eds.), *Family Violence: An International and Interdisciplinary Study*, Toronto, Butterworths, 1978; Christine Hallett and Olive Stevenson (eds.), *Child Abuse: Aspects of Inter-professional Co-Operation*, London, Allen and Unwin, 1980.
29 Erin Pizzey, *Scream Quietly or the Neighbours will Hear*, Harmondsworth, Penguin, 1974; Jean Renvoize, *Web of Violence*, London, Routledge and Kegan Paul, 1978.
30 M. D. A. Freeman, *Violence in the Home*, London, Saxon House, 1979: see also Murray A. Straus, ch. 5 of Eekelaar and Katz, *Family Violence.*
31 Goode, 'Force and violence in the family'.
32 Kate Millett, *Sexual Politics*, London, Rupert Hart-Davis, 1971, pp. 220–1, 228–33.
33 Juliet Mitchell, *Women's Estate*, Harmondsworth, Penguin, 1971, pp. 94–5, 114–20, 156, 160–1, 171.
34 Jessie Bernard, *The Future of Marriage*, New Haven, Conn., Yale University Press, 1972, pp. 4–5.
35 John Charvet, *Feminism*, London, Dent, 1982, pp. 128ff. For a more elaborate analysis, see Amanda Sebestyen, *Tendencies in the Movement: Then and Now in Feminist Practice*, London, Theory Press, 1979.
36 R. D. Laing, *Self and Others*, London, Tavistock, 1961; Harmondsworth, Penguin, 1971, p. 146.
37 R. D. Laing, *The Politics of Experience and The Bird of Paradise*, Harmondsworth, Penguin 1967, pp. 31–2, 95.
38 R. D. Laing and A. Esterson, *Sanity, Madness, and the Family*, vol. 1: *Families of Schizophrenics*, London, Tavistock, 1964, Introduction.
39 R. D. Laing, *The Divided Self*, London, Tavistock, 1969, p. 23.
40 *The Politics of Experience*, pp. 24, 50.
41 *Ibid*, p. 118; *The Divided Self*, p. 27.
42 Morgan, *Social Theory and the Family*, pp. 115, 124.

6 FAMILY LIFE AND MENTAL ILLNESS, ESPECIALLY SCHIZOPHRENIA

1 Erving Goffman, *Asylums: Essays on the Social Situation of Mental Patients and Other Inmates*, Garden City, NY, Doubleday Anchor, 1961.
2 J. K. Wing, *Reasoning About Madness*, Oxford, Oxford University Press, 1978, pp. 44ff.
3 John Wing (ed.), *Schizophrenia from Within*, Surbiton, National Schizophrenia Fellowship, 1975; 'Elizabeth L. Farr' (pseud.), introduction to Ming T. Tsuang, *Schizophrenia: The Facts*, Oxford, Oxford University Press, 1982.
4 This characterization of schizophrenia is compounded from those of Kurt Schneider (1959) and the World Health Organization (1978). See Anthony Clare, *Psychiatry in Dissent: Controversial Issues in Thought and Practice*, 2nd edition, London, Tavistock, 1980, p. 127; Wing, *Reasoning about Madness*, pp. 103–10; Tsuang, *Schizophrenia*, pp. 16–17.
5 National Schizophrenia Fellowship, *Living with Schizophrenia, by the Relatives*, Surbiton, 1974.
6 Quoted in Agnes Miles, *The Mentally Ill in Contemporary Society: A Sociological Introduction*, Oxford, Martin Robertson, 1981, pp. 5–10.
7 Laing and Esterson, *Sanity, Madness, and the Family*, p. 3.
8 Wing, *Reasoning about Madness*, pp. 109, 172–3, 189; David Taylor, *Schizophrenia: Biochemical Impairments, Social Handicaps?* London, Office of Health Economics, 1979, pp. 12–13.
9 Wing, *Reasoning about Madness*, pp. 103–9.
10 *Ibid.*, pp. 85, 113, 117; Tsuang, *Schizophrenia*, pp. 21–30.
11 Paul H. Wender and Donald F. Klein, *Mind, Mood, and Medicine: A Guide to the New Biopsychiatry*, New York, Farrar Straus Giroux, 1981, p. 136.
12 Clare, *Psychiatry in Dissent*, chs. 6 and 7.
13 Wing, *Reasoning about Madness*, pp. 209–10.
14 *Ibid.*, pp. 203–4, 213–5.
15 Thomas Scheff, *Being Mentally Ill: A Sociological Theory*, Chicago, Aldine, 1966; see also discussion in Miles, *The Mentally Ill*, pp. 13–19.
16 Clare, *Psychiatry in Dissent*, pp. 198–203; Tsuang, *Schizophrenia*, pp. 37–42; Wing, *Reasoning about Madness*, pp. 120–1; Wender and Klein, *Mind, Mood, and Medicine*, pp. 220–6.
17 Henry L. Lennard and Arnold Bernstein, *Patterns in Human Interaction*, San Francisco, Jossey-Bass, 1969.
18 *Ibid.*, pp. 61, 89, 128, 185.
19 Jules Henry, *Pathways to Madness*, London, Cape, 1972, p. 455.
20 Steven R. Hirsch and Julian P. Leff, *Abnormalities in Parents of Schizophrenics* (Maudsley monograph no. 22), London, Oxford University Press, 1975.

21 Tsuang, *Schizophrenia*, pp. 45–52.
22 G. W. Brown, E. M. Monck, G. M. Carstairs, and J. K. Wing, 'The influence of family life on the course of schizophrenic illness', *British Journal of Preventive and Social Medicine*, vol. 16, 1962, pp. 55–68; G. W. Brown, J. L. T. Birley, and J. K. Wing, 'Influence of family life on the course of schizophrenic disorders: a replication', *British Journal of Psychiatry*, vol. 121, 1972, pp. 241–58; Wing, *Reasoning about Madness*, p. 128.
23 C. E. Vaughn and J. P. Leff, 'The influence of family and social factors on the course of psychiatric illness', *British Journal of Psychiatry*, vol. 129, 1976, pp. 125–37.
24 Jacqueline Grad and Peter Sainsbury, 'Mental illness and the family', *Lancet*, 1963, i, pp. 544–7; 'The effects that patients have on their families in a community care and a control psychiatric service – a two-year follow-up', *British Journal of Psychiatry*, vol. 114, 1968, pp. 265–78.
25 Wing, *Reasoning about Madness*, pp. 128, 137, 221.
26 National Schizophrenia Fellowship, *Schizophrenia: The Family Burden*, 1973; reproduced by permission of the National Schizophrenia Fellowship who hold the copyright.

7 EXOGAMY AND THE AVOIDANCE OF INCEST

1 Claude Lévi-Strauss, *The Elementary Structures of Kinship* (orig. French, 1949), English trans. by J. H. Bell and J. R. von Sturmer, R. Needham (ed.), London, Eyre and Spottiswoode, 1969, pp. 18, 24–5.
2 I was still under the same misapprehension in 1981 when revising *An Introduction to Sociology*, 3rd edition, Cambridge, Cambridge University Press, 1985, p. 91.
3 Christopher Bagley, 'Incest behaviour and incest taboo', *Social Problems*, vol. 16, 1969, pp. 505–19; 'The varieties of incest', *New Society*, 21 August 1969, pp. 280–2.
4 Joseph Shepher, *Incest: A Biosocial View*, New York, Academic Press, 1983, pp. 125–32.
5 *Ibid.*, pp. 34–5.
6 Norbert Bischof, 'Comparative ethology of incest avoidance', in Robin Fox (ed.), *Biosocial Anthropology*, London, Malaby Press, 1975, pp. 37–67.
7 H. G. Wells, Julian Huxley, and G. P. Wells, *The Science of Life*, London, Cassel, 1938, p. 566.
8 G. P. Murdock, *Social Structure*, p. 296.
9 Morton S. Adams and James V. Neel, 'Children of incest', *Pediatrics*, vol. 40, 1967, pp. 55–62.
10 Bischof, 'Comparative ethology of incest avoidance', pp. 56–7;

Robin Fox, *The Red Lamp of Incest*, London, Hutchinson, 1980, p. 10.

11 Shepher, *Incest*, pp. 87–104.

12 Edward Westermarck, *The History of Human Marriage*, London, Macmillan, 1891, p. 320.

13 Murdock, *Social Structure*, p. 291.

14 Sigmund Freud, *Introductory Lectures on Psycho-Analysis* (orig. German, 1916–17); standard English edition, trans. James Strachey *et al.*, London, Hogarth, 1963, vol. 15, p. 210, vol. 16, pp. 334–5; *Totem and Taboo* (orig. German 1913), standard edition, vol. 13, 1955.

15 Jane van Lawick-Goodall, *In the Shadow of Man*, London, Collins, 1971, p. 168.

16 Arthur P. Wolf, 'Childhood association, sexual attraction, and the incest taboo: a Chinese case', *American Anthropologist*, vol. 68, 1966, pp. 883–98; 'Adopt a daughter-in-law, marry a sister: a Chinese solution to the problem of the incest taboo', *American Anthropologist*, vol. 70, 1968, pp. 864–74.

17 Melford E. Spiro, *Children of the Kibbutz*, Cambridge, Mass., Harvard University Press, 1958.

18 Bruno Bettelheim, *The Children of the Dream*, New York, Macmillan, 1969.

19 Yonina Talmon, 'Mate selection in collective settlements', *American Sociological Review*, vol. 29, 1964, pp. 491–508. Shepher, *Incest*, pp. 56–62.

20 J. R. Fox, 'Sibling Incest', *British Journal of Sociology*, vol. 13, 1962, pp. 128–50; see also his *Kinship and Marriage*, Harmondsworth, Penguin, 1967, ch. 2, and his *The Red Lamp of Incest*, ch. 2.

21 Shepher, *Incest*, pp. 112–13.

22 *The Red Lamp*, p. 6.

23 A. R. Radcliffe-Brown, Introduction to A. R. Radcliffe-Brown and Daryll Forde (eds.), *African Systems of Kinship and Marriage*, London, Oxford University Press, 1950, p. 70.

24 H. A. Junod, *The Life of a South African Tribe*, 2nd edition, London, Macmillan, 1927, vol. 2, p. 68.

25 E. J. Krige and J. D. Krige, *The Realm of a Rain-Queen*, London, Oxford University Press, 1943, pp. 5, 98, 308.

26 Pierre van den Berghe, quoted in Shepher, *Incest*, p. 130.

27 Russell Middleton, 'Brother–sister and father–daughter marriage in ancient Egypt', *American Sociological Review*, vol. 27, 1962, pp. 603–11.

28 Keith Hopkins, 'Brother–sister marriage in Roman Egypt', *Comparative Studies in Society and History*, vol. 22, 1980, pp. 303–54.

29 *New Catholic Encyclopaedia*, New York, 1967, art. 'Consanguinity'; Goody, *The Development of the Family and Marriage in Europe*, p. 33.

30 Anthony H. Manchester, 'Incest and the law', ch. 33 of Eekelaar and Katz, *Family Violence*; see also *ibid.*, chs. 32 and 35.

31 *Report of a Committee on the Marriage Law of Scotland*, Cmnd 4011, Edinburgh, HMSO, 1969, p. 16; T. B. Smith, *A Short Commentary on the Law of Scotland*, Edinburgh, Green, 1962, p. 316; David M. Walker, *Principles of Scottish Private Law*, Oxford, Clarendon Press, 1970, pp. 203–5.

32 *Sexual Offences: 15th Report of the Criminal Law Revision Committee*, Cmnd 9213, London, HMSO, 1984.

33 Lars-Göran Engström, 'New penal provisions on sexual offences proposed in Sweden', *Current Sweden*, no. 118, Stockholm, The Swedish Institute, 1976.

34 *Sexual Offences*, p. 69.

35 Ingrid K. Cooper, 'Decriminalization of incest – new legal–criminal responses', ch. 34 of Eekelaar and Katz, *Family Violence*.

36 Solomon Kirson Weinberg, *Incest Behaviour*, Secaucus, NJ Citadel, 1976; Susan Forward and Craig Buck, *Betrayal of Innocence: Incest and its Devastation*, Harmondsworth, Penguin, 1981; Jean Renvoize, *Incest: A Family Pattern*, London, Routledge and Kegan Paul, 1982.

8 AGE-MATES AND ADOLESCENT SOCIALIZATION

1 Kurt Danziger, *Socialization*, Harmondsworth, Penguin, 1971, esp. ch. 9 on 'Extra-familial influences.'

2 Philip Abrams and Alan Little, 'The young voter in British politics', and 'The young activist in British politics', *British Journal of Sociology*, vol. 16, 1965, p. 95–110, 315–33.

3 Michael Argyle, *Religious Behaviour*, London, Routledge and Kegan Paul, 1958, pp. 39–70.

4 V. Zaslavsky and Z., 'Adult political socialization in the USSR', *Sociology*, vol. 15, 1981, pp. 407–23.

5 E.g. among the Kikuyu of Kenya; see Carl G. Rosberg, Jr, and John Nottingham, *The Myth of 'Mau Mau': Nationalism in Kenya*, New York, Praeger, 1966, pp. 112–25.

6 Audrey I. Richards, *Chisungu*, London, Faber, 1956, p. 140.

7 Jeremy Tunstall, *The Fishermen*, London, MacGibbon and Kee, 1962, pp. 107–18.

8 Leopold Rosenmayr, 'Towards an overview of youth sociology', *International Social Science Journal*, vol. 20, no. 2, 1968, pp. 286–315, esp. pp. 302–3 on 'Aspects of adolescent consumer behaviour'.

9 Urie Bronfenbrenner, *Two Worlds of Childhood: US and USSR*, Harmondsworth, Penguin, 1974, pp. 103–4.

10 *Ibid.*, pp. 36–7

11 *Ibid.*, p. 45

12 *Ibid.*, p. 13.
13 *Ibid.*, p. 118
14 *Ibid.*, p. 104
15 Charles E. Bowerman and John W. Kinch, 'Changes in family and peer orientation of children between the fourth and tenth grades', *Social Forces*, vol. 37, 1959, pp. 206–11.
16 Bronfenbrenner, *Two Worlds*, pp. 101–2.
17 James S. Coleman, *The Adolescent Society*, New York, Free Press, 1961, p. 11; *Equality of Educational Opportunity*, Washington, US Department of Health Education and Welfare, 1966, p. 325.
18 Bronfenbrenner, *Two Worlds*, pp. 107–8.
19 Muzafer Sherif, 'Superordinate goals in the reduction of intergroup conflict', *American Journal of Sociology*, vol. 43, 1958, pp. 349–56; Bronfenbrenner, *Two Worlds*, pp. 145–7.
20 *Ibid.*, pp. 165–6.

9 WOMEN IN EMPLOYMENT

1 Laslett, *Family Life and Illicit Love*, pp. 72, 75.
2 Macfarlane, *English Individualism*, pp. 131–5.
3 Williams, *Sociology of an English Village*, p. 42.
4 Banks, *Prosperity and Parenthood*, pp. 70–85.
5 D. C. Marsh, *The Changing Social Structure of England and Wales*, London, Routledge and Kegan Paul, 1958, pp. 126, 135.
6 David Lockwood, *The Blackcoated Worker*, London, Allen and Unwin, 1958, pp. 36–7, 133.
7 *Royal Commission on Population Report*, Cmd 7695, London, HMSO, 1949, p. 97.
8 Pearl Jephcott, Nancy Seear, and J. H. Smith, *Married Women Working*, London, Allen and Unwin, 1962.
9 *United Nations Demographic Yearbook, Historical Supplement*, 1979, p. 903.
10 UK Central Statistical Office, *Social Trends*, nos. 10, 1980, pp. 121–2, and 12, 1982, pp. 62–3.
11 Alva Myrdal and Viola Klein, *Women's Two Roles: Home and Work*, London, Routledge and Kegan Paul, 1956, revised edition 1968, pp. 31–8.
12 Simon Yudkin and Anthea Holme, *Working Mothers and their Children*, London, Michael Joseph, 1963.
13 J. W. B. Douglas and J. M. Blomfield, *Children Under Five*, London, Allen and Unwin, 1958, pp. 125–6.
14 T. Ferguson, *The Young Delinquent in His Social Setting: A Glasgow Study*, London, Oxford University Press, 1952, pp. 24, 145.
15 Audrey Hunt, *A Survey of Women's Employment*, 2 vols. (Government

Social Survey Report no. SS 379), London, HMSO, 1968.

16 Hilary Land, *The Family Wage*, 25th Eleanor Rathbone Memorial Lecture, University of Leeds, 1979.

17 *Social Trends*, no. 5, 1974, pp. 16–17.

18 Edward Gross, 'Plus ça change? The sexual structure of occupations over time', *Social Problems*, vol. 16, no. 2, 1968, pp. 198–208, reprinted in Athena Theodore (ed.), *The Professional Woman*, Cambridge, Mass., Schenkman, 1971, pp. 39–51.

19 US Bureau of the Census, cited by Jeff B. Bryson and Rebecca Bryson, 'Salary and job performance differences in dual-career couples', ch. 12 of F. Pepitone-Rockwell (ed.), *Dual-Career Couples*, Beverly Hills, Calif., Sage, 1980, p. 242.

10 CAREERS AND COUPLES

1 John H. Goldthorpe and David Lockwood, 'Affluence and the British class structure', *Sociological Review*, vol. 11, 1963, pp. 133–63; John H. Goldthorpe, David Lockwood, Frank Bechhofer, and Jennifer Platt, *The Affluent Worker in the Class Structure*, Cambridge, Cambridge University Press, 1969, pp. 50, 96–108.

2 Michael Young and Peter Willmott, *The Symmetrical Family: A Study of Work and Leisure in the London Region*, London, Routledge and Kegan Paul, 1973, esp. pp. 258–62. See also the review symposium by Colin Bell, Raymond Firth, and Chris Harris, *Sociology*, vol. 8, 1974, pp. 505–12.

3 J. M. and R. E. Pahl, *Managers and Their Wives: A Study of Career and Family Relationships in the Middle Class*, London, Allen Lane, 1971.

4 Martha R. Fowlkes, *Behind Every Successful Man: Wives of Medicine and Academe*, New York, Columbia University Press, 1980, esp. pp. 47–9, 79, 125.

5 William L. O'Neill, *Everyone Was Brave: The Rise and Fall of Feminism in America*, Chicago, Quadrangle, 1969; *The Woman Movement: Feminism in the United States and England*, London, Allen and Unwin; New York, Barnes and Noble, 1969, pp. 89, 96.

6 Judith Hole and Ellen Levine, *Rebirth of Feminism*, New York, Quadrangle/New York Times, 1971, p. 17.

7 Matina Horner, 'Fail: bright women', *Psychology Today*, vol. 3, no. 6, 1969, reprinted in Athena Theodore (ed.), *The Professional Woman*, Cambridge, Mass., Schenkman, 1971, pp. 252–9.

8 Rhona Rapoport and Robert N. Rapoport, 'Three generations of dual-career family research', ch. 1 of Fran Pepitone-Rockwell (ed.), *Dual-Career Couples*, Beverly Hills, Sage, 1980.

9 Political and Economic Planning, *Women in Top Jobs: Four Studies in Achievement*, London, Allen and Unwin, 1971; Michael P. Fogarty,

Rhona Rapoport and Robert N. Rapoport, *Sex, Career and Family*, London, Allen and Unwin, 1971.

10 Rhona Rapoport and Robert N. Rapoport, 'The dual-career family: a variant pattern and social change', *Human Relations*, vol. 22, 1969, pp. 3–30; *Dual-Career Families*, Harmondsworth, Penguin, 1971; *Dual Career Families Re-examined*, London, Martin Robertson, 1976; and many others. See also Harold Benenson, 'Women's occupational and family achievement in the US class system: a critique of the dual-career family analysis', *British Journal of Sociology*, vol. 35, 1984, p. 19–41.

11 Lotte Bailyn, 'Career and family orientation of husbands and wives in relation to marital happiness', *Human Relations*, vol. 23, no. 2, 1970, pp. 97–113, reprinted in Theodore (ed.), *The Professional Woman*, pp. 545–67; Fogarty *et al.*, *Sex, Career and Family*, chs. 7 and 8.

12 Fogarty *et al.*, *Sex, Career and Family*, pp. 337, 483–96; Rapoport and Rapoport, *Dual-Career Families*, p. 302.

13 Margaret M. Poloma and T. Neal Garland, 'The myth of the egalitarian family: familial roles and the professionally employed wife', paper presented to the American Sociological Association, Sept. 1970, reprinted in Theodore (ed.), *The Professional Woman*, pp. 741–61.

14 Lynda Lytle Holmstrom, *The Two-Career Family*, Cambridge, Mass., Schenkman, 1973.

15 Jeff B. Bryson and Rebecca Bryson, 'Salary and job performance differences in dual-career couples', ch. 12 of Pepitone-Rockwell (ed.), *Dual-Career Couples*.

11 SOCIAL CLASS, SOCIAL MOBILITY, AND FAMILY LIFE

1 World Bank, *World Development Report 1984*, p. 273.

2 John Haskey, 'Social class patterns of marriage', *Population Trends*, no. 34, London, Office of Population Censuses and Surveys, Winter 1983, pp. 12–19.

3 Derek Llewellyn-Jones, *Human Reproduction and Society*, London, Faber, 1974, p. 420.

4 Ann Cartwright, *Recent Trends in Family Building and Contraception*, London, Office of Population Censuses and Surveys, studies on medical and population subjects no. 34, HMSO, 1978.

5 Ann Cartwright, *The Dignity of Labour? A Study of Childbearing and Induction*, London, Tavistock, 1979, p. 66.

6 Jean Thompson and Malcolm Britton, 'Some socio-economic differentials in fertility in England and Wales', in R. W. Hiorns (ed.), *Demographic Patterns in Developed Societies*, London, Taylor and Francis, 1980, pp. 1–13.

7 Colin Gibson, 'The association between divorce and social class in England and Wales', *British Journal of Sociology*, vol. 25, 1974, pp. 79–93.

8 Peter Townsend, *Poverty in the United Kingdom*, Harmondsworth, Penguin, 1979, pp. 170–1.

9 Peter Townsend and Nick Davidson (eds.), *Inequalities in Health: The Black Report*, Harmondsworth, Penguin, 1980, pp. 51–3.

10 *Ibid.*, pp. 56–7.

11 John Fox and Peter Goldblatt, 'Socio-demographic differences in mortality', *Population Trends*, no. 27, London, Spring 1982, p. 10.

12 John and Elizabeth Newson, *Infant Care in an Urban Community*, London, Allen and Unwin, 1963; *Four Years Old in an Urban Community*, London, Allen and Unwin, 1968, Harmondsworth, Penguin, 1970; *Seven Years Old in the Home Environment*, London, Allen and Unwin, 1976 and Harmondsworth, Penguin, 1976.

13 A. H. Halsey, A. F. Heath, and J. M. Ridge, *Origins and Destinations: Family, Class, and Education in Modern Britain*, Oxford, Clarendon Press, 1980.

14 J. W. B. Douglas, *The Home and the School*, London, MacGibbon and Kee, 1964; Panther, 1967.

15 Gerhard E. Lenski, *Power and Privilege: A Theory of Social Stratification*, New York, McGraw-Hill, 1966, p. 391.

16 D. V. Glass (ed.), *Social Mobility in Britain*, London, Routledge and Kegan Paul, 1954.

17 John H. Goldthorpe *et al.*, *Social Mobility and Class Structure in Modern Britain*, Oxford, Clarendon Press, 1980.

18 John H. Goldthorpe, 'Women and class analysis: in defence of the conventional view', *Sociology*, vol. 17, 1983, pp. 465–88. See also Michelle Stanworth, 'Women and class analysis: a reply to John Goldthorpe', *Sociology*, vol. 18, 1984, pp. 159–70; Anthony Heath and Nicky Britten, 'Women's jobs do make a difference: a reply to Goldthorpe', *ibid.*, pp. 475–90; John Goldthorpe, 'Women and class analysis: a reply to the replies', *ibid.*, pp. 491–9; Robert Erikson, 'Social class of men, women and families', *ibid.*, pp. 500–14.

12 FAMILY LIFE AMONG ETHNIC MINORITIES

1 K. Ishwaran (ed.), *The Canadian Family*, revised edition, Toronto and Montreal, Holt, Rinehart and Winston, 1976, p. 15.

2 Philippe Garigue, 'The French-Canadian family', in Bernard R. Blishen *et al.* (eds.), *Canadian Society: Sociological Perspectives*, abridged edition, Toronto, Macmillan, 1971, pp. 126–41; 'French-

Canadian Kinship and Urban Life', *American Anthropologist*, vol. 58 (1956), pp. 1090–101, reprinted in Ishwaran (ed.), *The Canadian Family*, pp. 518–30.

3 Ralph Piddington, 'A Study of French-Canadian Kinship', *International Journal of Comparative Sociology*, vol. 2, no. 1, 1961, pp. 3–32; reprinted in C. C. Harris (ed.), *Readings in Kinship in Urban Society*, Oxford, Pergamon, 1970, pp. 71–98; also in Ishwaran (ed.), *The Canadian Family*, pp. 555–74.

4 John Reid, 'Black America in the 1980s', *Population Bulletin*, vol. 37, no. 4 (Population Reference Bureau, Inc., Washington DC, 1982).

5 Thornton and Freedman, 'The changing American family', *Population Bulletin*, vol. 38, no. 4, 1983.

6 William F. Pratt *et al.*, 'Understanding US Fertility: Findings from the National Survey of Family Growth, Cycle III', *Population Bulletin*, vol. 39 no. 5, 1984.

7 E. Franklin Frazier, *The Negro Family in the United States*, Chicago, University of Chicago Press, 1939; revised and abridged edition, New York, Dryden, 1948; reprinted by Chicago University Press, 1966. See also his 'The Negro Family in America', in Ruth Nanda Anshen (ed.), *The Family: Its Function and Destiny*, New York, Harper, 1949; revised edition, 1959; G. Franklin Edwards (ed.), *E. Franklin Frazier on Race Relations: Selected Writings*, Chicago, University of Chicago Press, 1968.

8 Gunnar Myrdal, *An American Dilemma: The Negro Problem and Modern Democracy*, New York, Harper, 1944, pp. 695–7, 930–5.

9 Melville J. Herskovits, *The Myth of the Negro Past*, New York, Harper, 1941, pp. 167–71. See also Stanley M. Elkins, *Slavery: A Problem in American Institutional and Intellectual Life*, Chicago, University of Chicago Press, 1959, pp. 93–4n.

10 E. Franklin Frazier, *The Negro in the United States*, New York, Macmillan, 1949; revised edition, 1957, ch. 1 and p. 367.

11 Lee Rainwater and William L. Yancey, *The Moynihan Report and the Politics of Controversy* (including the full text of *The Negro Family: The Case for National Action*, by Daniel Patrick Moynihan), Cambridge, Mass., MIT Press, 1967.

12 Hylan Lewis, Agenda Paper, November 1965, in Rainwater and Yancey, *ibid.*, pp. 314–41.

13 Jessie Bernard, *Marriage and Family among Negroes*, Englewood Cliffs, NJ, Prentice-Hall, 1966.

14 Rainwater and Yancey, *The Moynihan Report*, pp. 184–6.

15 William Ryan, *Blaming the Victim*, New York, Random House, 1971; revised and updated edition, 1976. See also Rainwater and Yancey, *The Moynihan Report*, pp. 197–9, 220–32, 457–66.

16 Andrew Billingsley, *Black Families in White America*, Englewood Cliffs, NJ, Prentice-Hall, 1968.

17 John M. Mogey, 'The Negro Family System in the United States', in Reuben Hill and René König (eds.), *Families in East and West*, Paris and The Hague, Mouton, 1970, pp. 442–53.

18 Carol B. Stack, *All Our Kin: Strategies for Survival in a Black Community*, New York, Harper and Row, 1974.

19 Robert William Fogel and Stanley L. Engerman, *Time on the Cross: The Economics of American Negro Slavery*, 2 vols., Boston, Mass., Little Brown, 1974, p. 5.

20 Laslett, *Family Life and Illicit Love*, p. 253.

21 Eugene D. Genovese, *Roll, Jordan, Roll: The World the Slaves Made*, New York, Pantheon, 1974.

22 Herbert G. Gutman, review of *Time on the Cross*, in *Journal of Negro History*, vol. 60, 1975, pp. 53–227; reprinted as *Slavery and the Numbers Game: A Critique of Time on the Cross*, Urbana, University of Illinois Press, 1975.

23 Herbert G. Gutman, *The Black Family in Slavery and Freedom, 1750–1925*, New York, Pantheon, and Oxford, Basil Blackwell, 1976, pp. 153–4.

24 *Ibid.*, pp. 455–6.

25 Goode, *World Revolution and Family Patterns*, pp. 238–47.

26 Roger Ballard, 'Family organization among the Sikhs in Britain', *New Community*, vol. 2, no. 1, 1972–3, pp. 12–24; Roger and Catherine Ballard, 'The Sikhs: the development of south Asian settlements in Britain', ch. 2 of James L. Watson (ed.), *Between Two Cultures: Migrants and Minorities in Britain*, Oxford, Blackwell, 1977; Catherine Ballard, 'Arranged marriages in the British context', *New Community*, vol. 6, no. 3, 1977–8, pp. 181–96; Catherine Ballard, 'Conflict, continuity, and change: second-generation south Asians', ch. 5 of Verity Saifullah Khan (ed.), *Minority Families in Britain: Support and Stress*, London, Macmillan, 1979; Roger Ballard, 'South Asian families', ch. 8 of British Family Research Committee, *Families in Britain*, London, Routledge and Kegan Paul, 1982.

27 Verity Saifullah Khan, 'The Pakistanis: Mirpuri villagers at home in Bradford', ch. 3 of Watson (ed.), *Between Two Cultures*; 'Migration and social stress: Mirpuris in Bradford', ch. 2 of her *Minority Families in Britain*.

28 Muhammad Anwar, *The Myth of Return: Pakistanis in Britain*, London, Heinemann, 1979.

29 Arthur Wesley Helweg, *Sikhs in England: The Development of a Migrant Community*, Delhi, Oxford University Press, 1979.

30 In Verity Saifullah Khan (ed.), *Minority Families in Britain*, p. 121.

31 *New Community*, vol. 6, no. 3, p. 181.

13 MARITAL ADJUSTMENT, MARITAL BREAKDOWN, AND DIVORCE

1 Ernest W. Burgess and Harvey J. Locke, *The Family: From Institution to Companionship*, New York, American Book Company, 1945, pp. 456–7.

2 Ernest W. Burgess and Leonard S. Cottrell, 'The prediction of adjustment in marriage', *American Sociological Review*, vol. 1, 1936, pp. 737–51; reprinted in Paul F. Lazarsfeld and Morris Rosenberg (eds.), *The Language of Social Research*, New York, Free Press, 1955, pp. 268–76.

3 Lewis M. Terman, *Psychological Factors in Marital Happiness*, New York, McGraw-Hill, 1938.

4 Harvey J. Locke, 'Predicting marital adjustment by comparing a divorced and a happily married group', *American Sociological Review*, vol. 12, 1947, pp. 187–91; *Predicting Adjustment in Marriage: A Comparison of a Divorced and a Happily Married Group*, New York, Holt Rinehart and Winston, 1951.

5 Harvey J. Locke and Muriel Mackeprang, 'Marital adjustment and the employed wife', *American Journal of Sociology*, vol. 54, 1949, pp. 536–8.

6 Ernest W. Burgess and Paul Wallin, *Engagement and Marriage*, Chicago, Lippincott, 1953, pp. 618–9.

7 Robert F. Winch, *Mate-Selection: A Study of Complementary Needs*, New York, Harper, 1958; see also his *The Modern Family*, 3rd edition, New York, Holt Rinehart and Winston, 1971, chs. 10 and 18.

8 William J. Goode, *Women in Divorce* (originally *After Divorce*, 1956), New York, Free Press, 1969.

9 Egon Vielrose, *Elements of the Natural Movement of Population*, Oxford, Pergamon, 1965, p. 118.

10 According to British official usage, 'a marriage is either dissolved or annulled after a petition has been filed and a decree granted. The divorce statistics include annulments and dissolutions. In England and Wales the latter outnumber the former by over 100 to 1'. – Office of Population Censuses and Surveys, *Marriage and Divorce Statistics, England and Wales, 1981*, London, HMSO, 1984, p. 3. However, in the usage of some other countries, and internationally, divorce is distinguished from annulment; while in the United States it is conventional to refer to the dissolution of marriages by divorce or death.

11 Griselda Rowntree and Norman H. Carrier, 'The resort to divorce in England and Wales, 1858–1957', *Population Studies*, vol. 11, 1958, pp. 188–233.

12 Rachel M. Pierce, 'Marriage in the fifties', *Sociological Review* (new series), vol. 11, 1963, pp. 215–40.

13 Griselda Rowntree, 'Some aspects of marriage breakdown in Britain during the last thirty years', *Population Studies*, vol. 18, 1964, pp. 147–63.

14 *Report of the Committee on One-Parent Families* (the Finer report), Cmnd 5629, London, HMSO, 1974, pp. 224–5.

15 Glass, 'Divorce in England and Wales', *Sociological Review*, 1934.

16 Colin Gibson, 'The association between divorce and social class in England and Wales', *British Journal of Sociology*, vol. 25, 1974, pp. 79–93.

17 M. J. Murphy, 'Marital breakdown and socio-economic status', *British Journal of Sociology*, vol. 36, 1985, pp. 81–93.

18 Robert Chester, 'Contemporary trends in the stability of English marriage', *Journal of Biosocial Science*, vol. 3, 1971, pp. 398–402; 'Divorce and legal aid: a false hypothesis', *Sociology*, vol. 6, 1972, pp. 205–16.

19 The rise in early divorce was particularly vividly illustrated in Office of Population Censuses and Surveys, *Marriage and Divorce Statistics, England and Wales, 1977*, fig. 8 on p. 75. According to *ibid., 1981*, the median duration of marriage to divorce fell from 12.2 years in 1972 to 10.1 in 1981.

20 Barbara Thornes and Jean Collard, *Who Divorces?*, London, Routledge and Kegan Paul, 1979.

21 Robert Chester, 'The duration of marriage to divorce', *British Journal of Sociology*, vol. 22, 1971, pp. 172–82.

22 Laslett, *Family Life and Illicit Love*, p. 184.

23 Nicky Hart, *When Marriage Ends: A Study in Status Passage*, London, Tavistock, 1976, pp. 148–58.

14   DEPARTURES AND REJECTIONS

1 UK Central Statistical Office, *Annual Abstract of Statistics*, 1984, p. 72; *Social Trends 13*, 1983, pp. 26–7.

2 Arland Thornton and Deborah Freedman, 'The changing American family', *Population Bulletin*, vol. 38, no. 4, Washington DC, Population Reference Bureau, 1983, pp. 8, 10, 33.

3 *Report of the Committee on One-Parent Families*, Cmnd 5629, London, HMSO, 1974, pp. 95, 99.

4 Goode, *Women in Divorce*, pp. 221–31.

5 Peter Ambrose, John Harper, and Richard Pemberton, *Surviving Divorce: Men Beyond Marriage*, Brighton, Wheatsheaf, 1983, pp. 56, 133, 139, 143–5.

6 Hart, *When Marriage Ends*, ch. 7.

7 Jessie Bernard, *Remarriage*, New York, Dryden, 1956, repr. Russell, 1971.

8 Thornton and Freedman, 'The changing American family', p. 10.

9 CSO, *Social Trends 14*, pp. 35–6.
10 Paul Bohannan, 'Divorce chains, households of remarriage, and multiple divorcers', in Bohannan (ed.), *Divorce and After*, New York, Doubleday, 1970, pp. 127–39.
11 Lucile Duberman, *The Reconstituted Family: A Study of Remarried Couples and Their Children*, Chicago, Nelson Hall, 1975.
12 Bohannan, *Divorce and After*, pp. 133–7; Margaret Mead, in *ibid.*, pp. 124–5.
13 Rosabeth Moss Kanter (ed.), *Communes: Creating and Managing the Collective Life*, New York, Harper and Row, 1973.
14 Bruno Bettelheim, *The Children of the Dream*, New York, Macmillan, 1969.
15 Lionel Tiger and Joseph Shepher, *Women in the Kibbutz*, Harmondsworth, Penguin, 1975.
16 Rosabeth Moss Kanter, 'Commitment and social organization: a study of commitment mechanisms in Utopian communities', *American Sociological Review*, vol. 33, 1968, pp. 499–518; *Commitment and Community*, Cambridge, Mass., Harvard University Press, 1972.
17 John W. Bennett, *Hutterian Brethren*, Stanford, Calif., Stanford University Press, 1967: John A. Hostetler, *Hutterite Society*, Baltimore, Md., Johns Hopkins University Press, 1974.
18 Andrew Rigby, *Alternative Realities*, London, Routledge and Kegan Paul, 1974; *Communes in Britain*, London, Routledge and Kegan Paul, 1974.
19 Philip Abrams, Andrew McCulloch, *et al., Communes, Sociology, and Society*, Cambridge, Cambridge University Press, 1976.
20 *Ibid.*, pp. 131–2.
21 *Ibid.*, p. 144.
22 *Ibid.*, p. 145–50.
23 Nigel Nicolson, *Portrait of a Marriage*, London, Weidenfeld and Nicolson, 1973.
24 Quoted from memory from a letter to a newspaper which I unfortunately failed to keep.
25 Bertrand Russell, *Marriage and Morals*, London, Allen and Unwin, 1929, ch. 12.
26 Margaret Mead, 'Marriage in two steps', *Redbook*, July 1966, reprinted in Herbert A. Otto (ed.), *The Family in Search of a Future*, New York, Appleton-Century-Crofts, 1970, pp. 75–84.
27 Thornton and Freedman, 'The changing American family', pp. 11–12.
28 UK Central Statistical Office, *Social Trends 14*, 1984, p. 34.
29 *Current Sweden*, no. 263, Stockholm, The Swedish Institute, December 1980.
30 Jack Goody, *Production and Reproduction*, Cambridge, Cambridge University Press, 1976, p. 4.

31 *UN Demographic Yearbook, Historical Supplement*, 1979, p. 903.
32 Roger W. Libby, 'Creative singlehood as a sexual lifestyle: beyond marriage as a rite of passage', in Libby and Robert N. Whitehurst (eds.), *Marriage and Alternatives: Exploring Intimate Relationships*, Glenview, Ill., Scott Foresman, 1977, pp. 37–61.
33 Victor Kassel, 'Polygyny after sixty', in Otto (ed.), *The Family in Search of a Future*, pp. 137–43; George S. Rosenberg, 'Implications of new models of the family for an aging population', *ibid.*, pp 171–81.
34 Libby, 'Extramarital and comarital sex: a critique of the literature', in Libby and Whitehurst, *Marriage and Alternatives*, pp. 80–111.
35 Nena and George O'Neill, *Open Marriage*, New York, 1972; 'Open marriage: a conceptual framework', in James R. Smith and Lynn G. Smith, *Beyond Monogamy*, Baltimore, Md., Johns Hopkins University Press, 1974, pp. 56–67.
36 Jacquelyn J. Knapp and Robert N. Whitehurst, 'Sexually open marriage and relationships: issues and prospects', in Libby and Whitehurst, *Marriage and Alternatives*, pp. 147–60.
37 Lonny Myers and Hunter Leggitt, *Adultery and Other Private Matters*, Chicago, Nelson-Hall, 1975; Lonny Myers, 'A couple can also be two people', in Libby and Whitehurst, *Marriage and Alternatives*, pp. 335–46.
38 Brian C. Gilmartin, 'Swinging: who gets involved and how?' in *ibid.*, pp. 161–85; Robert R. Bell, 'Swinging: separating the sexual from friendship', in Nona Glazer-Malbin (ed.), *Old Family/New Family: Interpersonal Relationships*, New York, Van Nostrand, 1975, pp. 150–68; Duane Denfield and Michael Gordon, 'The sociology of mate swapping: or the family that swings together clings together', in Smith and Smith, *Beyond Monogamy*, pp. 68–83.
39 Larry L. Constantine and Joan M. Constantine, 'Sexual aspects of group marriage', in Libby and Whitehurst, *Marriage and Alternatives*, pp. 186–94.
40 Charles F. Westoff and Norman B. Ryder, *The Contraceptive Revolution*, Princeton NJ, Princeton University Press, 1977, p. 31.

Index